W9-AXA-826

F01
pb

Great American Mansions

and THEIR STORIES

By MERRILL FOLSOM

edited and revised
by Rachel Borst

HASTINGS HOUSE
Norwalk, Connecticut

EAU CLAIRE DISTRICT LIBRARY

BÅT 6-26-01 $32.00

T 122844

The main hall of the Art Gallery of the Huntington (page 244) with the bronze statue Diana Huntress, c. 1782, by Jean-Antoine Houdon (1741-1828).

For Merrill

Copyright © 1963, 2000 by Merrill Folsom

All rights reserved. No part of this publication may be reproduced, stored in a retrieval system, or transmitted in any form or by any means, electronic, mechanical, photocopying, recording or otherwise, without the prior permission of the copyright owner or the publishers.

ISBN: 8038-9417-1

Printed in Germany
Interior Layout by Susan Winters Graphic Design
Cover by Ziga Design

CONTENTS

FOREWORD

THE LATE MERRILL FOLSOM once wrote of the 'special mansion in the heart of every man' - the privilege to build imaginatively for oneself as the completion of the American dream. With the advance of the new millennium this special dream is still cherished by most Americans; and for many - both men and women alike - it is becoming a reality. A booming economy and growing computer age are largely responsible; it is now even possible to search for homes and obtain a mortgage online. As newspapers indicate, today's creative householders may also purchase thousands of dollars worth of valuable furnishings with the click of a mouse. These new trends mark a major contrast to former years, when the nation's elite made frequent trips abroad to buy furniture, doors, ceilings, artwork, collectibles, and, on rare occasions, the entire home itself. Yet despite the changes that are rapidly occurring in America's style of living, the mansions and plantations of yesterday remain an integral part of our diverse cultural heritage and an everlasting reminder that the best things in this world often begin with years of planning.

The builders of yesterday were of all types and backgrounds. Some were educated and genteel, some were illiterate and uncouth, many were self-made and more than a few were women. A goal that many shared was a desire to impress friends and business rivals with elegance and size, and of course the finest architect money could buy. For the most ambitious, the intention was to leave a legacy for future generations. Marjorie Post spent a lifetime turning her home into a public repository of Russian art, while collector of Americana, Electra Havemeyer Webb, recreated an entire village. Transportation magnate Henry E. Huntington, owner of the largest private library in America, summed up a common attitude when he stated: "The ownership of a fine home, a fine collection and a fine library is the swiftest and surest way to immortality." Today, over 2,000 scholars per year use the Huntington library's research materials - testimony to the late travel magnate's statement.

Not to be forgotten are the architects who brought to fruition the magnificent and original designs of these homes, using the singular opportunities provided them by America's elite to create legends of their own. Richard Morris Hunt (1828-95), considered the nation's most respected architect of the Gilded Age, designed and executed some of the most fabulous mansions in this volume, including the Breakers, Marble House and George Vanderbilt's Biltmore. Most persons of wealth considered a home designed by him to be a badge of social position. Hunt's predecessors were equally creative, particularly Benjamin Latrobe (1766-1820) and Thomas Jefferson (1743-1826), who also happened to be this nation's third President. Long before he drafted the Declaration of Independence, Jefferson, whose lifelong passion was architecture, helped draw up detailed plans to remodel the governor's palace at Williamsburg. His beloved home, Monticello, was a singular achievement sixty years in the making. Women also played a major role in the planning of the nation's great homes. Julia Morgan, who designed the Hearst Castle between 1919-1939, worked eighteen -hour days and left a legacy of over 700 buildings. Isabella Stewart Gardner was principal in overseeing the design of the Gardner Museum in Boston's Fenway Court, and Alva Vanderbilt, wife of George Vanderbilt, worked directly with architects in overseeing the design of Newport's Marble Palace - which under her jurisdiction later became a center for suffragettes.

Amidst a variety of theories, Merrill Folsom once expressed the belief that a true mansion must be "the brick-mortar-and-timber image of a fascinating person or family." In keeping with the original author's viewpoint, Hastings House has been careful to select former homes that are not only large and luxurious, but also contain a unique historical and inspirational element behind them. The choices were difficult, owing to the incorporation of choice pieces from the author's later *More Great American Mansions* (1967) with the finest stories from his first edition. Five new stories have been added: The White House of the Confederacy, Vermont's Shelburne Farms and Shelburne Museum, Tennessee's Belle Meade Plantation (formerly the nation's largest Thoroughbred Stud), and the Lockwood-Matthews Mansion, considered one of Connecticut's most treasured historic sites. Each story is filled with historical drama, with special emphasis on the biographical element that Folsom considered to be of unique importance. All mansions represented in this volume are open to the public, with websites and travel directions provided to the reader.

Le Corbusier, the famous French architect, said "I am like a lightning conductor - I attract storms." So it is with interesting persons in public life, and so it is with pace-setting homes. Thanks to a widely assorted group of benefactors and the ongoing efforts by preservationists, many of the nation's most outstanding mansions have been saved from certain destruction. It is to these spirited individuals whom this volume is finally dedicated, as well as the public who continues to care about its past.

Rachel Borst
Editor

Great American Mansions

and THEIR STORIES

Mosaic decorated Lower Loggia. Decorated by sculptor Karl Bitter (1867-1915), the spacious area was used as an extension of The Breakers living quarters.

A Seventy-Room "Cottage"

The Breakers of Cornelius Vanderbilt

THE MAGNITUDE and the extravagances of Newport as a summer citadel of high society have seldom been approached elsewhere. The fame of the watering place began to grow in 1880 and continued to expand into the 1920s. Mansions of extraordinary size were built, some with the dimensions of railroad terminals, Florentine palaces, English castles and French châteaux. All of them were called "cottages" and were occupied only two months a year. The largest mansion on Newport's sumptuous Bellevue Avenue, the Breakers, epitomizes the architectural extravagance and reckless spending characteristic of this Golden Era, as well as the social supremacy of its inhabitants, the Vanderbilts.

Southern planters started the social rush to Newport, followed by wealthy Bostonians. Then came the Wall Street tycoons and Mrs. John Jacob Astor's famous "four hundred" - literally referring to the number of guests she could fit comfortably into the reception rooms of her New York home. She could handle more at Newport. Social competition was a fact of life in this region, where the prevailing attitude was to live for the moment. Some estates had parties for 3,000 guests, and hundreds of thousands of dollars might be spent for one ball. Powder-haired English butlers in kneebritches would serve ten-course dinners on ornate solid-gold service - with lavish forms of entertainment continuing well into the night.

Among the vanguard of the wealthy elite arriving in Newport were several of the Vanderbilts. They included Cornelius II (1843-99), the favorite grandson of the Commodore, who had founded the family's railroad and steamship fortune in America, and son of William (1821-85), who had greatly enhanced the family fortune. Considered the family patriarch, Cornelius II was the first Vanderbilt to settle in Newport. He bought a previous Breakers, built for tobacconist Pierre Lorillard, in 1878. Designed by Boston architects Robert Swain Peabody and John Goddard Stearns, the mansion's central features were duplicated in a children's cottage which still stands on the grounds today. Cornelius' younger brothers soon followed him to Newport, erecting their own mansions: Rough Point and Marble House, between 1891-1892. Cornelius II summered at his new vacation home with his wife Alice and their children until 1892, when the house was completely destroyed by a kitchen fire. The Vanderbilt family, in residence at the time, barely escaped with their lives.

As his architect for the new "Breakers," Mr. Vanderbilt hired Richard Morris Hunt (1828-95), who had designed several Newport mansions and was widely known as the country's premier architect. After extensive study in Europe, Hunt had come to Newport to visit a brother and had become so fascinated that he remained to play a chief role in replacing wooden mansions with marble and granite palaces. Hunt conceived of the Breakers resembling a Palazzo of the Italian Renaissance period; as models he chose sixteenth-century style villas near Genoa and Turin.

Importing marbles and alabaster from Italy and Africa, Caen stone from France and rare woods and mosaics from five continents, Hunt completed the second Breakers in two years. Although the Vanderbilts had originally requested a two-story villa, the plan was expanded to four stories, perhaps as much to satisfy Hunt's desire to create a great work than to fulfill the family's requirements. The result was a seventy-room cottage with thirty baths. It has thirteen acres of lawns and gardens inside the massive wrought-iron fence that surrounds the estate.

Not a stick of timber was used in the main structure of The Breakers, since Mr. Vanderbilt wanted a house that would be completely fireproof. The walls are of brick, stone and tile. Steel beams support vaulted arches and slabs of marble, mosaic, terrazzo and tile. An enormous heating plant beneath the caretaker's cottage was joined to the basement of the house by a tunnel large enough for a team of horses. Engineers say that even today the house could not have been made more effectively fireproof.

After passing through the ivy-covered porte-cochère, visitors come to massive carved oak front doors that are so carefully balanced that a touch of the finger will move them. Hand-wrought iron doors with glass panels are just inside, providing visitors with a hint of the lavish scale and sumptuous ornamentation of the interior.

Off the entrance hall is the galleried great hall, rising forty-five feet to a decorated ceiling that appears to be a distant, cloud-swept sky. Across the hall is a wall of glass providing an unobstructed view of gardens and the Atlantic. The walls of the other three sides are faced with French Caen stone, a cream-colored limestone that lends itself to decorative carving. Huge fluted pilasters, supporting an ornate cornice, are decorated with oak leaves and acorns in stone, a symbol of the Vanderbilt family found in decorations throughout the estate.

A grand staircase rises from the hall, breaking into two curving sections at the first landing. Wrought-iron and bronze railings, marble columns, fountains and tapestries add to the spectacle. A rare Flemish tapestry produced by Karl van Mander the younger in 1619, is twenty-four by eighteen feet in length. It is illuminated from above by a multi-stained glass skylight thirty-three feet in length, created by American artist John LaFarge (1835-1910). Eight great bronze candelabra are patterned after Italian sixteenth-century originals.

The library in the south wing has panels of Circassian walnut and bas-relief carvings in the style of the High Renaissance. The coffered ceiling and embossed green Spanish leather panels enhance the setting for the Vanderbilts' extensive rare book collection. An antique French fireplace is from the Château d'Arnay-le-Duc and dates from the sixteenth century. Engraved on it is an inscription which is freely translated as: "Little do I care for riches, since only cleverness prevails in the end."

The music room, used for recitals and dancing, was designed by the French architect Richard Bouwens Van der Boyen and executed by Allard and Sons, French cabinetmakers. The paneling, columns, and appointments of this room were made in France and shipped to this country, with French craftsmen accompanying them for installation. The decorations of the morning room were similarly produced and installed.

The dining room is generally considered the most magnificent of the rooms. Said by architects to be as ornate as any in the palaces of Italy and France, it is fifty-eight feet long and rises two stories to a ceiling painting of Aurora, goddess of Dawn. Twelve monolithic shafts of red and cream rose alabaster, topped with gilded bronze Corinthian capitals, support a gold cornice decorated with garlands and masks, which provide a setting for life-size figures carved in the arches of the ceiling. Lighting is provided by two twelve-foot crystal chandeliers and twelve crystal wall sconces. The chandeliers were executed by the French glassmakers Cristalleries Baccarat, an organization founded in 1765. Each is composed of thousands of crystal balls and beads. The mansion was built at a time when electricity was unreliable, so the wall sconces are not only wired for electricity but also piped for gas. The sixteenth-century oak dining room table could be extended to seat up to thirty-four people.

Bright and spacious, the nearby kitchen with its white tile walls was built with no

The Breakers great hall rises forty-five feet and is illuminated from above by a multi-stained glass skylight by artist John LaFarge.

rooms above or around it to reduce the risk of any kitchen fire spreading to the rest of the house. It contains an original wood and coal-burning stove, more than twenty feet in length. In the center of the two-story high space is a long worktable with a zinc-covered top and drawers for utensils along the sides. The original gaslight fixtures and clock are still in place. Glass-fronted cupboards in the kitchen and flower room hold an unusual collection of iron and copper food molds, many of them made in France. A small, cool, north-facing room off the kitchen was used exclusively for pastry-making; its iceboxes and work-places appear just as they did at the turn of the century.

Boston native Ogden Codman (1863-1951), architect and interior decorator to New York and Newport society, planned several of the second and third floor rooms of The Breakers. The restrained elegance of these family bedrooms is representative of the cool, neoclassical style Codman would employ in his book *The Decoration of Houses*, written with novelist Edith Wharton. Each of the tiled bathrooms adjoining the Breakers' bedrooms was provided with hot and cold fresh and salt water, pumped up from the ocean below.

The wrought-iron fence surrounding the grounds is one of the most beautiful examples of ornamental ironwork to be found in the world. Each of the main panels of the fence is thirty-one feet wide and eight feet high. Each panel is located atop a tooled limestone wall four feet high, and between the panels are large limestone pillars. Outstanding features of the fence are iron gates twelve feet high, ornamented with forged clusters of oak leaves, acorns and the monogram "CV." The gates were inspired by earlier ones in Italy.

Located a mile from the mansion are the Vanderbilt stable and carriage hall complex. Before a 1970 fire destroyed an upper story, the brick stables had room for twenty-six horses, a variety of carriages, and guest accommodations. It has since been reopened to the public on weekends in season. A carriage hall has sleighs, victorias, broughams, cabriolets, phaetons, and an omnibus. There are twenty-eight luxury stalls, some monogrammed, as well as displays of coachman's liveries, silver-trimmed harness and garments for horses.

It was perhaps the irony of life that Mr. Vanderbilt, who was a handsome man and full of vitality, could not fully enjoy all that he had created. He suffered a paralytic stroke in 1896 - a year after The Breakers was completed - and died three years later, leaving chairmanship of the New York Central to his brother William. Other tragedies also overtook the family. Their oldest son William Henry II, designated heir to the

The Breakers dining room is generally considered the most magnificent room in the house. The chandeliers were executed by Cristalleries Baccarat, French glassmakers founded in 1765.

family business, died of typhoid fever at the age of twenty-two while a student at Yale; his parents had Vanderbilt Hall built there in his memory. Their daughter Alice Gwynne died of scarlet fever at the age of five. Another son, Alfred, died on the *Lusitania* when it was sunk in World War I.

Of the daughters, Gertrude became Mrs. Henry Payne Whitney, who aided hundreds of New York artists and built the Whitney Art Museum in New York. Gladys, the youngest child, became the Countess Laszló Széchényi. When Mrs. Vanderbilt died at age eighty-nine in 1934, she inherited The Breakers.

In 1948, Countess Széchényi made it possible for the Breakers to be opened to the public as a museum by leasing the house to The Preservation Society of Newport County for a symbolic fee of $1.00 per year. The Countess continued to pay major expenses on the property until her death in 1965. The Preservation Society then leased the house from her heirs, taking on responsibility for taxes and maintenance. In 1973, the Preservation Society purchased The Breakers and its grounds, stables, and greenhouses. In 1995 the mansion celebrated its centennial and was listed as a national historic landmark. Today, it remains Newport's most frequently visited "cottage." Its fascination lays in its history but mainly in its magnificent and imposing presence.

• • • • •

The Breakers is located on Ochre Point Avenue. The mansion is open daily from April through the end of October from 10:00 a.m. to 5:00 p.m. Admission is charged. The stables, open at the same hours from June through Labor Day, charge a $3.50 fee for adults. Children are admitted free. For further information call: (401) 847-1000, or visit The Breakers website at http//www.NewportMansions.org.

Photos courtesy of the Preservation Society of Newport County.

The Shelter of the Publisher and the Show Girl

William Randolph Hearst's La Cuesta Encantada™

SAN SIMEON • CALIFORNIA

When they are buried and their final scores are tallied, few men leave more than a ripple on the surface of life's ocean. William Randolph Hearst was one of the exceptional few to make waves - big ones - primarily in journalism but also in the areas of motion pictures, art collecting and politics. Admired and reviled, the spirit and character of this great man endures in the architectural pile of rock, mortar, and timber that he spent twenty-eight years assembling atop a hill above the once thriving hamlet of San Simeon; located midway between Los Angeles and San Francisco in California's Santa Lucia Mountains.

San Simeon - also known as La Cuesta Encantada and popularly as Hearst Castle -

*Above: At his feudal barony of 250,000 acres, William Randolph Hearst built
La Cuesta Encantada as a personal home.*

is a combination palace-museum that has attracted over twenty-million visitors since it opened to the public in 1958. The famous Mr. Hearst called his vast properties "the ranch." Like a feudal barony, it once sprawled across 250,000 acres of mountains and valleys, an area one-third the size of Rhode Island. Today, the publicly owned property has been whittled down to 137 acres surrounding the estate. An additional thirty acres has been set aside for a visitor center complex at the base of the hill adjacent to state Highway 1. Now anyone may travel to the summit of La Cuesta Encantada and tour San Simeon's 146 rooms.

To comprehend the motivations of Mr. Hearst in building his fantastic castle, one must understand his family background, boundless vitality, enigmatic personality and ceaseless thirst for power. A man who could have led a life of leisure, he vigorously managed a publishing and media empire for sixty-five of his eighty-eight years. He is commonly remembered for fomenting war against Spain at the turn of

Casa del Sol - guest house and garden

the twentieth century, yet he opposed American entry into World War I in 1914 and again in 1939. His publications extolled the virtues of American family life, yet he was estranged from his wife for most of their marriage.

William Randolph Hearst was of Scotch, English and Irish ancestry. He was born on April 29, 1863 in a San Francisco hotel room, near the Barbary Coast's brothels and gambling emporiums. The only child of George and Phoebe Apperson Hearst, his father was a self-made man, whose first fortune came from the silver mines of the Comstock Lode in 1859. An uncouth murderer of syntax who loved gambling, bourbon and chewing tobacco, George Hearst made his fortune in mining and other business enterprises. His frequent travels left the majority of child rearing to his wife Phoebe during his son's formative years.

Mr. Hearst's mother, the former Phoebe Apperson Hearst of Missouri, was gentle, cultured and aristocratic. She was a nineteen-year-old schoolteacher when George, then forty-one, met her while traveling in that state. Pheobe's parents considered him too old and rough-mannered to be an acceptable match for their daughter, so the couple eloped. After traveling to New York and Panama, they chose California as their home. The Hearsts were in their element in early San Francisco, for George Hearst sought economic opportunity as assiduously as Phoebe courted culture. Their son would inherit their determination and love of both worlds in equal measure throughout his life.

The family's wealth allowed Phoebe Apperson Hearst to take her son Willie on two grand traveling tours of Europe by the time he was sixteen. Under his mother's influence, Hearst's fondness for art collecting began at age ten, and came to be a compelling and ultimately indispensable part of his adult life. The records of his purchases as an adult show that over a course of fifty years he spent $50,000,000 on art. This included interior panels, iron gates, tile floors, tapestries, paintings and other objects - largely from castles, monasteries, churches and palaces in Europe. Many of these items are now at La Cuesta Encantada.

In 1882 Will enrolled at Harvard College where he successfully managed the college humor magazine and displayed great interest in entertainment and theater. Will did not devote as much time to his formal studies as he did to his initial exposure to the field of journalism and theater as a contributor to the *Harvard Lampoon* and the Hasty Pudding Club. He was asked to leave Harvard by his junior year.

In 1887 Hearst returned to the West Coast, where his father, then a United States Senator, gave him proprietorship over the *San Francisco Examiner,* an unprofitable Democratic newspaper that he had purchased years earlier. William successfully applied his own enormous energy, his father's substantial financial backing, and the sensational journalistic style of New York publisher George Pulitzer to create the nation's first media conglomerate. In the years following his father's death in 1891, young Hearst proceeded to purchase or begin papers in New York, Chicago, Seattle, Los Angeles, Boston, and twenty other American cities. He further enlarged his publishing empire by buying or founding such magazines as *Motor Connnoisser, Good Housekeeping,* and *Cosmopolitan.*

Hearst did not limit his activities to publishing. In 1902 he sought and won a seat in the House of Representatives, serving two terms. Later political bids for mayor of New York City in 1905 and 1909, the governorship of New York State in 1906 and the presidency in 1908 and 1912, were doomed to failure.

Following this misfortune, Hearst expanded his media empire into cinema, forming a motion production company that would become officially known as Cosmopolitan Productions. Following a separation from his wife in 1925, William moved his studio to California, where along with his new companion, actress Marion Davies, and other stars under Cosmopolitan contract, he forged an alliance with movie mogul Louis B. Mayer of Metro-Goldwyn-Mayer.

Miss Davies, née Marion Douras, was the blond daughter of a minor New York politician, Bernard J. Douras. Born in Brooklyn in 1897, she abandoned her studies for the stage while barely more than a girl. After appearances in two minor stage engagements, she was discovered by theatrical producer Florenz Ziegfield, who put her in the chorus of his Follies of 1917. Apparently it was here that Hearst met her, although there is often debate on this point.

Friends who saw them at La Cuesta Encantada claimed it was one of the great loves of all time and that marriage did not take place only because of Mr. Hearst's inability to divorce his wife. Mr. Hearst's wife, Mrs. Millicent Wilson Hearst, who had been a dancer in Broadway shows before marrying him in 1903, gave birth to five sons. In the years following their public separation, she lived in a palatial New York City apartment as well as another Hearst castle on Long Island - the former home of Mrs. Oliver H.P. Belmont. While feverishly developing La Cuesta Encantada, Mr. Hearst talked to his wife by telephone almost every day. She and her sons sometimes visited there.

Phoebe Apperson Hearst contracted influenza in the worldwide epidemic of 1919 and died in April, leaving the entire Hearst fortune, most of her art collections, and widespread real estate and business holdings to her only child. Those close to him claim that motivation for erection of the castle were forged from the Hearst's desire to combine fine architecture - in this case the architectural style in vogue in California at the time, Mediterranean Revival - with fine art, in a setting that he loved. Indeed, Hearst had many sentimental attachments to this property. He had already spent much of his early youth on this property after his father acquired it in 1870. Early in his marriage, Mr. Hearst took his wife and five sons to the top of the hill on camping trips. The family called the hilltop site Camp Hill.

The building plan of the estate, which Hearst would name La Cuesta Encantada (The Enchanted Hill), resembled that of a Mediterranean town. Features included a broad circular walk, an elaborate garden design featuring terraces, paths and statuary, with a central open space dominated by Casa Grande and three smaller guest houses.

To plan his castle, Hearst retained Julia Morgan, a San Francisco architect, to direct the design and construction of the extraordinary estate that hosted a wide circle of famous guests in the 1920s and 1930s. Born in San Francisco in 1872, Julia was one of the first women to graduate with a degree in civil engineering from the University of California at Berkeley. In 1902, after two attempts by the French to keep her out of the school, Julia became the first female to graduate from the École des Beaux-Arts in Paris - long recognized as one of the finest architectural institutions in the world. She later would open her own office in San Francisco, where many of her clients "were women and institutions for women."

Immersed in her work for over fifty years, Julia Morgan designed and built more than 700 structures-yet she never published any of her designs, declined interviews, and accepted but one honorary degree. In marked contrast to William Randolph Hearst, she was a modest woman who avoided the public spotlight.

Morgan herself hired, oversaw, and paid the many artisans and laborers who worked at San Simeon - sometimes as many as 150. She dealt with stonecasters, ornamental plasterers, woodcarvers, tile designers, tapestry workers, and others. She maintained work on the project until 1947, when illness forced Hearst to leave the estate once and for all. Her obsessive dedication to her profession benefited W.R.

EAU CLAIRE DISTRICT LIBRARY

The Neptune pool took twelve years to perfect. On the pediment of the Greco-Roman temple are statues of Neptune and Nereids.

Hearst, who was also familiar with eighteen-hour days packed with details and decisions. As sources close to the senior Hearst would later reveal, the two "had an extraordinary adventure together."

Early in 1920, Hearst and Morgan had decided that the architecture of the estate would be the soft and graceful Renaissance architecture of Southern Spain. Three palatial guest houses were built first at la Cuesta Encantada; and the large, centrally located main house - the Casa Grande, followed. The guest houses are Casa del Mar, facing the sea; Casa del Monte, facing the mountains; and Casa del Sol, facing the sunrise. La Casa Grande, the centerpiece of San Simeon, was begun in 1922. It was first occupied in 1926, though some later sections were not completed until the 1930s or even at all.

Mr. Hearst's plans for La Casa Grande were so fluid that he sometimes requested changes even after the work had been successfully completed. These included additional wings to the north and the south of the house in 1929, and the addition of a three-lane bowling alley in the basement underneath the movie theater (a change which was never completed). After ordering $25,000 worth of carillon bells for a newly constructed bell tower, Hearst nearly canceled the idea, despite the fact that the imported bells had already arrived in California.

At the time of its completion in 1947, La Casa Grande, San Simeon's main structure, stood 137 feet tall. It would contain approximately 115 rooms, four floors and around 60,000 square feet of space. Julia Morgan's design provided guests with thirty-nine bedrooms, forty-one bathrooms, fifteen sitting rooms, a main library, a mammoth dining hall, thirty fireplaces, a billard room, and a movie theater.

Hearst shared a private suite of rooms located on the third floor with Marion Davies.

The upstairs area of the main house included a relatively small and modestly decorated bedroom for himself, a handsome sitting room overlooking the Pacific, a second bedroom for Davies, and two baths. Directly across the hall is the suitably imposing Gothic Study, the command post of his media empire and repository of his finest books and manuscripts.

Plenty of space was needed for entertaining and most of the downstairs rooms are enormous. A baroque portal stands at the entrance to the Casa Grande and leads across an ancient mosaic to a large main vestibule. In a single sweep guests immediately catch a glimpse of the Assembly room, which includes a French fireplace sixteen feet high, Flemish tapestries, Italian-carved Renaissance choir stalls and ceilings, timeless wall reliefs, bronze and European sculptures.

The vestibule's mosaic floor, portraying "Mermen and Fishes," dates from the third century A.D. Mr. Hearst bought the tile in Rome and sent a crew of Italian artisans to La Cuesta Encantada to lay it. They also worked on the extravagant white and green Neptune Pool, perhaps the most splendid outdoor pool Morgan ever designed. A design which took twelve years to perfect, it was surrounded by statuettes of white marble and a Greco-Roman temple. Artisans were also vital to the Roman pool, a remarkable indoor swimming pool lined with mosaics of tile made from 22-carat hammered gold and delicate Venetian glass. The ideas for this pool came from Morgan.

Wherever a visitor turns in the castle he is confronted with objects of art, some 2,000 years old. One of the most outstanding collections at San Simeon is the Greek vases, which range from early eighth century to the end of the fourth century B.C., and illustrate Greek figure painting at its finest. Upon Hearst's death, the Metropolitan Museum of Art in New York purchased eighty of them - 155 currently remain in the Main Library at La Casa Grande. Within the Assembly Room, the largest of rooms, rare wool

When at San Simeon, W.R. Hearst conducted business from his third-floor Gothic Study. A rare book vault is concealed behind a wall to the right of the photo.

and silk Flemish tapestries by sixteenth-century artist Giulo Romano depict the struggles of Roman general Scipio Africanus during the Punic Wars. A variety of paintings, such as Duccio di Buoninsegna's *Madonna and Child*, Guilio Campi's *Portrait of A Woman*, and other masterpieces are also to be found.

Hearst also collected rare books and manuscripts from abroad. A collection of his once included an Egyptian papyrus manuscript of *The Book of the Dead* (circa 600 B.C.), the largest collection of letters and documents related to the Revolutionary War, as well as dozens of illuminated manuscripts from thirteenth-century Flanders and sixteenth-century France, Italy, and Spain. The library still houses a large literary collection related to Charles Dickens, Hearst's favorite author, and signed copies of novels and autobiographies by Edna Ferber, Somerset Maugham, H.G. Wells, Faith Baldwin and others who contributed pieces to his magazines or visited San Simeon.

Mr. Hearst's passion for exotic beauty extended far outside of the interior of his estate. The gardens of the castle have flowers and trees from many parts of the world. Drives are lined with citrus and there are plantings of pomegranate, oleander, acacia, and eucalyptus as well as tangelo lime, lemon, grapefruit, and tangerine trees. There is a mile-long pergola espaliered with grapevines and fruit trees. Thirty-three Italian cypress trees, twenty-eight to thirty feet tall, were brought across the mountain from Paso Robles and planted because Mr. Hearst hated to see them cut down to make room for a housing development.

At peak operation, five greenhouses designed by Julia Morgan were in use. Since Hearst liked to see a complete change of garden for each season, three gardeners were devoted to the propagation of 700,000 annuals year-round. Even this did not satisfy each season's need, so extra orders were filled from nurseries within the San Francisco Bay area.

The zoo of La Cuesta Encantada once contained one of the largest wild animal collections in the world. In it were zebras, gnus, seven varieties of deer, bison, elephants, tigers, leopards, lions, llamas, ostriches, yaks, chimpanzees, kangaroos, and antelopes. A separate section was reserved for 1,500 birds. Although most of the animals have been sold, the estate still maintains some aoudads, zebras, bobcats, red-tail fox and deer.

Guests of Mr. Hearst who experienced this splendor included Sir Winston Churchill, George Bernard Shaw, Calvin Coolidge, Aldous Huxley and Amelia Earhart. On all occasions the Casa Grande and its three satellite houses were ready for the arriving celebrities. Maids and valets greeted them- even at late hours. Guests were free to motor up to San Simeon themselves. They could also fly to Hearst's private airstrip or feel free to use his private train- complete with chef, kitchen, dining room and club car. When Eleanor Medill (Cissy) Patterson, one of his favorite newspaperwomen, arrived on her own special train, he had a brass band waiting for her.

Mr. Hearst, who loved youth and glamour, also sought the company of movie folk. Invitations to San Simeon, located just 250 miles north of the Hollywood studios, were the aspiration of most in the film colony. Some were hired to perform in pictures with Miss Davies. A few luminaries who were often invited included Louis B. Mayer, Sam Goldwyn, Flo Ziegfeld, Jack and Henry Warner, Sonja Henie, Claudette Colbert, Ginger Rogers and Fred Astaire, Errol Flynn, Bing Crosby, Clark Gable, Ava Gardner and Gary Cooper. They were free to spend the weekend - with pools, tennis courts, bridle paths and a zoo at their disposal.

While on his travels inside and outside the castle, Mr. Hearst always had a telephone close at hand. Eighty telephones were strategically placed in rooms, in the gardens, at the swimming pools, and at the tennis court. The switchboard had three operators and was open twenty-four hours a day. Visitors were free to do as they pleased throughout the day but at 7:00 p.m. they were expected to be in the Assembly Room to greet Mr. Hearst when he came down from the Gothic Suite on a small elevator and entered from an unobtrusive door half hidden in the paneling. The guests were permitted one cocktail before dinner. Mr. Hearst, although not a teetotaler, disapproved of heavy drinking and imposed limits - largely to keep Marion free from temptation. Those who over-imbibed would find their bags packed and taken to the door. Actor Errol Flynn and author Dorothy Parker were but two visitors who were "sent down the Hill."

Dinner generally was served at 9:00 p.m. with Hearst on one side of the long table and Miss Davies opposite him. Printed menus permitted a choice of food and listed the movies to be shown that night. The table and the china were elegant but the table bore only paper napkins and plain bottles of mustard, ketchup and pickles - treasured reminders of Hearst's camping days on the hill.

After dinner, everyone was invited to the movie theater. Hearst sat in the front row with Marion Davies, a telephone beside him, where motion pictures not yet available to the public could garner some early publicity among Hollywood's elite. Following these occasions, Hearst would retreat upstairs to the Gothic Study to work until 3:00 or 4:00 a.m. - telephoning publishers throughout the country as he wrote some of the editorials that were to be printed the next day. Miss Davies often joined him there, since he appreciated her opinions and outlook on world problems.

In 1947, Mr. Hearst's doctor advised him to leave the altitude and problems of La Cuesta Encantada for a simpler place due to heart problems. Ms. Davies bought for $120,000 a Spanish stucco house on eight acres in Beverly Hills and she and Mr. Hearst moved into it. He remained there until his death in 1951 at the age of eighty-eight.

The bulk of Mr. Hearst's personal estate and his interest in the multi-million dollar Hearst publishing empire were left to his wife, sons and charitable trusts. However, La Cuesta Encantada was soon found by heirs to be something of a drain on the pocketbook. In his will Hearst had suggested that it be given to the University of California as a memorial to his mother, but the regents of the University looked askance at the idea because of operating costs.

In 1954 the Hearst sons invited Goodwin Knight, at that time the governor of California, to spend a weekend at the castle and talk about methods of transferring the property to the state. Knight finally referred the problem to Newton B. Drury, the

The Assembly Room at Christmas. The room has antique choir stalls, Flemish tapestries and a ceiling from Europe.

state Director of the Division of Beaches and Parks. Drury advocated the property's acquisition by the state; the California park commissioners and legislators took a look at it and in 1957 it was voted into the state park system with only two legislators objecting. The public immediately clamored for a chance to see the castle. In 1976 the U.S. Department of the Interior designated La Cuesta Encantada a National Historic Landmark. It was thus enrolled in the National Register of Historic Places. San Simeon remains today a lasting and unique tribute to the collaboration of architect Julia Morgan and her best-known client, William Randolph Hearst.

• • • • •

The Hearst San Simeon Historical Monument™, as La Cuesta Encantada is officially known, is located near California Highway 1 and is open from 8:20 a.m. to 3:20 p.m. daily except Christmas, Thanksgiving and New Year's Day. There are four daytime tours and one evening tour available in the Spring and Fall. For further information contact the Hearst information line at: (800)444-4445 or visit their website at http://www.hearstcastle.org.

Photos courtesy of Hearst Castle™/Hearst San Simeon State Historical Monument™

A Blue Ridge Château

George W. Vanderbilt's Biltmore

ASHEVILLE • NORTH CAROLINA

A FRENCH RENAISSANCE château of 250 rooms in the Blue Ridge Mountains, Biltmore Estate was begun by George Washington Vanderbilt - youngest grandson of the Commodore - when he was a twenty-six year old bachelor. Motivated by family competition and a keen sense of enterprise - his vision for a country retreat and show-case soon evolved into the largest private residence in America.

On emigrating to America from Holland around 1650, the family changed its name to Vanderbilt. Biltmore derived its name from Bildt, the town in the Netherlands whence the van der Bildts had come, and "more," an English word for rolling, upland country. Visitors there today still find it a fairyland principality with a strange

Biltmore 19

The library at Biltmore contains more than 10,000 books which George W. Vanderbilt really read. A spiral staircase leads to the balcony.

Graustarkian flavor of grandeur, romance and adventure.

The ambitious Vanderbilt had plenty to plan his dream with - namely grounds of 125,000 acres. The family has now disposed of the majority of property, leaving 8,000 acres. The shortest drive from the massive front gates to the residence is still more than three miles long, circling through a carefully land-scaped wonderland of majestic conifers, hardwoods, rhododendrons and 40,000 azaleas of 500 different varieties.

Asheville was a popular health resort in the late nineteenth century, when train service brought tourists into the southern Appalachians to enjoy the mineral springs, fresh air, and pleasant climate. When George first visited the area in 1888 with his mother, he was captivated by the rugged beauty of the rural region and found it the perfect setting for a new home. He had a lively imagination and millions of dollars to implement his wishes. The nucleus of the family fortune had been gained from transportation by George's grandfather, Commodore Cornelius Vanderbilt. It had been increased many-fold by the varied enterprises of William Henry Vanderbilt, a son of the Commodore and the father of George. All the Vanderbilts were builders; but George, in addition, was a scholar and the only non-businessman of the clan.

Forsaking New York and Newport society, George Vanderbilt assembled the Biltmore acreage. Construction of Biltmore got under way in 1889; it was a massive undertaking that included a mansion, gardens, farm, and woodlands. Construction would require a thousand artisans, from local laborers who earned fifty cents a day to acclaimed craftsmen, such as the Viennese sculptor Karl Bitter (1867-1915). A rail line was installed to expedite delivery of supplies, while an on-site kiln and wood-working factory were created to produce bricks and process oak and walnut for floors and paneling.

George Vanderbilt conceived his new mansion on a scale and to a plan reminiscent of vast baronies erected in Europe hundreds of years earlier. Celebrated architect

Richard Morris Hunt drew as his inspiration the richly ornamented style of the French Renaissance for the exterior, while the rooms of the interior are based in upon an eclectic variety of European architectural tradition. George was also influenced by his family's tradition of extravagant homes and by the 3,500-acre model farm, called Shelburne Farms, that his sister Lila had constructed in 1886 with her husband, William Seward Webb.

Mr. Vanderbilt had a reading knowledge of eight languages, traveled extensively throughout the world, and was a student of architecture. His friend, Richard Morris Hunt, had studied at the École des Beaux Arts in Paris and had been a founder and president of the American Institute of Architects. Hunt had built several fine mansions at Newport, office buildings in New York and university structures for Yale and Princeton.

Frederick Law Olmsted, a master of natural landscape architecture, was hired to lay out the grounds of the estate; he had designed New York's Central Park, other public parks and several university campuses, including Stanford University. Chauncey Delos Beadle was superintendent of Biltmore for sixty years and developed the gardens. Gifford Pinchot, later governor of Pennsylvania, directed the reafforestation of Biltmore's woodlands.

The French châteaux of Chambord, Chenonceaux and Blois inspired the architecture of Biltmore but many of Mr. Vanderbilt's own ideas also were incorporated in the structure. While the walls were rising he traveled widely in Europe to buy paintings, tapestries, sculptures, porcelains, woodwork, an entire palace ceiling canvas and other objects. The rooms at Biltmore were designed to accommodate them.

In 1895 Biltmore formally opened with a big Christmas party at which Mr. Vanderbilt's mother presided. It was the first of many gala affairs on the Estate, which played host to such luminaries as the novelists Edith Wharton and Henry James, as well as the society painter John Singer Sargent. When George later married, he brought his bride, the former Edith Stuyvesant Dresser of New York, to the mansion. Their only child, Cornelia (1900-76), was born and grew up at Biltmore.

Adjacent to the Biltmore tract was the nearby small town of Best, which George purchased in 1889 and renamed Biltmore Village. Originally populated by local farmers, Mr. Vanderbilt enlarged the town over the next twelve years to include a school, a hospital, a church, shops and cottages outfitted with plumbing and heating, as well as a railroad station for the families. He also introduced innovative farming techniques to the area and gave jobs to most of the men, some of whose descendants still work on the estate. The village that Mr. Vanderbilt constructed for his employees has now been absorbed by Asheville.

As the years passed by the estate grew increasingly productive. The farms yielded meat and dairy products, fruits and vegetables and honey from forty-one beehives. The nearby forest produced over 3,000 cords of firewood annually which were processed at Biltmore's own mill. And a 300-acre nursery offered for sale about five million plants - one of the most complete stocks in the country until it was destroyed by flood in 1916.

The Rose Garden, in front of the Conservatory at Biltmore, contains thousands of rose bushes and vines.

George was actively involved with the operation of Biltmore until his unexpected death in March, 1914 following an emergency appendectomy in Washington, D.C. Following his untimely death, part of the estate was sold to the national government for the Pisgah National Forest. Other parts were converted into modern home sites and a long stretch was used for the Blue Ridge Parkway. In 1925, his widow Edith married Senator Peter G. Gerry of Rhode Island and moved to that state. When daughter Cornelia married John Francis Amherst Cecil of London in 1924, Biltmore became their official residence. Acting on a request by the city of Asheville to revitalize the Depression- ridden local economy with tourism, Mr. and Mrs. Cecil opened the estate to the public in March, 1930.

Mr. Cecil, a son of Baroness Amherst of Hackney and Lord William Cecil, had been the First Secretary of the British Embassy in Washington and was eleven years his wife's senior. They produced two heirs, George Henry Vanderbilt Cecil and William Anherst Vanderbilt Cecil, who were born on the Estate in 1925 and 1928. Together, these two men would be responsible for the successful large-scale preservation of Biltmore in recent times as full owners of the estate.

Following a separation from her husband, Cornelia Vanderbilt-Cecil went to London in 1932, taking her two sons with her. She obtained a Paris divorce soon after. Fifteen years later she married a British bank clerk, and they lived unpretentiously together in London's staid Kensington Square. The sons served in the British Royal Navy in World War II. Biltmore House also served in the war: its huge music room was used as a secret storage vault for paintings from the bomb-threatened National Gallery of Art in Washington.

Cornelia's father left her $5,000,000, and asked that she spend at least one-half of every year in the mansion, but Mrs. Cecil relinquished her interest in Biltmore after she chose England as her home. The estate is now managed by a board of directors, of which Cornelia's son William A.V. Cecil serves as chairman. His son, Bill Cecil Jr., is currently CEO and president of The Biltmore Company and Biltmore Estate Wine Company, which has become the most visited wine-making facility in America.

Visitors to Biltmore House are vividly reminded of the glorious gilded age. More than ninety rooms, faithfully preserved and filled with thousands of original furnishings, suggest that the Vanderbilts are still in residence. Biltmore is particularly memorable in winter-each Christmas season nearly forty trees decorate the interior.

The Winter Garden is a sunken area of marble with glass roofs near the entrance hall; in all seasons it is filled with palms and bright flowers, many of which come from

The 102-step Grand Staircase rises four floors. The 1,700 pound chandelier in the center hangs from one pin.

Biltmore's own greenhouses. Complementing the garden setting is a marble fountain with a bronze statue of a boy with geese by Karl Bitter, the now-famous Viennese sculptor and carver who had just arrived in this country at the time Biltmore was started.

Paintings by Whistler, Renoir, Sargent, Zorn and Zuloaga are among the art masterpieces adorning the mansions walls. At all locations throughout Biltmore House, portraits of family members may be found, including works commissioned by John Singer Sargent (1856-1925) and Giovanni Boldini (1842-1931), an Italian artist of international renown in the late nineteenth century. An ivory chess set that Napoleon Bonaparte used while imprisoned on St. Helena is displayed in the salon on the main floor. Other furnishings include an 800 B.C. Chou dynasty sacrificial vessel, rare Persian rugs, exquisite Wedgwood china, Dürer prints, Spanish and Italian chests, sixteenth-century tapestries and French walnut library panels.

A massive stone spiral staircase comprising 102 steps rises four floors. The grand staircase is a copy of the famous one in the Château de Blois, except that it spirals in the opposite direction from the original. It has no side supports as it winds around a gigantic 1,700 pound wrought-iron chandelier that is seven stories high and is said to be the largest one in the world suspended from a single iron pin.

Biltmore's library shelves hold more than 10,000 books, many of them with valuable leather bindings and some containing original documents. An avid reader and book lover, George acquired an original collection of 23,000 books in eight languages during his lifetime. The ceiling painting of this room was acquired from the ballroom of the Pisani Palace located in Venice, Italy. Attributed to Giovanni Antonio Pellegrini (1675-1741), the sixty-four foot long masterpiece is considered allegorical; and resembles a ceiling still in the Palazzo Labia of Venice. A circular staircase in the library leads to an attractive balcony, and adjacent to the library is a private room to which Mr. Vanderbilt retreated for study and meditation.

In keeping with George Vanderbilt's vision, Biltmore, which was named a National Historic Landmark in 1963, is entirely self-sustaining, receiving neither government subsidies nor private grants. Its operations and preservation efforts are supported by a variety of ventures, including farming, wine production, The Biltmore Estate Collection (a line of reproduction furnishings available for sale), and guest admissions. The estate maintains a staff of over 1,000 employees. Although figures vary somewhat, the estate attracts around 900,000 visitors per year from all parts of the world.

• • • • •

Biltmore Estate is open to the public from 9:00 a.m. to 5:00 p.m. every day of the year except Thanksgiving and Christmas. The gates of the estate are located on U.S. Highway 25, accessed from exit 50 or 50B off Interstate 40. For ticket information, call (800) 543-2961, or visit the website at http://www.biltmore.com.

The Most Revered House in America

George Washington's Mansion House Farm

MOUNT VERNON • VIRGINIA

GEORGE WASHINGTON WAS described in Congress by Henry "Light Horse Harry" Lee, as the man who was "first in war, first in peace, and first in the hearts of his countrymen." Although his remarkable military and political accomplishments made him the most eminent American figure of the eighteenth century, Washington preferred private life at Mount Vernon to public life. As the place he called home, this elegant Georgian-style home on the banks of the Potomac River served as his refuge throughout active years of duty in two wars, a seat in the House of Burgesses, and two terms as the first president of the United States. Now more than a million visitors a year come to tour the house, gardens and lawns, enjoy the panoramic views and learn things about the

Father of His Country that they never took time to understand.

The territory comprising Mount Vernon had long been held in the Washington family's name. George Washington's great-grandfather was a pioneer settler of the Northern Neck (the area between the Potomac and the Rappahannock rivers). The 5,000-acre estate was part of a family grant to Washington's great-grandfather, John. Washington's father, Augustine, built a house on it. In 1843, Washington's elder half-brother, Lawrence, also built a house for his bride, Anne Fairfax. He named it Mount Vernon (after British Admiral Edward Vernon, under whom he served in the Caribbean). George went to live there at the age of sixteen. When Lawrence died of tuberculosis in 1752, the estate went to his wife and daughter, but Lawrence's widow vacated

The founders of the nation sat on this piazza, an innovation that entitles Washington to a niche in the architectural world.

the property and George Washington gained clear title to it in 1761.

During forty-five years of ownership, George Washington tirelessly devoted much energy to the enlargement, adornment, and management of his estate. Mount Vernon was subject to a great deal of architectural change throughout his tenancy there. What began as a modest one and one-half story farmhouse kept growing in size, as its owner did in physical and political stature. Now - as when Washington was there - the mansion contains eighteen main rooms and fourteen auxiliary buildings, including the kitchen, wash house, and other dependencies.

From 1752-1758, George Washington's military career, as aide to General Edward Braddock and as colonel of the Virginia regiment, permitted only infrequent visits to Mount Vernon. During this period the plantation was managed with the assistance of his younger brother, John Augustine. George's marriage to Martha Dandridge Custis in January 1759 meant that he would need to enlarge the house for his family. Between 1757 and 1759, Washington's workers carried out several major construction projects, including raising the house to a full two and one-half stories, putting on a new roof, reinforcing the foundations, adding weather-boarding, and plastering the upstairs chamber.

Mount Vernon became- and still is - one of the most distinguished examples of Colonial architecture. The indications are that Washington himself was largely responsible for the basic design as now presented. Architecture was not a common profession in his day and the property owner often did his own planning. Washington was apparently influenced in this manner by several colonial structures such as the Governor's Palace at Williamsburg, as well as English books of architecture found in his library. Tools and hardware used in building the mansion were imported from England.

All the cooking at Mt. Vernon was done in the kitchen house, near the mansion. An oven is located to the right of the fireplace.

During the time he began to alter the appearance of the house Washington acquired new furnishings to accord with the latest architectural fashions. Orders to agents in London requested beds, "a doz. Best mahogany Gothik back" chairs, and tables for the larger house; in addition to silver, glass, ceramics, prints, rugs and window hangings. Visits to nearby plantations such as Belvoir and Gunston Hall as well as his own travels to colonial capitals helped Washington to keep abreast of evolving trends.

The relative economic success of this plantation and awareness of his increasingly prominent position among the colonial gentry led Washington to initiate another major construction phase in 1774. He undertook additional rooms to the north and south of the house, the decoration of the family dining room, and the construction of

The Little Parlor contains the English harpsichord of Nelly Custis, Washington's youngest granddaughter, and a member of the Mount Vernon household from childhood.

the piazza. Although he also had expectations of early retirement, Washington's hopes would be denied. The beginning of the Revolutionary War abruptly took him away from Mount Vernon in 1775 and the management of the construction fell to his distant cousin and trusted friend Lund Washington. George returned to his plantation only once during the next eight years.

Despite Washington's affection for Mount Vernon, he was ready to sacrifice it to the cause of the American Revolution. While the general was at war, the British man-of-war *Savage* anchored offshore the Potomac demanding provisions, in return for which the property would be spared. In his absence, Washington was horrified to learn that his estate manager had gone onboard the ship and met their demands, and that, in addition, twenty servants had been carried off. Washington wrote back angrily: "This will be a precedent for others… It would have been a less painful circumstance to me…that in consequence to your noncompliance with their request, they had burnt my House, and laid the Plantation in ruins."

Upon Washington's triumphant return to private life in 1783, most of the planned work to the mansion had been completed, including the addition of a private study and master bedroom, the addition of a piazza, and the paneling of the small dining room. Only the "new room," or large dining, room remained unfinished. While construction was proceeding, Washington received a marble chimney piece from admirer Samuel Vaughan. Washington feared that it was "too costly by far, I fear for my own room and republican style of living." Nevertheless it was installed, thereby setting the tone for the neoclassical embellishments of this room, including the magnificent "Venetian" window. Two years later, Washington had a cupola placed on top of the roof and crowned it with an ornate "dove of peace."

One of the dominant features of the mansion - and perhaps the most copied feature in new houses of Colonial design - is the high-columned piazza that extends across the front, overlooking the Potomac. This piazza was an innovation when first built and it entitles Washington to a niche in the architectural world.

The large dining room was built during the Revolution by Lund Washington, who had been managing the mansion in Washington's absence. Detailed directions for its construction were written by the General while he was entrenched at Harlem Heights in New York and various other headquarters where he was stationed during the war. It was in this room that Washington received Charles Thomson in April 1789; Thomson having been delegated to inform Washington that he had been unanimously elected to the presidency of the newly formed United States. The new President barely had time to enjoy the completed state of his home before departing for New York and later Philadelphia.

The mansion's first floor contains a center hall, a little parlor, a formal parlor, a study, a small family dining room and a downstairs bedroom. Twenty-five to thirty-five percent of the present furnishings were Washington's and the percentage steadily increases. Original family portraits and landscapes, original sideboards and desks, a key to the Bastille given by the Marquis de Lafayette, Nelly Custis' English harpsichord, china, silver, and hundreds of other items are displayed. An exhaustive search for original objects based on early documents, photographs, and oral traditions has led to the discovery of many items in public and private collections.

Five bedrooms on the second floor include George Washington's, which contains the bed in which he died in 1799. The bed appears to be unusually short because of its exceptional width and height, but actually it is six-feet-six inches long. Washington was six-feet-two inches tall, and at the age of fifty-four, weighed 190 pounds. He was sixty-seven at the time of his death.

The harmonious union of architecture and furnishings within the mansion was further reinforced by careful manipulation of the natural elements in the surrounding landscape. While Washington contemplated changes to the mansion in the 1750s, he also began an ambitious redesign of the property that he had inherited. He first removed four dependency buildings radiating from the entrance to the mansion, replacing them with a servants' quarters and a kitchen, which he built perpendicular to the house. A lane running between these buildings serviced an increasing number of "outbuildings," including a greenhouse; servants' quarters; blacksmith shop; spinning house; salt house; gardener's house; storehouse; smokehouse; wash house; a stable; a carpenter shop; and a dung repository. These structures were essential in supporting the self-sufficiency of the plantation.

Beyond these buildings, Washington developed an ornamental landscape. He transformed the lane intersecting the mansion into an expansive lawn, or bowling green; a planted "wilderness" of trees and shrubs outlined and defined it. Serpentine paths flanking the lawn were laid out leading to the house's west entrance. A narrow, elliptically-shaped pleasure garden and kitchen garden were also installed on either side of the lawn. Washington cultivated an unencumbered view of the Potomac River and the Maryland shore through clever landscaping and the planting of a hanging garden on a steep slope leading to the river. The result of his landscaping efforts resulted in a unified and visually regular configuration still apparent today.

Despite the fact that public duty took Washington away from his home off and on for twenty-three years, he is still considered one of the most progressive farmers in eighteenth-century America. He was continuously experimenting with a variety of farming techniques, desiring to set a standard for farmers across the country. In an effort to gain economic success in agriculture, Washington tried raising a number of products, including tobacco, wheat and mixed grains. In addition he operated a fishery, produced cloth and developed plantation crafts, including carpentry, cooperage, and blacksmithery. A model of self-sufficiency, Mount Vernon also grew and manufactured its own cotton, wool, and silk products; corn and wheat was raised and milled, tobacco grown and cured, wine pressed and whiskey distilled. Washington was able to achieve these lofty ends largely through his ability to avoid dependency on the failing system of transatlantic trade. Indeed he once stated proudly in 1789: "I use no porter or cheese in my family, but such as is made in America."

George Washington's successful transformation of Mount Vernon from a modest holding to a sprawling plantation did not, however, prepare for the decades ahead. On December 14, 1799, the former President died suddenly of a throat infection in the privacy of his upstairs bedchamber. He was buried - at his request - three days later in the family vault a short distance from the mansion. Mount Vernon then entered the custody of his widow Martha until her death shortly after in 1802. In accordance with the terms of his will, George's nephew Bushrod Washington inherited the mansion and approximately 4,000 acres of surrounding land. Some of Washington's servants and slaves, manumission of whom he had favored since the 1770s, were also freed. A series of auctions at Mount Vernon following Martha's death resulted in the dispersion of most of the furnishings that Washington had accumulated during nearly half a century.

Mt. Vernon's banquet hall has a Palladian window. The wall decorations resemble Wedgewood pottery. The furniture was Washington's.

Under Bushrod Washington's management - an Associate Justice of the Supreme Court who had little interest in agronomy- the mansion and its farms fell into a severe decline. Upon his death in 1829, Bushrod bequeathed the remainder of the estate to his nephew, John Augustine Washington, who survived him by only three years. The latter's widow possessed Mount Vernon until 1850, until it became the property of her son John Augustine Washington, Jr., the last Washington to own the estate. The unfortunate heir had little time to enjoy his new fortune before his death in an early skirmish of the Civil War.

Unchecked deterioration of the plantation resulted in the immediate decision by John A. Washington, Jr. to sell Mount Vernon. After both the federal government and the Commonwealth of Virginia refused the burden of restoring and maintaining it, preservation fell upon the newly established Mount Vernon Ladies' Association of the Union. Between 1853 and 1858 this energetic organization, under the inspired leadership of Ann Pamela Cunningham and orator Edward Everett, raised the $200,000 necessary to purchase the estate.

Since then, the Mount Vernon Ladies' Association, the oldest historic preservation organization in the nation, has served as the faithful steward of George Washington's historic estate and gardens. Miss Cunningham's injunction to "see to it that you keep [Mount Vernon] the home of Washington" has inspired the Association's mission to preserve the estate. Over past decades, such notable philanthropists as Phoebe Apperson Hearst, J.P. Morgan, Henry Ford, and Thomas Edison have recognized the merit of this activity through ingenious forms of benevolence. J.P. Morgan and his son donated Washington's dress and sash, Henry Ford gave motor-driven fire-fighting apparatus to the estate, and Thomas Edison designed a power system for its buildings. Today, individuals and foundations also support a growing number of educational programs associated with the mansion. "I have no objection," wrote Washington in 1794, "to any sober or orderly person's gratifying their curiosity in viewing the buildings, Gardens &c about Mount Vernon."

• • • • •

George Washington's Mount Vernon Estate & Gardens, is located approximately 16 miles from Washington, D.C., at the southern terminus of the George Washington Memorial Parkway. Mount Vernon welcomes visitors every day of the year. For further information call: 703-780-2000 for visitation hours, a listing of special events and programs as well as admission fees, or visit the mansion website at http://www. mountvernon.org.

Photos courtesy of the Mt. Vernon's Ladies Association

"Vermont's Smithsonian"

The Shelburne Museum

AT FIRST GLANCE, the Shelburne Museum appears to be a particularly well-preserved Vermont town. A covered bridge leads to a cluster of houses and barns; nearby buildings include a meeting house, schoolhouse and general store. A closer look, however, reveals such unexpected sights as a covered bridge, a landlocked lighthouse, and the steamboat *Ticonderoga*, relocated from Lake Champlain to become the centerpiece of the museum. The museum is now home to some 80,000 objects which span three centuries.

It was not just coincidence that Vermont was chosen to be the home to Shelburne Museum. The site's founder, Electra Havemeyer Webb, said the happiest times of her life were spent here, and she wanted to use her collections of art and Americana to "do something special for the people of Vermont." Born in 1888, Electra was the third child of millionaire H.O. Havemeyer, the so-called "Sugar King." Electra frequently traveled as a child with her parents to Europe as they built their fabulous collections of European and Impressionist art, Asian textiles, bronzes and ceramics; which they eventually donated to the Metropolitan Museum of Art in 1929.

Electra began her own art collection at the age of eighteen, soon after the death of her father. Few Americans would have shared her conviction that she had "bought a work of art" when a transition from classical interests led to the acquisition of her first piece of Americana in 1907, a cigar store figure of a native American woman, covered with layers of paint now worn and faded from years of weathering. Electra Havemeyer was one of the few people who appreciated such pieces, both for their aesthetic strength and because they embodied a link to America's vanishing handicraft traditions.

In 1910, Electra married J. Watson Webb, the eldest son of retired railroad executive William Seward Webb, whose wife Lila was a Vanderbilt. The Webbs did not collect art, but were known for elegant entertaining at their magnificent 4,000-acre Vermont country seat, Shelburne Farms. Although reputed to be a bit intimidated by her future in-laws, Electra had an ebullient side to her nature and was able to balance her artistic nature with the Webbs' enthusiasm for sports, hunting and the countryside.

For thirty-five years following her marriage, Electra led a busy life raising five children and managing households in Vermont, Long Island and New York City. Her interests were wide ranging; in addition to collecting Americana, she loved the outdoors. The family summered in the Adirondacks, and sometimes traveled as far as Alaska and Scotland to hunt big game. In World War I, Electra contributed to the War effort by driving ambulances in New York City, only a short time after the birth of her four children between 1910 and 1916. In 1942, she joined the Civilian Defense Volunteer Organization and eventually became Director of Blood Donor Development in New York. Despite her outside concerns, however, Electra's wish from early in her marriage was to start a museum.

Over the years, Electra's collection of antiques and Americana grew far beyond the necessity of furnishing her home. All available space was soon crammed with antiques and folk art, including the attic, a tennis court building, and soon an entire tennis court. Electra justified this later by saying: "... I just couldn't let good pieces go by... pottery, pewter, glass, dolls. Quilts, cigar store Indians, eagles, folk art. They all seemed to appeal to me."

Family tradition encouraged her desire to share her collections with the public. . Electra's mother, Louisine Havemeyer had once told her children, ". . . remember how blessed you are, and if opportunity ever offers, equalize the sum of human happiness, and share the sunshine that you have inherited." Mother and daughter did not however, share the same tastes in art. After one visit to her daughter's crowded home early in Electra's marriage, she exclaimed: "How can you, Electra, you who have been brought up with Rembrandts and Manets, live with such American trash?"

The steamboat Ticonderoga, c. 1906, and Colchester Reef Lighthouse, c. 1871.

In 1947, when her husband's retirement enabled them to make Vermont their principal residence, Electra Webb was at long last able to fulfill her dream of creating a museum. The catalyst which launched the project was the need to find a new home for a collection of carriages which had belonged to her father-in-law, William Seward Webb. As Electra told the story years later, "I couldn't bear to have those carriages go, and so I said, "Would you consider giving them to me if I had a piece of property and kept them in Shelburne where they could be seen by others and not go away from Shelburne? And they were all delighted...Now that was the spark that lit my fire and I had my opening. And that was the start of Shelburne Museum. I had dreamed of it all these years, but not until [then] had I been able to explain what I wanted to do. . . Well, from then on, there was no stopping me."

Electra Webb began a search in the village of Shelburne for property where she could house the twenty-eight carriages, sleighs and wagons from the Webb estate. Yet she also had her own collections in mind and so decided to seize an opportunity with the purchase of an eight-acre parcel of land-complete with farmhouse-near the town center. In May of 1947, a crew was hired to begin work on the museum's first building, a Horseshoe Barn, to hold the carriages. Electra never feared the incongruous; she saw the old barns, houses and public buildings of the Lake Champlain region as the perfect setting for her collections. During the this early period in the museum's history she rescued a two-lane covered bridge, a lighthouse that had once crowned a reef in Lake Champlain, a jailhouse and even an old 220-seat paddle wheeler, the

Ticonderoga. Long in service on Lake Champlain, the historic piece was now threatened with abandonment.

Of all her purchases, purchase of the *Ticonderoga*, was the most troublesome to Electra. She was certain her husband would disapprove highly of the expensive purchase and worried greatly about his response. Over breakfast one morning Mr. Webb's awaited reply was alarmingly casual: "I don't know that's so bad…a lot of other stuff you bought is much worse." Extensive planning followed his approval, and the boat was moved two miles overland to its current berth on museum grounds. Declared a National Historic Landmark in 1960, the *Ticonderoga* now stands near the entrance.

The museum opened to the public in 1952 after years of exhaustive planning and legal negotiations. It contained ten buildings filled with carriages and sleighs, quilts, dolls, toys, folk sculpture and furniture. By 1960, eighteen buildings had been moved to the grounds. Other buildings have since been constructed to serve the specialized needs of the collections. Following Electra Webb's death in that year, her son, James Watson Webb, Jr., assumed leadership of the museum. Over the next seventeen years he expanded the scope of the collections and oversaw the addition of nineteen new exhibition buildings, which continue to grow through gifts and purchases.

Architectural diversity is echoed and amplified within the museum's thirty-seven buildings. Buildings dating from the eighteenth century to the present house a variety of folk sculpture, practical items, and household goods; including quilts, costumes, and handmade rugs. The Hat and Fragrance Textile Gallery, donated to the

Kirk Brothers Circus, c. 1910-1956. Handcarved and painted by Edgar Kirk.

museum in 1947, was originally constructed as a Vermont distillery around 1800. It contains Electra Webb's outstanding collection of hatboxes. Four one-story rooms were added in 1950 to provide additional space for her collections. Electra's interest in textiles extends itself to the viewer in the Weaving Shop, built for the museum in 1955. Here, craftspeople demonstrate the complete process of transforming raw wool and flax into woven cloth using historic spinning wheels and looms.

A select group of buildings recreate lost eighteenth and nineteenth century village culture, with heavy emphasis on mercantile life. The Apothecary Shop, constructed on site in 1959, contains dried herbs, spices, drugs, and labeled glass bottles of an earlier period, as well as professional tools common to a druggists's shop between 1870 and 1900. The fully stocked General Store, originally constructed in 1840, contains a post office, barber shop, and tap room. The museum also features an eighteenth-century sawmill, complete with waterwheel, a blacksmith shop (built circa 1800) and a printing shop. These two exhibitions also feature authentic demonstrations of the trade as they existed in the earliest years of the twentieth century.

A central attraction of the museum is the heavy emphasis on bygone forms of transportation. An authentic nineteenth-century covered bridge, circa 1845, marks the entrance to the museum property. The Railroad Station and Freight Shed, built in 1890 by Dr. William Seward Webb, the original owner of nearby Shelburne Farms, displays telegraphy systems, railroad memorabilia and maps; completing a picture of Victorian era rail travel. Adjacent to this exhibit is the Rail Car Grand Isle, a private luxury rail car, built by Dr. Webb's railway concern, the Wagner Palace Car Co. Built in 1890, the car features a mahogany-paneled parlor, a dining room, staterooms and plush furnishings typical to luxury cars of that period. The Rail Locomotive No. 220, a full-scale steam locomotive housed underneath a shed, escorted U.S. presidents Calvin Coolidge, FDR, Herbert Hoover and Dwight D. Eisenhower, on many trips across the country.

Electra Webb's interest in Americana has an appeal to all age groups, especially children. The Variety Unit, added to the museum in the 1950s, contains over 1,000 antique dolls from all over the world, as well as dollhouses, music-boxes and miniature transportation toys popular in the Victorian era. The magic of its appeal extends itself to the adjacent Toyshop, which contains miniature dolls, miniature cars and bicycles, trains and wagons. Across the museum property, the Circus Building reveals two miniature circuses containing over 5,000 hand-carved pieces, as well as painted panels made by the Gustave Dentzel Carousel Company of Philadelphia, circa 1900. This parade, which completely replicates a three-ring circus, stretches for 500 feet.

The museum's fine art galleries contain American paintings, prints and drawings, including formal portraits and landscapes. The Electra Havemeyer Webb Memorial Building, a handsome Greek revival building, houses the founder's collection of European and Oriental paintings, sculpture and decorative art. The Webb Gallery, constructed in 1960, includes a collection of nineteenth-century portraits, landscapes, and genre scenes by such artists as William Prior, Erastus Salisbury Field, Winslow Homer, and

The Electra Havemeyer Webb Memorial Building contains her collection of paintings, including works by Rembrandt, Corot, Manet, Monet and Degas.

Fitz Hugh Lane. Works by twentieth century painters Anna Mary Robertson Moses (also known as Grandma Moses) and Andrew Wyeth are also on view. The museum's Stagecoach Inn, built in 1783, contains a variety of sculptural folk art, including tobacconists' trade signs, ship figureheads and patriotic carvings.

Shelburne Museum's grounds and gardens rival the other collections for the enjoyment and fascination they offer the viewer. Large maples and locust trees are original to the property. Pines, hemlocks, spruce and cedar trees suggest the forests of the neighboring Adirondack Mountains. At least five varieties of apple trees and 200 flowering crabtrees enliven open spaces, while 400 lilac bushes of ninety varieties are situated all throughout the grounds. While these gardens serve to bring pleasure, the museum also features a variety of thematic gardens to instruct the viewer. Medicinal herbs are found in the Apothecary Herb Garden and plants once used in the preparation of food and fabric are located outside the Hat and Fragrance Textile Gallery. The Electra Bostwick Memorial Garden, built in memory of the former artist, is arranged by color to represent a painter's palette.

Today the Shelburne Museum works to interpret and preserve for future generations the buildings and collections of the property as well as the traditions they represent. The museum's programs and exhibitions encourage visitors to explore the central themes of ingenuity, craftsmanship, and creativity through objects as varied as a blacksmith forge, a pastel portrait by Impressionist painter Mary Cassatt, and a hand-stitched Vermont quilt.

"My interpretation of folk art is a simple one," Electra Webb wrote in 1955. "Since the word 'folk' in America means all of us, folk-art is that self-expression which has welled up from the hearts and hands of the people. The creators can be kin or strangers, and they can be rich or poor, professional or amateur, but in America, particularly Vermont and New England, they are still known as folks." Electra Webb's message to the public was that above all, art is part of daily life, and should be enjoyed by everyone.

• • • • •

Shelburne Museum is located seven miles south of Burlington, VT on Route 7. The museum is open daily from 10 a.m. to 5 p.m., from late May through mid-October. Admission is charged for adults and youth ages 6-14. Price of admission includes a second consecutive day free. Select buildings are open mid-October through December 31 and April 1 until late May. The museum is closed on major holidays or in cases of severe weather. Accommodations for people with disabilities are possible. For more information call (802) 985-3346, ext. 3389, or visit the museum website at http://www.shelburnemuseum.org.

Photos courtesy of Shelburne Museum, Inc.

An Italian Renaissance Villa

Vizcaya, the Winter Home of James Deering

MIAMI • FLORIDA

IN 1914, INDUSTRIALIST James Deering began construction of a self-sufficient, Renaissance-style Italian villa in the Florida wilds. The bayfront villa and its formal gardens became the winter retreat of the visionary Deering and his notable friends. Completed in just two years, Vizcaya Museum and Gardens provides a window to both the history of the city and the Italian Renaissance, represented in the museum's architecture. Originally an estate of 180 acres, the mansion was designed to resemble a Northern Italian village with modern day conveniences. Today the home remains Miami's most well-known edifice.

Mr. Deering was born in 1859 in South Paris, Maine, a descendant of Roger

Deering, a shipwright from Dartmouth in Devonshire. When James Deering was a youth the family moved to Evanston, Illinois, where his father William founded the Deering Harvester Company, which was merged in 1902 with a McCormick family concern to form the International Harvester Company. After graduating from Northwestern University and attending M.I.T., Mr. Deering sold reapers, binders, and tractors to farmers throughout the West. A lifelong bachelor, Deering was vice-president of International Harvester until 1919 when he switched most of his energies to the upkeep of his villa. From a distance, however, Deering served as a director of International Harvester until his death.

A linguist, Mr. Deering spoke French, Italian and German, which helped in his search for a site and new furnishings. His charitable gifts were numerous, and in the United States Deering generously supported a number of philanthropic causes. An elegantly dressed man, with mixed-gray hair, pince-nez, penetrating pale-blue eyes and a kindly voice, Deering often carried a Malaaca cane and sported pearl-gray suits, occasionally switching to white linens. He owned 600 neckties.

Vizcaya's entrance loggia has an early Roman bath from Pompeii, surmounted by a statue of Bacchus and infants aside sea monsters.

The name Vizcaya came from the early Spanish adventurers who sailed from Biscay, Spain to the harbor in Florida which they named Biscayne Bay, close to the shoreline Mr. Deering later bought. The name Vizcaya is a Basque word for "elevated place."

As a site for his new home, Mr. Deering chose the flat Florida jungle, mangrove swamp and low limestone cliffs on the shore of Biscayne Bay, near the southern boundary of Miami. Henry M. Flagler's railroad extended there and Miami had grown by this time from an Indian trading post into a burgeoning community of 10,000 people. Deering had already examined other possible sites, including the French Riviera, Monte Carlo, southern Italy, North Africa, Egypt and the semitropical resort areas of the United States. He chose Miami as the site of his tropical winter home because of the location's ideal climate. Deerings parents wintered in Coconut Grove since 1901 and his brother Charles also possessed extensive properties in this area.

As architects for Vizcaya, Mr. Deering retained F. Burrall Hoffman, Jr. (1882-1980) and Paul Chalfin (1873-1959). A graduate of Harvard, Hoffman studied architecture and received a diploma from the École des Beaux Arts in Paris. While he was responsible for designing the buildings, the actual concept of the house came from Mr. Chalfin, a young New York painter, designer and art lecturer retained to advise Deering and direct and supervise the creation of his winter home. All three traveled to Italy at various times during the planning of the estate to study examples of the Italian country villas that would serve as the models for Deering's winter residences. The intention of the three men was to create a sixteenth-century Italian-style estate that appeared to have stood in existence for over 400 years.

Money was of no concern either in the search or purchase of art objects for the projected mansion. Before the first stone of the dwelling was laid, Mr. Deering had acquired enough paintings, statues, furniture, old roofs, tile floors, doors and ceilings from castles around Europe to fill several warehouses. For the most part, however, the furnishings are Italian. Even the Biedermermeir-style bedroom is named for the nineteenth-century Venetian president Manin (1804-57), famous for his resistance to Austrian rule. The house contains one of the finest collections of European decorative arts from the Renaissance to the present, yet Deering would be careful to add all twentieth century conveniences available.

The building created by Hoffman to match Chalfin's images is three stories high. However, except for the obvious towers in each corner of the building, the house appears to be only two stories. Between, on an intervening level, are twelve rooms for servants and service, a feature used in the early sixteenth century as builders made the transition from medieval to modern lifestyles. Dictating exterior contours of the mansion are the formal gardens, which were planned by Columbian-born Diego Suarez (1888-1974) to rival those of the Villa d'Este in Tivoli and Villa Albini in Rome.

The house is arranged around a central courtyard in the fashion of a sixteenth-century villa, with the reception room, Renaissance hall, music room, tearoom, banquet room, and library on the main floor. There are three loggias: one to the east, one to the west, and one to the south, which provide views across the courtyard to the bay and the gardens. The floor of the courtyard is paved with cuts of Florida quarry keystone and planted with tropical vegetation and palm trees. The vaulted arcades along the north and south sides of the courtyard use Cuban tile combined with the native limestone for the floor.

Above the courtyard, galleries look down from three sides around upon the master bedroom suite and guest bedrooms, as well as the upstairs dining room and kitchens. Here, the flooring is of Cuban tile while cypress beams support the ceiling of the galleries. Mr. Deering's bedroom, which has a balcony view of Biscayne Bay, is of a restrained classical design, comparatively simple. The bathroom, in contrast, includes gold fixtures, a marble tub, silver urns and a tentlike linen ceiling canopy. The modern-day kitchen, notable for its porcelain sinks, is located on the second floor. A second-floor dining room favored by Mr. Deering has large doors and windows that provide a panoramic view for a quarter of a mile across the ten acres of formal gardens, pools, cascading stairs, ornate fountains and grottoes. On the other side of the house are former service rooms and servants' quarters. Not open to the public,

The great Renaissance hall of Vizcaya features furnishings from the Italian Renaissance. The organ, still in use, is framed by a 17th century alter screen.

Tea House, Vizcaya

they currently function as the administrative offices of the museum.

The entrance doors of Vizcaya are circa 1800, of The Empire style. Two urns near the door are of Egyptian Rose granite, made during the craze for Egyptian art that followed Napoleon's African campaign. In the entrance loggia is a late second-century Roman bath of yellow marble, with an Italian seventeenth-century statue of Bacchus, the Roman God of Wine, above it. Flanking the bath are carved putti astride sea monsters. The combination seems incongruous until actually seen.

In the entrance hall, visitors view a remarkable pale green coffered ceiling and matching green marble floor. This is the first of many spectacular examples of design to be found on the ceilings, three of which are antique. This area also features hand colored wallpaper panels that were made in the Paris workshop of Joseph Dufour in 1814.

The Adam-style library is typical of

The music room contains a harpsichord from Cortona, Italy, c. 1619, a dulcimer, c. 1700, and a French harp, c. 1790.

the best work of the Adam brothers of England, who developed a classic design that has strong Roman influences. The chairs in the room are early nineteenth-century Italian neoclassic. They are upholstered with French tapestry of the same period, probably from the looms of Beauvais. A remarkable eighteenth-century rug is from a loom set up in Madrid by Bourbon kings to emulate those of La Savonnerie in Paris. The room has a great mahogany bookcase in the George III style and a portrait signed by Richard Livesay, dated 1787.

The reception room is in the style of Louis XV, with carved, painted and gilt bois-erie. The style is typical of Northern Italy in the mid-eighteenth century. The antique plaster ceiling is from the Palazzo Rossi, built in Venice circa 1750. The North Hall, located adjacent to this room, features Italian chairs from the seventeenth century. It also contains two Spanish chests and carved walnut columns of the sixteenth century.

Located in the northeast corner of the ground floor is the Renaissance hall, a formal room complete with a sixteenth-century fireplace and tapestries. The lofty wood ceiling is in the style of the Renaissance, and was designed for Vizcaya by Paul Chalfin. It is plaster, modeled and painted to resemble carved wood. The chandeliers, from the Charles Deering estate, are seventeenth-century in origin. Lions appear in the carvings of the room, also in the rugs and tapestries. One of the tapestries, woven in 1550 for Duke Ercole II of Ferrara, shows Hercules killing a lion. The long Spanish rug of the great hall is one of the finest existing Hispano-Moresque of the fifteenth century. It was made for the Admiral of Castile, the grandfather of King Ferdinand V and patron of Columbus.

Another notable ground floor room is the East Loggia, which, as the tourist will particularly appreciate, has a sweeping view of the bay and Key Biscayne. The doors and frames in this room are from the Palazzo Torlonia in Rome. The music room,

Although James Deering was retired at the time he lived at Vizcaya, he still handled many business matters in his sitting room.

which is located next to the East Loggia, has walls and a ceiling from a palazzo of the Borromeo family of Milan, circa 1760. In this room the visitor will find a harpsichord which bears the inscription and date of its maker, Giovanni Battista Boni (GIO. BTA. BONI), of Cortona, Italy, 1619. Visitors to the music room will also find on display a dulcimer, circa early eighteenth century, and a French harp circa 1790.

Located in the north side of the house is an unusual swimming pool that is partly under the mansion and partly outdoors. The ceiling, designed by the famous American artist Robert Chandler (1872-1930), provides an underwater grotto effect. It depicts murals and concrete walls embedded with thousands of sea shells.

In his own yacht, the *Nepenthe*, Mr. Deering arrived at Vizcaya on Christmas Day, 1916, to open the mansion. As the craft was moored between the shore and a great stone barge serving as a breakwater, two antique Italian cannons were fired, liveried servants stood at attention and a celebration began.

Guests recall the mansion as an elegant home. Meals were prepared by a French chef and his assistants, and Mr. Deering was shaved by a liveried valet in front of a gold-framed mirror. A frequent guest, the noted painter John Singer Sargent (1856-1925) made a water color of Mr. Deering that now belongs to the family. Other visitors included William Jennings Bryon, Lillian and Dorothy Gish, and Bryan Paderewski.

Mr. Deering equipped his mansion with ultra-modern conveniences such as electricity, a telephone, an elevator and central vacuum cleaning systems. The building is constructed of steel-reinforced concrete. The exterior walls are stuccoed and painted to appear weathered and aged. Several different types of limestone were used, excavated either on the grounds, in local quarries, or imported from Cuba. To provide instant antiquity, handmade roof tiles from old buildings in Cuba were acquired and reinstalled.

One of the features that most identifies Vizcaya with an Italian Renaissance villa are its fountains. Splashing water is seen and heard all over the grounds. A variety of theme gardens are located on several levels. The Secret Garden is completely enclosed in sculptured walls with stairs leading to a high platform; one of the many elevated vantage points for seeing the Formal Gardens. The Theater Garden has a raised stage. The Maze Garden, a familiar feature in European gardens from the time of the Renaissance, is circular and is formed by hedges of orange jasmine. The Fountain Garden has a seventeenth-century Italian fountain at its center, surrounded by waterways leading to smaller fountains. The Casino, a miniature house on some of the highest ground of the gardens, provides views of colorful scenery in all directions.

A peacock bridge, otherwise known as the O Bridge, has twisted columns surmounted by stone peacocks, designed by the American sculptor Gaston Lachaise (1882-1935). Another noted artist, A. Stirling Calder (1870-1945), also created sculpture for the estate, including the symbolic figures on the great stone barge at the waterfront.

Mr. Deering enjoyed this luxury for just nine years before his sudden death from heart failure in 1925 at the age of sixty-six. He had been suffering from pernicious anemia, which prompted someone to observe that he probably would have enjoyed a longer life "if he had had a wife to tell him what to eat." Vizcaya was inherited by Mr. Deering's two nieces: Mrs. Marion Deering McCormick of Chicago and Mrs. Barbara Deering Danielson of Boston.

After Deering's death in 1925, a minimal staff maintained the house. The powerful hurricane of 1926, which devastated much of Miami, extensively damaged the surrounding grounds and formal gardens. Deering's heirs attempted to operate the estate as a museum for a time, but eventually most of the land was sold off for development. The mansion now has a plot of twenty-eight acres, the rest of the original 180 having been donated or sold. In 1952, Dade County purchased the remaining complex for $1,000,000 and opened it as The Dade County Art Museum. Since that time, extensive restoration has brought the villa and the remaining acres of the gardens back to the way they appeared in Deering's day. The mansion has since served as the sight of a historic meeting place between former U.S. President Ronald Reagan and Pope John Paul II in 1987, and the historic Summit of the Americas in 1994, where thirty-four leaders of the Western Hemisphere met with President Clinton. Vizcaya is currently accredited by the American Association of Museums and is designated a national Historic Landmark.

• • • • •

Located at 3251 South Miami Avenue in Miami, Florida, the Gardens of Vizcaya are opened to the public every day from 9:30 a.m. to 4:30 p.m., except Christmas. Admission is $10 for adults, $5.00 for children ages 6 to 12, and $8.00 for senior citizens. Children five and under are admitted free. For additional information call: (305)250-9133.

Photos courtesy of Vizcaya.

Every President Added Something

The White House - A Montage

WASHINGTON • D.C.

OF ALL THE MANSIONS in America, the White House is the most well-known. Visitors stream through it at a rate of 1.5 million per year. The oldest federal structure in Washington, its large portals and interior elegance are an everyday sight to millions of others who read the paper and watch television. The stately structure is the only residence of a head of state open to the public on a regular basis free of charge. It is also the home of the President of the United States, where pressing matters of government are conducted even as tourists visit nearby, admiring the many treasures from the past.

But there is a dramatic behind-the-scenes saga of the evolution of the White House

The President's dining room, which serves as a convenient place for family meals and private entertainment, is furnished in the style of the Federal period.

that is generally overlooked. . . it is a mansion of memories.

The individual imprint of every President is indelibly ledgered in the walls, the adornments, the gardens and the customs of the 132 room structure. These imprints overlap and blend into a unit for the modern home life of First Families, providing mute evidence that every President possessed strong personal tastes and did not hesitate to exercise them.

Located on the edge of a swamp, in the new Federal City that was excessively hot in the summer, cold in winter and dank most of the time, the site for the executive mansion was intended as a compromise; it was the only geographically area acceptable to the northern and southern segments of the new nation. Spartan by today's standards, the original mansion was a sandstone residence of twenty rooms; without baths, running water, electricity, gas, elevator, or even a service bell.

Design of the White House was initiated in 1792 through competition. George Washington (1789-97) - then living in a rented Philadelphia home - shared in choosing James Hoban (1762-1831), an unknown Irish immigrant of Charleston, South Carolina, as the winner of a $500 prize for best design of the residence. The plan was Georgian, inspired by the Duke of Leinster's Palace in Dublin and pictures of English gentlemen's houses in an architectural book by James Gibbs, a disciple of Sir Christopher Wren. A plan submitted anonymously by Thomas Jefferson for a Greco-Roman classical structure was rejected. The house was to be grander than any house, state-house, or meeting-house built in America up until that time.

Washington, who died before the building was completed, never lived in the White House during his tenure as the nation's first leader. John Adams (1797-1801) and his wife Abigail, arrived in Washington during the middle of his term in the autumn of

1800. They found a house only partially complete; smelling of new plaster (mixed with hog hair and horse hair), wallpaper paste (made with white flour and beer), unfinished mahogany flooring and lead paint and varnish. Debris littered the outside grounds and construction shacks were not yet removed. The first couple had no firewood - "because people cannot be found to cut and cart it," and no bell to summon a servant. Luckily, they were free to leave Washington after four months.

Although Jefferson had lost the contest for designing the mansion, he had a fling at planning revisions of the structure when he moved in as President in 1801. Jefferson, an accomplished builder, must have been impatient to speed up construction. In 1803 he hired American architect Benjamin Latrobe (1766-1820), who planned a new roof for the White House, provided a new entryway into the basement kitchen, and drew up designs for the stately north and south porticos, which were added to the White House in the 1820s. Jefferson also converted the drawing rooms into informal reception centers and built terraces and colonnades resembling those of Monticello, his home in Virginia. A man known for his ingenuity, Jefferson designed rotating clothes closets and hidden cabinets that held official documents and his carpenters' tools.

When President James Madison (1809-17) took office in 1809, his wife Dolley, a famous hostess, got rid of the carpenters' tools and restored the drawing room. Callers to the White House in 1810 praised the new room as "immense and magnificent." Dolley was unprepared, however, for the British sailors who arrived without invitation in 1814 while her husband was absent. She fled for her life as the mansion was set afire. Someone procured a wagon; in it she carried a Gilbert Stuart portrait of George Washington as well as the government's silver. Today, the portrait is the only remaining item from the original furnishings.

Hoban took charge of rebuilding the crumbling exterior walls and stripping out fire-damaged stone. Moving into the restored mansion in 1817, President James Monroe installed huge chandeliers, rich brocades, French Empire furniture and Hannibal and Minerva clocks. In 1824, he also added the south portico, which was also designed by Mr. Latrobe. Items from the Monroe restoration have formed the heart of the White House historic collection and the former French diplomat's concern with gentility established a new standard of elegance and social form in the Executive mansion.

The gardens of the White House became spectacular only when President John Quincy Adams (1825-29) arrived. An ardent gardener, he extended the original west wing garden with gravel paths and arbors. Adams is said to have planted an elm tree that still stands in the south grounds. Soon after, the north portico, providing the imposing entrance on Pennsylvania Avenue, was added by President Andrew Jackson (1829-37). He planted the famous magnolia trees on the grounds and piped the first water into the mansion. In 1829, President Jackson decorated the East Room in grand style, at a cost to taxpayers of more than $9,000. In 1837, President Van Buren (1837-41) redecorated the oval salon and began the tradition of a "blue room." Highly criticized by certain members of Congress for the "regal splendor of the Presidential palace" during a time of great economic depression, Van Buren lost a bid for a second term in office. Until the arrival of James Polk (1845-49) from Tennessee, money for White House furnishings would not be available again.

While Victorian fancy dominated the household furnishings, gaslight would make its first appearance in the White House. The first stationary source of illumination, its arrival in 1848 meant that furnishings could now remain in place, attractively arranged.

Millard Fillmore (1850-53), the nation's thirteenth president, could not find a dictionary when he assumed the Presidency in 1850. He added not only a dictionary but a $2,000 library of rare and antiquarian books. His successor, Franklin Pierce (1853-57) installed the first full central heating system as well as installation of the first comprehensive plumbing system.

The administration of Abraham Lincoln (1860-65) saw only one major physical change to the White House. Lincoln added a private passage on the second floor from the library through the reception room to his office. Since eliminated, it enabled the popular president to reach his private quarters unseen by waiting strangers. President and Mrs. Lincoln bickered over what he considered "flubdub" decorations. After his assassination, many of the valuable furnishings vanished. Some historians assert that Mrs. Lincoln stole them; in truth no one really supervised the White House during the five weeks she lay mourning in her room, and vandals helped themselves. Items that were found missing were never returned to the White House.

Andrew Johnson (1865-69), the one-time tailor from Tennessee, completed the high wrought-iron fences of the grounds, while his daughter, Martha Patterson, oversaw extensive cleaning and refurbishing. By 1866, the White House fairly shone with her improvements. Ulysses S. Grant (1869-77), installed elaborate false timbers and cut-glass chandeliers in the East Room. Other presidents made changes but it remained for Chester Arthur (1881-85), to install an elevator and auction off twenty-four van loads of furniture that he considered objectionable. Arthur called in the famous Louis C. Tiffany of New York to redecorate the state rooms in a style that later resembled Art Nouveau.

Early in the Civil War, Union soldiers camped on the grounds and slept on the floor of the East Room. Also the site of weddings and funerals, seven presidents have lain in state in this room, including President Lincoln, and President John F. Kennedy in November 1963. The six lively children of Theodore Roosevelt (1901-09), used the room for jujitsu, their various pets, and even for roller skating.

A bathtub large enough for four people was installed by William Howard Taft (1909-13), a man of imposing girth. Under his administration, construction began on a new West Wing, where the current Oval Office is located. Taft was the first president to perform business in this room, which he used every day from October 1909. Through the influence of his wife, Taft also oversaw the addition of cherry trees to the nearby Tidal Basin, a gift of the mayor of Tokyo.

New construction work was enhanced in 1913 by the addition of gardens planted by Ellen Axson Wilson, the first wife of Woodrow Wilson (1913-21). An artist, Mrs.

The Green Room, a first-floor parlor, was completely refurbished in 1971. Its furniture, in the style of the Federal period, includes many pieces by the famous New York cabinetmaker Duncan Phyfe.

Wilson set up a studio in the mansion and was the first to plant roses in the now famous White House Rose Garden.

Cramped quarters and a crumbling roof structure led to the demolition of the attic and its replacement with a third floor under the Coolidge Administration (1923-29). A White House fire on Christmas Eve of 1929 led soon after to the rebuilding of the executive office under the administration of Herbert Hoover (1929-33). Franklin D. Roosevelt (1933-45) added a remodeled Oval Office, a movie theater, a swimming pool, a bomb shelter and an eastward addition to the East Wing. An amateur architect and lover of old houses, FDR was fascinated with improving the White House. Due to the Depression and World War II, changes to the interior of the White House were delayed. The chance to make a real difference would not occur until Harry S. Truman's succession to the presidency in 1945.

All the Presidents kept adding more pipes, wiring and conduits until the honeycombed timbers sagged dangerously and the foundations, on soft clay, settled several feet. At a reception in the Blue Room in 1948, Mr. Truman heard strange creaking sounds. He had already been disturbed by noises in the structure at night and by odd sounds of movement. He suspected, fearfully, that the White House was falling down.

The Lincoln Bedroom. In it is a large quantity of furniture Mrs. Lincoln purchased in 1861, including an oversize rosewood bed. Lincoln used this room as his office and study.

That same year a structural survey was carried out. Lorenzo S. Winslow, the White House architect, and other officials reported that the White House was standing upright "just through sheer force of habit." While broken timbers and sagging stairs were still being examined, a leg of the piano in Margaret Truman's room broke through two floorboards into the family dining room below.

Most experts thought the least costly thing to do would be to tear down the mansion and build anew, but the public demanded that the old White House be preserved. A total reconstruction of the interior, with modern steel and concrete, marbles and fine woods, was undertaken at a cost of 5.8 million dollars. The house of sixty - five rooms became one of 132, with only thirty-three of these on the ground, main and second floor levels. The renovation has often been criticized by preservationists, as many of the original architectural elements of the early White House - including plaster, paneling, and flooring - were discarded.

Upon his move into the rebuilt White House in 1952, Truman converted Lincoln's old cabinet room into the Lincoln Room. In it is a large quantity of furniture Mrs. Lincoln purchased in 1861, including an oversize rosewood bed, a matching marble-top rosewood table, patterned Brussels carpet and a late Empire marble-and ormulu clock. Overlooking the Washington Monument, Lincoln used this room as his office and a place to escape his wife's extensive redecorating.

The advent of television precipitated a particular interest in the interior design of the White House, and most of the changes since Truman's time have been in the form of interior decoration. The most famous redecoration of the White House took place during the brief administration of John F. Kennedy (1961-63), under the auspices of his wife Jacqueline Kennedy. The White House Historical Association was established as a private nonprofit organization to enhance the appearance of the White House. Its purpose ever since has been the acquisition of historical furnishings as well as the production of publications. A special committee on paintings soon followed. Mrs. Kennedy was also responsible for the restoration of the White House Rose Garden, which had been largely neglected since 1913.

By Executive Order, President Lyndon B. Johnson (1963-69) established the Committee for the Preservation of the White House. The order also provided for a permanent curator. Mrs. Johnson acquired paintings by such famous artists as Thomas Sully, John Singer Sargent, and Winslow Homer. In 1969, President Nixon (1969-74) ordered the Roosevelt swimming pool floored over and the present broadcast and press room built. Over the course of his administration, all the principal rooms on the State Floor and Ground Floor were redecorated. A major redecoration of the second and third-floor rooms also took place under the administration of Ronald Reagan (1981-89), while a televised tour of the second-floor living quarters during the Bush administration (1988-92) introduced to the public a part of the White House rarely seen. Under the Bush administration, the second-floor Treaty Room was converted into a private study, and it is now President Clinton's office and sitting room. Shortly before Clinton took office, a twelve-year preservation effort of the White House exterior grounds was completed. The exterior walls were stripped of over forty-two coats of old paint and conservation of the original stone walls took place. The White House also received thirty-four American paintings for its permanent collection.

The White House has served forty-two presidents, only ten of which have served in the mansion that stands today. Its durable legacy, stalwart through three fires, a Civil war and two World Wars, remains a tribute to American endurance and national dignity. As a fulfillment of George Washington's hope, the White House looks "beyond the present day."

• • • • •

The White House is located at 1600 Pennsylvania Avenue N.W. but the tourists' entrance is around the corner on East Executive Avenue. The East, Red, Blue, Green and State Dining rooms are open from 10:00 a.m. to noon Tuesday through Saturday, except on holidays. Admission is free. For further information, call: 202-456-1414 or visit the White House website at http://www.whitehouse.gov.

Photos courtesy of the White House Collection, copyright White House Historical Association.

An Organic Innovation

Taliesin, The Home of Frank Lloyd Wright

SPRING GREEN • WISCONSIN

IT WILL BE MANY A DAY before people stop arguing whether Frank Lloyd Wright was the greatest architect in the modern world. There is little doubt, however, that of all the geniuses identified with the visual arts in America, he has had a greater influence on the daily lives of more people than any contemporary.

A legacy of his creative thinking, Wright's home at Taliesin is a celebration of art into naturalism. Genius is reflected in the low-ceiling of the entrance hall that opens dramatically into a soaring cathedral-like room; a clerestoried window that casts soft light on an inviting lounge, eaves that lack downspouts so that long icicles dangle from them like stalactites, rooms that flow freely together, and a picture window that overlooks treetops.

*Frank Lloyd Wright's study at Taliesin shows the organic design of
the structure and the blending of indoors and outdoors.*

A revolutionist in architecture, Mr. Wright undertook to tear America away from
its traditional square, regimented housing, as well as from its conventional museums, office structures and schools. He felt Washington, D.C. should be razed and
once called New York City's Metropolitan Museum a barn, the United Nations
Secretariat a gravestone, Rockefeller Center a crime against humanity and Wall
Street the plague spot of America. He also undertook to fight the common concepts
of personal morality, although he had a set of ideals based solely in Wrightian logic
considered overtly radical for his time. Ultimately, his nonconformist activities
merged to produce Taliesin, a fifty-room home in the wooded hills of dairy country
at Spring Green, Wisconsin. Although not the most spectacular of the over 400 structures Wright built, it is considered by some experts to be his greatest and most interesting. It incorporates his basic architectural concepts and was steadily revised
throughout Wright's forty-eight years of residence.

The living room of Taliesin includes a high and irregular ceiling, clerestoried windows, built-in bookcases, picture windows, and furniture made by Taliesin craftsmen. Native stone masonry in this room was an architectural innovation.

The revisions in his thinking at Taliesin were punctuated by two major fires. One of the fires was accompanied by seven murders, committed by a distraught employee when Mr. Wright was out of town. The other one found Mr. Wright on the roof with blistering feet, while lightning crackled around his head and he recalled the punishments of Job.

Mr. Wright was born in 1867 near Taliesin, the son of William R.C. Wright, an Amherst College graduate, preacher, medical scholar, musician and teacher. Frank's father abruptly abandoned his family when the architect was still a boy, never to be seen again by his wife and children. Frank's mother, Anna, decided she wanted her son to be an architect from earliest infancy. To give force to her sense of determination she hung pictures of majestic English cathedrals in the boy's nursery. She also stimulated his sense of independent creativity through educational toys, such as Froebel Blocks, designed by Friedrich Froebel of educational fame. Through the blocks, Frank learned about color and form, and during the building of Taliesin he commented that those blocks seemed to stay in his hands all his life.

The evolution of Taliesin stemmed from many influences. Important ones were Mr. Wright's mother and three women he loved throughout the course of his life. His mother, Anna Lloyd Jones Wright, a schoolteacher, was a descendant of Welsh preachers and farmers who had settled in the lush countryside of Wisconsin because of its resemblance to Wales. The Lloyd Jones clan was proud of its independence. One of its mottoes was "Truth Against the World."

One of the earliest principles of Wright's career was self-reliance. Working for nineteen dollars a month on his Uncle James' farm, Mr. Wright learned another Lloyd Jones motto that is symbolized in Taliesin: "Add tired to tired." He later worked for a contractor in Madison, forty miles from Spring Green, and then in Chicago for Louis Sullivan, the noted architect. Shunning the traditional concepts of Richard Morris Hunt and Charles Follen McKim, who were building castles in the East, Wright created compositions with plain bricks, concrete masses and unpainted timber.

In 1889 Mr. Wright built his first personal home. It remains standing as a landmark at Forest and Chicago Avenues in the Oak Park area of metropolitan Chicago. Wright had recently married Catherine Tobin, who was to give him four sons and two daughters, but was not to remain an influential force in his life. Mr. Wright broke completely with convention to design for his bride a horizontal "house of the prairies" in a style that became known as Usonian. The twenty-room structure has many of the continuing Wrightian devices - low lines, deep eaves, walled gardens, windows in rows, and bricks and timbers of earthy colors. It originally had a large willow tree growing through the roof.

In this house Mr. Wright experimented with a dramatic scheme, later used at Taliesin and in hundreds of other houses, of having a mall entry suddenly open into a small, high room with a balcony and other points of interest. The effect was exhilarating to many of his local clients. This new design sought to do away with dull precedent, while emphasizing such themes as community, functionalism, and the harmony of a home with its surroundings. To offset his artistic efforts in these homes, Wright designed custom chairs, carpets, urns, and wall hangings.

The high room at Oak Park was designed as a playroom and in it Mr. Wright, his wife and six children played classical music together; he at the piano and the others on drums, horns and string instruments. Wright was a good father and an energetic provider and the house was a joyous one.

Just as he had broken with the architectural past, Mr. Wright effected a dramatic interruption of his personal life in 1909. Abandoning his wife and six children, Wright entrusted his work to a hastily selected colleague and fled to Europe with a woman by the name of Mamah Borthwick Cheney. She was the comely wife of one of his clients, Edward H. Cheney, a manufacturer of electrical equipment, and the mother of two young children. The event created an immediate sensation, as Mr. Wright's notoriety was already increasing at a rapid pace.

From this crisis in the life of Frank Lloyd Wright, Taliesin began to grow. When he and Mrs. Cheney returned from Italy a year later, the adverse publicity and the loss of contracts from local citizens convinced Wright that Oak Park was not the place to remain. His mother then gave him thirty acres that she owned in the Lloyd Jones family valley outside of Spring Green; a land holding that Mr. Wright would later increase to 2,700 acres.

Months before leaving Oak Park for good, Mr. Wright had already begun furious preparation on the house he and his new mistress would soon occupy. When the first part of the house was completed in late 1911, he invited the press to come and see it for themselves. Wright explained to reporters that Mrs. Cheney was his loyal comrade, and that he intended to be her protector for the rest of his life. Although Mr. Cheney divorced his wife, the first Mrs. Wright balked at a legal separation, so Mr. Wright would never marry the woman for whom Taliesin was first built.

The name Taliesin comes from a Welsh bard who sang the glories of the fine arts. The name means "Shining Brow" and Mr. Wright thought it especially appropriate for his home. No house, he said, should be built on top of the hill, else you lose the hill, but rather just on the brow, where he built Taliesin. A mansion of fifty rooms, a score of baths and a dozen fireplaces, it so harmonizes with the landscape that it seems to have grown there.

Mr. Wright often spoke of "marrying" his buildings to the ground, so that they could not "be intelligently studied apart from the environment." As Taliesin grew, it became apparent that the new owner intended to use his own dwelling place as a standard by which to test this function. Architecture should be in league with the land so that each could be happier because of the other.

Rock outcroppings on the brow of the hill were exploited to produce a "natural house" among the birches, the pines and the cedars. A stone quarry a mile from the house provided a sandstone of the yellowish, earthy color that Mr. Wright favored using inside and outside his houses. Local workmen, most of them novices in construction, were taught how to build the house walls and the gardens so they harmonized with the natural ledges of rock. Mr. Wright soon had country masons setting a few stones in place, then stepping back to view the effect as a sculptor might look critically at his creation. Taliesin became a home and a workshop inside a garden, with a mass of apple blossoms behind the house in spring and perfume from the orchard drifting down the valley.

The exterior wood trim and shingles were treated with preparations to blend with the silver-gray trees in the violet light at sunset. Chimneys of the great stone fireplaces were built to rise majestically through the house in rooms where socializing occurred. Outside, they remain quiet rock masses bespeaking strength. No gutters or downspouts were permitted on the house. Mr. Wright wanted Taliesin to be a frosted palace in the winter, with six-foot icicles hanging from the roof, glistening with prismatic colors as the sun struck them.

Mr. Wright designed each of the rooms so that the sun would stream in at some hour of the day, the windows of every room opening onto treetops to admit the fragrance of foliage and the singing birds of summer. Many have built-in bookcases, nooks, and other places of interest; all in woods of natural color, but they have little provision for paintings and etchings. "Pictures," Mr. Wright said, "deface walls faster than they decorate them."

A central feature of Taliesin is the Wrightian device of trees growing through roofs. Trademark designs also include floors made of broad cypress planks or slabs of stone, and plaster mixed with raw sienna to give the walls of both the interior and exterior a tone of natural tawny gold. The halls and the stairs also bear the Wright signature.

Frank Lloyd Wright's Taliesin studio. The architect's drafting table is located at the center.

Trimmed to his size, which Mr. Wright could claim was a slim five-feet-eight inches tall, they are not intended for the comfortable passage of taller and bulkier persons. Visitors to Wright houses often claim that the rapid fluctuations of heights and widths are oppressive. Others find them delightful. The variations and the points of interest they emphasized were a point of fascination to Mr. Wright.

The furnishings of Taliesin are generally simple and occasionally Asian. The lack of elegant furnishings is not apparent in the living room because of the many-faceted style of its construction, including a high and irregular ceiling, clerestoried windows, an inviting fireplace, lounges, picture windows, and furniture made by Taliesin craftsmen. For his extraordinary library and prized collection of Japanese prints, Mr. Wright installed a huge fireproof stone vault. The table silver and other valuables, however, did not have similar protection.

During the early years at Taliesin, Mr. Wright executed twenty-one commissions and two architectural masterpieces, including Tokyo's Imperial Hotel and Chicago's Midway Gardens. As new possibilities opened up to him, the creative benefits of the architect's self-designed lifestyle were becoming increasingly apparent. Then in August, 1914, tragedy struck. While Mr. Wright was away in Chicago on business, Mrs. Cheney, her two children, ages ten and twelve, and four Taliesin staff were brutally murdered. The responsible party was a Barbadian butler named Julian Carleton, who worked in the kitchen with his wife Gertrude. Carleton had been complaining about the hardship of working in the isolated Wisconsin countryside and had induced his wife to give notice. Soon after serving

Landscape, Taliesin. Mr. Wright once possessed one of the largest collections of Asian art in the West.

lunch to his co-workers and the three Cheneys on a screened terrace, he tossed a lit match to gasoline which he had sloshed throughout the kitchen. As the seven victims tried to escape the flames, Carleton killed at least three of them with a hatchet, including Mamah and her two children. Most of the house burst into flames, although some of it was ultimately saved by farmers who rushed to Taliesin with pumps and hoses. The killer was found soon after near death from muriatic acid that he had swallowed.

Mr. Wright received the tragic news in Chicago by telephone and boarded a train toward Spring Green. There a nightmare awaited him, for in the midst of the charred ruins of his home lay the bodies of those closest to him. Working without sleep for the remainder of the night, Wright, Mrs. Cheney's former husband, as well as various relatives and neighbors worked to put out the blaze and save a portion of Taliesin from flames. Soon after, Mr. Wright buried Mamah on the grounds of Taliesin in a simple yet moving garden ceremony. The murderer's deed was never satisfactorily explained, and Carleton died in prison days after.

Mr. Wright received thousands of letters, most of them sympathetic. One that especially impressed him was from Mrs. Miriam Noel, a sculptress of forty-three, with connections to southern high society. A divorcé with three grown children, Miriam was a self-consciously artistic woman whose substantial alimony afforded her a creative lifestyle. Wright summoned her to his Chicago office soon after first communicating with her. Less than six months later, she moved into the rebuilt Taliesin as its new mistress.

While often serving as a source of moral, creative, and even financial support to Mr. Wright, the former Mrs. Noel's relationship with the architect was doomed to failure. A combination of family and financial setbacks, as well as his continued devotion to Mamah Cheney's memory, made the chance of a successful union between the two impossible. Hoping that it would restore happiness, Mr. Wright married her in November, 1923, after his first wife finally consented to a divorce. The marriage lasted only five months before Miriam left Taliesin and moved to California, where she

Watergarden, Taliesin. The pond in the forefront was man-made.

started a series of lawsuits that were to pester Mr. Wright for many years.

At a performance of Russian dancing in Chicago, Mr. Wright met Olga Iovanova Lazovich Hinzenberg, a vivacious Montenegrin divorcé who had come to the United States with her daughter, Svetlana. He wooed her vigorously before moving her into Taliesin in February of 1925, where the couple produced Wright's third daughter, Iovanna. For the next thirty-five years, Olgivanna, as she called herself, was Mr. Wright's constant and devoted companion. The union met with much bitterness from Miriam; however, whose use of the press, courts, police, banks, and even the Wisconsin State Government, became an ongoing threat to Mr. Wright and his family. As Mrs. Noel's behavior became increasingly erratic, the long lost support of Wright's family, friends and the public returned. Miriam finally consented to a divorce in 1927; one year later Mr. Wright and Olgivanna were married.

A second big fire at Taliesin in 1925, was believed to have been started by defective wiring in Mr. Wright's bedroom. He joined with others in fighting the flames as a high wind fanned them. Trying to spur the firefighters to greater efforts to save the house, he climbed to the roof with a hose. His feet were burned, his lungs seared, his hair and eyebrows scorched. Suddenly the wind changed, thunder rumbled, and a torrent of rain put out the flames. Salvaging charred marble heads, Ming pottery and other relics from the ashes, Mr. Wright began weaving plans for another reconstruction of his home.

Meanwhile, Wright's burgeoning financial difficulties threatened to destroy Taliesin more effectively than fire ever did. To save the mansion from foreclosure in 1929, Wright needed $75,000, which he obtained with the help of friends. In 1955 the Wisconsin Supreme Court ruled that Taliesin, although used partly for training architects, was not an educational institution within the meaning of the law and was subject to normal taxes, of which Mr. Wright owed $18,000. Mr. Wright's reply to the state was: "Very well. I'll tear down Taliesin and leave the land idle. Let the tax people collect on that."

Friends organized a banquet, at which $10,000 was raised to save Taliesin. Deeply touched, Wright continued living and working there. When he died in 1959, he was buried in the family cemetery across the valley from his home. The simple grave site is marked by a slab of the native stone like that used in his home.

After bitter debate, the American Institute of Architects finally conferred its highest honor, the Gold Medal, on Mr. Wright, but many are still annoyed by the type of architecture Mr. Wright advocated and his acerbic pronouncements.

In 1932, Mr. Wright set up the Taliesin Fellowship for the training of apprentices in "essential architecture," a program still in existence. As part of their training, the apprentices also study philosophy, sculpture, painting, music, and the industrial arts. It was Wright's belief that education should be in the doing, not in the classroom. Wright added two dormitory wings as well as a drafting studio to the property outside his Spring Green home. The program, which drew an immediate following of students from around the world, is known today as the Frank Lloyd Wright® School of Architecture. It currently exists as a nationally accredited professional degree program. In 1976 the National Park Service declared Taliesin a National Historic Landmark. Visitors to the house and property are now estimated at 35,000 annually.

• • • • •

Taliesin is located at the intersection of State Highway 23 and County Highway C, near Spring Green. Tours of the house are offered seven days a week, May through October. All tours begin at the Wright-designed Frank Lloyd Wright Visitor Center, which is located adjacent to the Taliesin estate. Different tours are available ranging in price from $10.00 to $60.00. Discounts are available to children under 12 as well as senior citizens and students with ID. Some tours require reservations, so calling in advance is recommended. For further information, call: (608) 588-7900, or visit the Taliesin website at http//www.taliesinpreservation.org.

Photos courtesy of Pedro E. Guerrero, c. 1999.

The Plantation with A Pygmalion

Shadows-On-the-Teche

NEW IBERIA • LOUISIANA

"I HAVE NEVER CONSIDERED myself anything but a trustee of something fine which chance had put in my hands to preserve. Fine things are without value, in that they belong only to those rare people who appreciate them beyond any price. It is to those people that I would like to entrust this place." Thus wrote William Weeks Hall, descendant of the original owner of Shadows-on-the-Teche; the restoration of which he devoted more than three decades of his life.

The hauntingly beautiful historic plantation house known as Shadows-on-the-Teche stands on the banks of the Bayou Teche, fronting Main Street, in New Iberia,

Louisiana, one of twenty properties owned by the National Trust for Historic Preservation. A white-columned brick building constructed between 1831 and 1834, Shadows is both a survivor and reminder of a bitter time period in American history. Built for sugar planter David Weeks and his wife Mary Conrad Weeks, the house was home to four generations of the Weeks family for 125 years.

David's father William Weeks was born in England where he learned the trade of weaving before coming to the American colonies as a young man. At about the time of the Revolutionary War, William Weeks obtained a Spanish Land Grant for property near present-day St. Francisville, Louisiana, where he developed a cotton plantation. Near the end of the eighteenth century, William Weeks decided to buy more property in the region known as the Attakapas district west of the Mississippi

Dining room at Shadows-on-the-Teche. Portraits of John Moore and Mary Conrad Weeks Moore hang above the mahogany sideboard.

River. It was William's son David Weeks who completed the purchase of several thousand acres of land not far from New Iberia with easy access to the Gulf of Mexico for shipping purposes. While his father had concentrated on cotton, David focused his energies and resources establishing a sugar plantation, which became one of the highest producers of that product in the Teche County by the time he began construction of the house in 1831. David chose a site on the Bayou Teche, a beautiful stream that flows through the Evangeline country at New Iberia.

Invoices found in the extensive collection of Weeks Family Papers indicates that the two brothers, James and John Bedell, were in charge of most of the construction. One of only two brick houses on the Bayou Teche in the vicinity of New Iberia in the 1830s, Shadows was built in the Classical Revival style with eight two-story white columns across the front facade. Unlike other columned plantation houses being built across

The parlor at Shadows-on-the-Teche is restored to reflect the style and prosperity of the late 1850s. Portraits of Alfred Weeks and Charles Weeks, two sons of David and Mary Weeks, hang near the window and over the mantle.

the South in the same period, the new Weeks home had a Louisiana Colonial floor-plan with exterior staircases, wide galleries, no interior hallways, and numerous opposing windows and doors for good ventilation in the subtropical climate of southern Louisiana.

With its impressive columns and mélange of Tuscan influences, the structure made such an impression on other planters that before it was even completed they began construction of similar homes. Mr. Weeks' wife, the former Mary Clara Conrad, added plantings to enhance the exterior appearance of her new home. These included rows of live oaks as well as magnolias.

As the house approached completion in May 1834, David Weeks left on a sea voyage to the northeast in an attempt to find a cure for a recurring disease, referred to in family letters as "the complaint." In his absence, Mary and their six children moved into the new house. In a letter to her husband, Mary expressed her joy at the family's new living accommodations, stating, "….I never saw a more delightful airy house, any room particularly. I have all the children in it and open the doors and windows every night. Heaven only knows if my hopes will ever be realized but I hope in a house so well ventilated that they will be blest with health of late years they have not all enjoyed."

David Weeks died in New Haven, Connecticut, on August 25, 1834, never having lived in his new house in the Bayou Teche. An appraisal of the estate made after David's death valued the 158 acres on which the house was built, together with the house, furnishings, and other outbuildings on the property at $20, 700.

Following the death of her husband, Mary Weeks was kept very busy seeing to the management of the plantation and the education of her children. She received much advice about running her home from one of her deceased husband's oldest friends, Judge John Moore, whom she would eventually marry in 1841. Moore was a sugar planter and Louisiana politician who served two terms in the U.S. Congress as representative from Louisiana. A marriage contract signed on the day of their wedding legally kept their respective properties separate; thereby protecting the inheritance of Mary's children.

Throughout the bitter years of the Civil War, Mary Weeks Moore found herself alone again at Shadows as husband and children left the region to avoid confiscation of their property by advancing Federal troops. Plantation profits vanished and Union soldiers arrived in New Iberia in 1863 - soon after taking over Mary's home as uninvited guests. Yankee officers took over Shadows for about two months; using the first floor for quarters, and Mary's prized gardens as a camping ground.

Mary refused to desert her home, fearing her departure would bring further destruction to the property. Maintaining her composure in the face of adversity, she confined herself to the family living quarters on the second floor along with her sister-in-law, daughter-in-law, and a few servants. Mary had just received word that Judge Moore was on his way home in late December 1863 when she passed away in her sleep. Some of the people in town said she died of starvation, others, of a broken heart. She was buried on the property, beneath her beloved gardens, two weeks prior to the retreat of Yankee soldiers from her home.

Following the Civil War, Shadows became the home of William F. Weeks, the eldest son of David and Mary. William used the Shadows as home for his family while continuing to manage the sugar plantation on Grand Cote, now called Weeks Island. Williams and his daughters Lily and Harriet planted young oak trees and camellias and built a greenhouse. They also filled the front gallery with potted ferns and "modernized" the dining room and parlor with Victorian wallpaper, Acadian woven textiles at the windows and doors and rag rugs on the hardwood floors.

But after William's death in 1895, the two daughters vacated the property, and the house fell into disrepair. It was William's only grandchild, William Weeks Hall, born in 1894, who inherited the role of caretaker and undertook Shadows' restoration.

Hall, an indifferent student but a talented artist, won scholarships to study art at the Pennsylvania Academy for Fine Arts, where he was awarded travel scholarships to study art in Europe between 1920-1922. By the time he returned to New Iberia in May 1922, he was determined to restore the family home, and devoted the next thirty-six years of his life to ensuring that Shadows would be preserved and open to the public; a place where people could see a "picture of the life" from an earlier era.

In an attempt to attain public assistance with the preservation of Shadows, Hall worked to make the site known nationally by inviting famous people to visit, including movie producers D.W. Griffith and Cecil B. DeMille, writers Henry Miller and Harnett Kane, and even Walt Disney. Hall encouraged articles about his home in national publications, and invited Dave Garroway, host of "Wide, Wide World" to film a segment of his weekly T.V. show at Shadows, in his efforts to publicize the site.

Master bedroom at Shadows-on-the-Teche c. 1831-34.

All of this publicity attracted visitors to Shadows, where Hall welcomed restoration architects and historians to the property, enjoying their conversation and appreciation of his family home. During Hall's lifetime, only the gardens were open to the public, but often brazen visitors would invade even the most private areas of Mr. Hall's living quarters. He once commented that the public was "seeing more of me than of Gypsy Rose Lee."

Hall sometimes felt overwhelmed by the number of visitors, increasingly so, as he became older, leading him to acquire the reputation of an eccentric recluse among the local townsfolk. He sometimes took delight in making tourists the butt of his jokes. On one occasion he obtained life-size papier-maché figures of buxom women and placed them in dim light inside bedroom windows of the Shadows. His particular sense of humor only supported his reputation in the minds of many locals.

It is to Hall's credit that many noteworthy people recognized something special about him. In his travel book *The Air- Conditioned Nightmare*, Henry Miller states about Hall: "He had transformed the house and grounds…into one of the most distinctive pieces of art which America can boast of. He was living and breathing in his own masterpiece."

Weeks Hall died on June 25, 1958 but was able to die content in the knowledge that Shadows-on-the-Teche would be preserved. Just one day before, Hall had received word that the National Trust for Historic Preservation would accept Shadows as one of their historic properties, and make it available for public tours. After restoration of the home was completed, the Shadows opened to the public in 1961.

• • • • •

Shadows-on-the-Teche is located on 317 East Main Street, New Iberia, at the intersection of Louisiana highways 182 & 14, thirty minutes southeast of Lafayette, and three hours west of New Orleans. It is open form 9 a.m. to 4:30 p.m. daily, with the exception of Thanksgiving, Christmas, & New Year's Day. Admission is charged. For further information please call: (318) 369-6446. Visit their website at http://www. nthp.org

Photos by Ron Blunt, courtesy of Shadows-on-the-Teche, National Trust Historic Site.

Architecture and Landscape as Art

Frederic Church's Olana

HUDSON • NEW YORK

FREDERIC EDWIN CHURCH, a leader of the Hudson River School of landscape painters, gained acclaim as the first internationally admired artist in America. He thought nothing of attacking on canvas the Aurora Borealis, the highest peaks of the Andes, and the full sweep of Niagara Falls. Crowds stood in line in New York City to see his paintings. In 1849, when he was only twenty-two, the National Academy of Design elected him a full member. Collectors and museums competed to buy his pictures at prices up to $12,500 - a record for an American artist at that time.

The only son of wealthy Hartford businessman Joseph Church, the future artist descended from a family whose Puritan ancestors had sailed to America on the

Olana 67

Court Hall. Filled with Chinese porcelains, Mexican folk pottery and Persian armor, this room represented past civilizations brought to the new world.

Mayflower. Frederic's father was a successful businessman and had hoped his son would follow in his footsteps; however, the young Church had a gift for drawing and was determined to paint pictures. The father relented and, in 1844, at the age of eighteen, Church left for Catskill, New York, to study with artist Thomas Cole (1801-1848). The English-born Cole was then forty-three and at the height of his artistic fame. He would later be called the founder of the "Hudson River School" – a group of landscape artists who created for Americans a vision of their beautiful nation as a God-given Eden.

By the late 1850s, Church had become the preeminent American landscape painter, succeeding Cole, who died unexpectedly of pneumonia in 1848. Within this time, Church painted three pictures – *Niagara* (1857), *The Heart of the Andes* (1859), and *Twilight in the Wilderness* (1860) – that were celebrated in both America and Europe. These paintings secured Church's fame, both artistically and financially. His *Niagara*, a wall-sized painting some three-and-a-half feet high by seven-feet wide, portrayed the swirling power of Niagara Falls with a vividness never before depicted two-dimensionally. Thousands of New Yorkers paid to look at this painting, purchased from the artist by a gallery on Broadway for the unheard of sum of $4,500.

Church was a reserved man for whom painting was a private matter, and his resulting fame was not always without difficulties. A turning point in his life arrived when, in June 1860, he married Isabel Mortimer Carnes, a young woman from Dayton, Ohio, whom the artist had first met at the New York exhibit of his *Heart of the Andes*. Of their first encounter, the *Boston Evening Transcript* quipped: "Church has been successfully occupied with another heart than that of the Andes."

Several months before he married Isabel, Church took time away from his New York City studio to travel up the Hudson and purchase a 126-acre plot of land known locally as Wynson Breezy Farm. Located directly across the river from the village of Catskill, where Church had studied with Cole, this property would become part of a house, grounds, and ornamental farm that Church eventually would call Olana.

After purchasing the Wyson Breezy farm, Church began construction of a modest country cottage ("Cozy Cottage") designed by architect Richard Morris Hunt (1827-1896), the architect of fashionable mansions in Newport, R.I., Asheville, North

Carolina and New York City. The couple began a family soon after, and eventually had six children, two of whom died in a diphtheria epidemic of 1865.

In 1867, Church bought the summit on which Olana was built. The importance he attached to this property is evident in a letter to friend and sculptor Eratus Dow Palmer: "I have purchased the wood lot on the top of the hill recently at a high price but I don't regret it...I want to secure...every rood of ground that I shall require to make my farm perfect." To design the house for the summit, Church again engaged Hunt, who envisioned a "French manor." Late that year, Church and his family left on a journey to Europe and the Middle East that would last until 1869.

Church's journey to England and the Middle East radically affected his image of what his new house should be. In England, where Church's paintings and reputation had preceded him, the couple was welcomed by fellow artists and admirers. Church wrote: "...my antiquated dress coat has had a busy time of it." By the early 1860s, many European architects, artists, and designers espoused the belief that a beautiful domestic environment would promote moral and spiritual fulfillment. Artful houses and interiors formed the focus of this movement—pattern and ornamentation, hand work and an exploration of eclectic sources.

Church found himself captivated by Middle Eastern architecture and buildings. He wrote his friend Palmer, "The dwellings (of Beirut) are often quite grand. They have a large room called the court in the center often 30 x 50 feet or larger - and perhaps thirty feet high . . . I have got new and excellent ideas about house building since I went abroad."

In addition to a central courtyard, Church decided that his new house should have thick, fortress-like walls and the interior should reflect the ornamental intricacy that he and his wife had seen in many Moorish homes. In sum, the house would be, as Church wrote in a letter, "Persian, adapted to the Occident." He also referred to this style as "Personal Persian."

Upon his return, Church replaced Hunt with English-born architect Calvert Vaux (1824-95), who had worked for American architect Andrew Jackson Downing (1815-52). With Vaux's help on structural matters, construction of the house was begun in 1870, in accordance with Church's design. Two years later, the family—now including four children—moved into the second story of the incomplete building. By the time it was completed in 1876, Church was spending the majority of his time on the design and landscaping of his home.

Church's approach to house design paralleled the way he planned a work of art: pencil sketches followed by more finished oil sketches as his ideas coalesced. From these sketches, in turn, he produced a final work of art. For Olana, Church sketched hundreds of drawings delineating every exterior and interior element - for some elements there are as many as twenty-five individual drawings. Final watercolor and oil sketches guided building construction. In all of these designs, including the later work of interior decoration, Church solicited his wife's opinion.

A series of misfortunes-both public and personal-contributed to Church's signifi-

Dining room/picture gallery. Designed by the artist to recollect a medieval hall, the two-story room holds an important collection of European Old Master paintings dating from the 14th to the 19th centuries.

cant contributions to the design of Olana. The artist would ride on a crescent of success until the 1870s, when tastes in American art changed and the work of the Hudson River School fell from fashion. While the market for Mr. Church's paintings declined, so did his physical health, as his right and left hands and arms became disabled with rheumatoid arthritis. From 1877 until his death in 1900 Church painted with increasing difficulty, devoting his efforts instead to his estate.

Although the initial impression of the interior may seem to be a chaotic profusion of color, Church, in fact, thoughtfully composed all aspects of the mansion's design. Mixing paints on his palette, he prepared color swatches for the walls of the ceilings of each room. With the butt of his brush, he inscribed in the wet paint the names of the rooms and the pigments employed to tender the color. Each room reflects Church's unique affinity for pigmentation: the formal reception room is gray-brown with a peach-colored ceiling; the sitting room has gray walls, salmon trim, and a light green ceiling; the court hall's yellow walls and glazed blue-green ceiling contrast with its alcoves which, separated from the main space by turquoise Islamic arches, have bright pink ceilings.

The exotic furnishings in Olana illustrate Church's wish to create a repository for the objects of civilization. "The whole house," wrote a nineteenth-century journalist, "is a museum of fine arts, rich in bronzes, paintings, sculptures, and antique and artistic specimens from all over the world." The court hall alone is, in fact, a distillation of cultural and geographical diversity containing French and Chinese porcelains, Kashmiri chairs,

Church designed and built this studio between 1888 and 1891. It remains one of the most intact and important 19th-century artist's studios in America.

a Mexican Madonna in an Indian niche, pre-Columbian figures, a Japanese Buddha, Persian metal wares and vases, Turkish rugs and throws, Moroccan taborets, American chairs and tables, South American butterflies, mounted Quetzels and Birds of Paradise.

The court hall, one of the earliest examples of a "living hall" in America, forms the spatial, visual, and artistic center of the house. The central room of the house, it is encircled by the other major living spaces, including the east parlor, sitting room, library, and dining room/picture gallery, all of which open off the court hall. Its style, including gold and silver painted decorations, is thought to have resembled one of the Beirut interiors that Church and his wife observed on their Middle Eastern trip.

For Church and his family, Olana was a home and a retreat, especially after the 1870s when public taste for the Hudson River School waned. Their sentiments are reflected in the name they chose for the estate. The word is a variation on *olane*, a fortress-treasure house in ancient Persia supposedly overlooking the Garden of Eden.

Yet Olana was not a home that could be built anywhere. Keenly attuned to nature, Church carefully chose the location of the main house and how it should relate to its surroundings. A key to Church's siting of Olana is the experience of looking out at the landscape and seeing it panoramically. With its breathtaking views of the Hudson Valley and Catskill Mountains, Olana offered Church a series of real-world panoramas similar to the landscapes he painted in his wall-size pictures.

Church carefully designed Olana's landscaped grounds between 1860 and 1891, transforming the agricultural landscape of the Wynson Breezy property into a pleasure ground and ornamental farm. He shaped the landscape as consciously as he created a painting. At Olana, the river, mountains, and sky provided a sublime background,

This comfortable sitting room was the focus of family activity. The painting above the mantle: "El Khasne, Petra," was executed by Church in 1875.

for which Church created a foreground and middle ground.

The farm itself occupied one-half of the 250-acre property and was an important part of life at Olana. For the house, it produced food and cut flowers. As a practical Yankee, Church insisted that the farm pay for itself; hay oats, rye, corn, apples, cherries, grapes, peaches, plums, pears, and strawberries were produced and shipped to market. At the same time, Church made aesthetic use of the farmstead, creatively manipulating the views of pastures, fields, and orchards.

Thick woodlands surrounded the house, park and farmstead. From the 1860s to 1890, Church planted hundreds of maples, birches, hemlocks, chestnuts and oaks, both singly and in clusters, throughout the property. He also had his workmen dig a lake with edges carefully sculpted to echo the shape of the Hudson as it widened to form the lake-like expanse in "the bend in the river."

Seven and a half miles of roads traverse the property. In the nineteenth century, carriage riding was an important recreation. Thus between 1884 to 1887, Church designed a series of roads to delight the traveler, including dramatic views, shifts in landscape, and destination points. He created innumerable vignettes—for example, open pastoral views contrasting with dark enveloping forest, and the serene waters of lake and river set against sun-dappled woodlands. Shifts in the light, atmosphere, and weather caused daily, even hourly, changes in these scenes. Touring the carriage roads of Olana, a visitor could experience the scenery as if it were a series of paintings.

Church's final addition to Olana was a studio. Projecting to the west, this space featured extraordinary framed views, a large north window for light, and an assemblage of objects to provide visual pleasure for the artist and his family. The design and construction of this space helped to affirm Church's continuing role as an artist while providing him with a further creative diversion. Twenty years earlier Church had taken two years and $60,000 dollars to build the original house. For the studio extension with only two main rooms, he spent three years and $35,000. "I wonder," Church mused in a letter to a friend, "whether I shall work as hard in the new studio as I did in erecting it?"

Upon construction of the studio in 1891, Church lived another nine years. His wife Isabel died in 1899 and Church died one year later. Olana was inherited by their son Louis who, with his wife Sally, made few changes to the estate. After their deaths in 1943 and 1964, Olana passed to relatives who were not interested in preservation. In 1965, Olana and its contents were scheduled for auction. To save the estate from dispersal, local civic leaders, architectural and art historians, and nationally prominent supporters of the arts formed Olana Preservation. All recognized the rarity of a nineteenth-century American artist's home surviving intact. By 1966, after raising two-thirds of the purchase price, they persuaded the New York State Legislature to allocate the remaining funds and to accept Olana as a state historic site.

Olana State Historic Site is currently owned and operated by the New York State Office of Parks, Recreation, and Historic Preservation (OPRHP). This organization is committed to the preservation of the historic structure, its designed landscape, the views from the site, the historic collections, and the interpretation of Olana collections to the broadest possible audience. Assistance in their endeavors has been aided by the formation of Friends of Olana, a private not-for-profit education corporation, established in 1971. Their mission includes supporting and conducting ongoing preservation and development, as well as research and educational programs at Olana. In addition, they are engaged in private, state and national fund-raising for preservation of structures, collections, and education at the site.

• • • • •

The entrance to Olana is located on Route 9G, one mile south of the Rip Van Winkle Bridge near Hudson, New York. The estate's grounds are open throughout the year, from 8:00 a.m. to sunset. The house is open for guided tours April through October, Wednesday through Sunday, 10:00 a.m. to 5:00 p.m. It is also open on Memorial Day, Independence Day, Labor Day, and Columbus Day. The last tour begins at 5:00 p.m., after which there is no admittance. An admission fee is required. Tour reservations are not required, however tickets are limited. Group reservations are also available. For further information, call:(518)828-0135 or visit the website at http://www.olana.org.

Photos courtesy of the NYS Office of Parks, Recreation and Historic Preservation, Olana State Historic Site.

74 *The Governor's Palace*

Hanging in the ballroom are large portraits of George III and Queen Charlotte, painted by Allan Ramsey, the king's official portrait painter.

Rockefeller's Delight

The Governor's Palace

WILLIAMSBURG • VIRGINIA

ONE OF EARLY AMERICA'S most fascinating mansions is the Governor's Palace of Colonial Williamsburg. Symbol of the power and authority of the British crown in colonial Virginia, it stands out as a forerunner of the flowering of Virginia gentry style in the first half of the eighteenth century.

The Governor's Palace is a keystone feature of the Historic Area of Williamsburg, both as a museum and as a part of its history. From 1699 to 1780, Williamsburg had been the capital of Virginia, an area that extended North to the Great Lakes and West to the Mississippi River. Before the American Revolution, the Palace was the residence and headquarters for the British king's deputy. It later functioned as the official residence of

The supper room of the Governor's Palace with table set for a seated dessert. The room is distinguished by its hand-carved cornices and woodwork.

seven royal governors and the first two governors of the Commonwealth of Virginia: Patrick Henry and Thomas Jefferson. Situated on a large imposing lawn, the governor's residence, located directly perpendicular to the main axis of town and to the College of William and Mary, was once revered as a symbol of local authority.

The original Governor's Palace, of which the present one is an exact duplicate, was destroyed by fire in late December, 1781, while Jefferson was in residence and some rooms were being used as a temporary hospital for soldiers wounded at Yorktown. For the next 125 years, the once illustrious landmark and its immediate environs stood in a state of ruin. Altering the course of misfortune would prove to be a difficult, but significant, historical challenge.

In 1926, Dr. W.A.R. Goodwin, a local Episcopal rector, set out to persuade John D. Rockefeller Jr. to finance the restoration of an entire eighteenth-century town using modern research techniques. After a few walks through the neglected streets, Mr. Rockefeller decided that the historic part of Williamsburg should be restored because it had been an important training ground for leaders of American independence. This dream evolved into Colonial Williamsburg, where preservationists set out "to restore the setting of great historical events, and recover the great object lesson in monumental town planning." Rockefeller was determined to rebuild the palace and the capital completely, "preserving existing foundations wherever possible."

Rockefeller set up Colonial Williamsburg as a corporation to "recreate accurately the environment of the men and women of eighteenth-century Williamsburg and to bring about an understanding of their lives and times that present and future generations may more vividly appreciate the contribution of these early Americans to the ideals and culture of our country." Rockefeller gave the idea his full support for more than thirty years. He committed the necessary financing to accomplish the work and fully endowed its educational programs.

Three thousand surrounding acres were acquired as a buffer. Although it stretches for a mile through the heart of the community, the restoration is only part of modern Williamsburg. At one end of the village is William and Mary College, whose celebrated Christopher Wren building was also restored. By the time he was finished, Mr. Rockefeller had acquired 173 acres, restored eighty-eight original buildings, and reconstructed hundreds of others. Ninety acres of gardens were similarly restored and developed.

Many pre-existing elements contributed to the restoration of the Governor's Palace. Former president Thomas Jefferson, a one-time resident and accomplished self-taught architect, drew accurate measurements and rooms within the residence. A French military cartographer had drawn a layout of the town. After the death of one governor in 1770, a meticulously detailed inventory of household furnishings was discovered. For the Rockefeller reconstruction, researchers also had recourse to letters, wills, deeds, and maps to provide guidance. During excavations, builders found the original foundations of the palace; these were largely used for the new building, and so were the foundations of existing buildings.

Planning for the original palace began in 1706, a few years after the capital of Virginia had been moved from Jamestown to Williamsburg. The colonial assembly set aside 3,000 pounds for the construction of an "official residence" for governors. Henry Cary, a master builder who supervised the construction of other buildings for the Royal Crown, took charge of the project. Alexander Spotswood, then Governor, gave most of his time to the development of the palace and its garden. The building was not completed until 1722. By that time the costs had sky-rocketed far beyond the original appropriation. When the building was finally completed, one townsman referred to it as "a magnificent structure built at the publick expense, finished with gates, fine gardens, offices, walks, a fine canal, orchards, etc."

The Governor's Palace enjoyed a brief but illustrious history as the home to seven royal governors, beginning with Governor Alexander Spotswood, the first executive to reside in the building. By the late 1760s the increasing importance of Virginia's wealth to Britain and the deteriorating relationship between them brought the governor's office into greater prominence. As Virginia entered an age of unparalleled material consumption, the Governor's Palace became a primary meeting ground for merchants, diplomats, polite society and townsmen.

The red-brick architecture of the palace, usually described as Georgian, in many respects resembles that of pre-Georgian English country estates. No obvious local antecedent for the house has survived, nor did it have any imitators; no other mansion rivaled its elegance. Its official appearance is further enhanced by a stately cupola rising above the balustraded roof. For special occasions a lantern was, and still is, hung in the cupola at night. Dutch influences introduced into England by William III are discernible in this and other details.

The Renaissance is reflected in the formal gardens and in the regimented layout of subsidiary buildings. However, the broad chimneys of several buildings and the contours of the smokehouse, laundry, wellhead and salt house have a distinctive Virginia design. The floors of several rooms within the mansion are of weathered pine boards salvaged from old Virginia barns and houses.

Extensive repairs and expansion of the palace were undertaken around 1753. At this time, a ball and supper room were added to allow for increased entertaining. Parties served political purposes but also were a main source of pleasure to the Governors and First Ladies. Lord Botecourt wrote when he was governor that "52 dined with me yesterday and I expect at least that number today." Among the most elegant and up-to-date rooms in the building, the ballroom and supper room became a stage on

The bedchamber of Lord Botetourt, the last governor to reside in the palace, contains a Virginia-made mahogany bedstead dressed in "double drapery" curtains.

which the governor and his guests acted out the latest forms of etiquette and displayed themselves as being in touch with the world's most fashionable and civilized conversation and manners. Food was carried in great covered containers from the kitchen in an adjacent building to the dining rooms. Thousands of bottles of imported wines, brought by ship up the James River, were kept under lock in cellar vaults until needed.

The colony provided basic furnishings for the palace, but most Governors also had valuable treasures of their own - largely imported from England. Consequently, inventories were carefully kept in official archives. Later, these records proved invaluable to redevelopers in acquiring antiques of identical type. In all, over 16,500 objects, both practical and decorative, were itemized on the occasion of the first inventory in 1770.

The main entrance hall is paneled in black walnut; its floor is of black and white

A garden view at the rear of the Governor's Palace.

marble. In cabinets and on walls are collections of early muskets, swords, flintlock pistols and other weapons. The forecourt's castellated walls create something of a military effect; these walls, however, are decorative but so nonfunctional that the Earl of Dunmore took to his heels unhesitatingly when the colonists rebelled.

Hanging in the ballroom are large portraits of George III and Queen Charlotte, painted by Allan Ramsey (1713-84). Chinese Chippendale tables are under the portraits. A glass case contains a rare collection of miniatures presented to the restoration by Sir Campbell Stuart.

The parlor contains one of the palace's many Waterford crystal chandeliers. This room served as a waiting room, as well as a place for business or entertainment. Antique settees and smoking chairs upholstered with old needlework, looking glasses, as well as thirty-four scripture-prints (popular in that period) adorn this room.

The supper room is distinguished for its hand-carved cornices and woodwork that indicate the Chinese influence once so popular in England. An antique chandelier is of Irish glass. Chinese wallpaper in this room was stripped from an English house. Lord Botecourt would later add central heating to this room as well as to the ballroom.

The large middle room on the second floor recalls the intimate side of life in the palace. This setting was used for the reception of "ambassadors, courtiers, and other personages of high station." By mid-century the western side was used to accommodate the Governor's library and bedroom. Within this library the governors collected literature of their time, including the novels *Tom Jones* and *The Adventures of Joseph Andrews*, as well as traditional historical, legal and religious fare. Thomas Jefferson, an avid bibliophile, amassed 1,250 volumes during his stay.

About forty-five of the sixty interior spaces in Botecourt's inventory were servants' living quarters, not including the laundry, kitchen, and pantry. Status determined the locations of living quarters within the household; size and quality of furnishings also depended upon rank. Lower servants might share a room with upper servants or be assigned a space to share with work-related equipment. The lowest servants and the slaves slept in attics or were relegated to spaces that served as a guard function near valuable items, such as horses.

Only a few steps from the palace is a harmonious building that held the Governor's office, and another building that was the guardhouse. The unruliness of the colonists caused the last royal governor, John Murray, fourth Earl of Dunmore to keep marines close at hand both day and night. With the coming of the American Revolution, the Earl of Dunmore fled Williamsburg. The palace then served as a residence for the first two governors of the new Commonwealth of Virginia, Patrick Henry and Thomas Jefferson. Although Jefferson is known to have drawn up proposals to remodel the palace, his changes never materialized, as the seat of power in Virginia would be moved to Richmond in 1780.

The Rockefeller researchers were excavating one day south of the fruit garden when they discovered the bones of 156 men and two women - most likely the remains of soldiers and nurses who had been injured in the Yorktown campaign of 1781 and taken to the palace for treatment. Today, a simple stone tablet honors their sacrifice.

Just around the corner from the palace is the original George Wythe House. Wythe (1726-1806), a mild-mannered revolutionist who fought the British, was a leader of Virginia's plantation society. His home, now open to the public, served as one of George Washington's many headquarters near the end of the Revolutionary War. Several other houses are also open to visitors, each with its own distinctive features.

The Governor's Palace would set a precedent for future architects as well as become a leading Virginia cultural symbol. Today it remains a shrine that honors not only America's past, but the scholarship and hardwork of modern day restoration.

• • • • •

Colonial Williamsburg is located between Richmond and Norfolk on Interstate 64. Take exit 238, then follow the signs to the Visitor's Center. Hours of exhibition vary seasonally. Tickets necessary to tour the Governor's Palace and other Colonial Williamsburg exhibitions are available at the Visitor's Center and outlets in the Historic Area. For ticket information call 1-800-HISTORY or visit the Colonial Williamsburg website at http://www.Colonialwilliamsburg.org.

Photos courtesy of the Colonial Williamsburg Foundation

A Suffragette's Château

The Marble House Revisited

NEWPORT • RHODE ISLAND

THE MOST ELEGANT, although not the largest, resort house in America when it was first built, William K. and Alva Vanderbilt's former summer home, Marble House, overlooks the Atlantic Ocean on Newport's illustrious Bellevue Avenue. Some travelers say it still holds the distinction of being the area's most elegant and, because of economic and social transitions, it may never be equaled.

The Vanderbilts called it their "cottage" although it cost eleven million dollars to construct. It was their summer residence, used when they were not at their homes in New York City and Jekyll Island, Georgia, or traveling around the world on their palatial yacht, the *Alva*. They stayed at Marble House only six or seven weeks of the

The dining room at Marble House is inspired by the Salon of Hercules at Versailles. A full-length portrait of young Louis XV by Jean-Baptiste van Loo (1684-1745) hangs over the east wall in its original 18th century presentation frame.

year. Mr. Vanderbilt was a grandson of Commodore Cornelius Vanderbilt (1794-1877), founder of the clan and its fortune in America. Mrs. Vanderbilt was the former Alva Smith, the headstrong daughter of a cotton planter from Mobile, Alabama. By 1892 she was known as one of the foremost hostesses of New York and Newport society, thanks largely to the privilege her marriage had accorded her.

The couple built Marble House in time for the debut of Consuelo, one of their three children. Just a year after their daughter's marriage in 1895 to the Duke of Marlborough, the couple were divorced. The outspoken Mrs. Vanderbilt stated, "I blaze the trail for the rest to walk in. I was the first girl of my set to marry a Vanderbilt. Then I was the first society woman to ask for a divorce, and within a year ever so many have followed my example." In the divorce settlement, Mrs. Vanderbilt received ownership of Marble House. Soon after, however, she married a neighbor, Oliver H.P. Belmont, and at his insistence began residence at his own mansion, Belcourt, which was located down the street.

The Marble House, with its great collection of art treasures from many parts of the world, was boarded up for years. When Mr. Belmont died suddenly in 1908, the militant and energetic Alva Vanderbilt Belmont returned to the mansion and started it on a new life as a center for suffragettes. An imaginative woman, Alva was the first one to wear bloomers in Newport, the first female to drive an automobile there, and the

The Gold Ballroom features some of the richest ornamentation in the house. The fleur-de-pèche marble fireplace holds large bronze figures of Old Age and Youth and a mask of Dionysus, all by Jules Allard.

first woman anywhere to be elected to membership in the American Institute of Architects. She shocked Newport by cutting her hair short, speaking of God as "She," and finally by using her property as a base for "radical" activity. Tiring of the America scene however, Alva boarded up the mansion again in 1924 and moved to Paris, where she spent the remainder of her life.

Richard Morris Hunt (1828-95), the celebrated designer of many mansions in New York City and Newport, was the architect hired by the Vanderbilts. He completed the structure in 1892 after four years of planning, including detailed inspections of Versailles and other palaces of Europe that he admired.

So much imported marble was used in the mansion's construction that the general contractor, Charles E. Clarke, built a wharf, warehouse and stone-carving center at

The small, colorful Chinese Teahouse was designed by the sons of Richard Morris Hunt on the basis of their own research in the Orient. It was used primarily for entertaining.

the harbor at Newport. The largest quantity of white marble used on the exterior of the mansion came from a quarry at Tuckahoe in Westchester County, New York. Batterson, See & Eisele handled the masterful marble installations. Mr. Vanderbilt became so enthused about the beauty of the marble work that he commissioned Austro-American sculptor Karl Bitter (1867-1915) to carve a bas-relief of Mr. Hunt to hang beside one of Jules Mansart (1646-1708), the architect of Versailles. Both carved portraits are in the Marble House today for everybody to see. Following his work at Newport, Bitter was rewarded with municipal commissions in New York. These included the creation of a fountain in front of the Plaza Hotel, the bronze doors of Trinity Church and sculpture on the façade of the Metropolitan Museum of Art.

Mr. Vanderbilt kept the construction of the mansion a guarded secret, and it is believed that men working on different aspects of the building were sequestered and forbidden to discuss the project. Marble Palace was the first mansion built in Newport by the Vanderbilt family and its erection was eagerly anticipated in the press and in artistic circles.

Grillwork for the mansion was made by the John Williams Bronze Foundry of New York City. Before being shipped to Newport it was exhibited publicly with the fanfare of a great art show. The ornamental grille that now screens the entrance hall is sixteen feet high, twenty-five wide and weighs ten tons. Unrivaled in America in terms of composition, forging and texture, the grille contains four posts in the shape of Corinthian pilasters. They divide the grille into bays. In a center bay is a door eleven feet high. So heavy that they swing on pivots instead of hinges, the doors are a masterpiece of craftsmanship. Among the ornaments of the grille are masks of the boy

Apollo set against a sunburst (symbol of Louis XIV), and plaques monogrammed "WV."

The entrance hall is twenty-feet high and is lined and paved with yellow Sienna marble from Monte Arenti, a quarry near Montagnola, Italy. The ceiling has stucco relief in the form of masks and arabesques of fruit, foliage and animals.

Located in the entrance hall are two tapestries from Gobelins, one of France's renowned tapestry works. One woven in 1791 on the cartoon of Joseph-Benoit Suvee depicts Admiral Gaspard de Coligny, the Protestant leader, about to be assassinated. The other one, woven in 1790 on the cartoon of Barthelmy, depicts Etienne Marcel, Provost of Paris, being murdered by Jean Maillard. French antiques of past centuries are in the hall, along with ornamental furnishings bearing the "WV" monogram and elaborate cabinets made under Mr. Hunt's supervision by J. Allard et Fils of Paris. Huge mirrors are framed in the Venetian manner.

The Gold Room, which also served as a ballroom, contains some of the richest ornamentation. Its fabulous beauty once prompted a guest in the 1890s to liken it to a jewel box, "far ahead of any palace I have ever seen...or dreamed of." The walls are lavishly gilded and have arched bays for doors and windows. Carved panels are again the work of Karl Bitter. The mantle holds bronze figures set on Fleur de Pèche marble: Old Age and Youth hold candelabra while in between is the mask of Dionysus with garlands of ormolu flowers. Above the mask, a glass globe of the earth revolves to tell the hour, the day and the month. Inside the fireplace, between panel of fleur-de-lis, is a fireback depicting Hades, king of the underworld, seizing Persephone as his future queen. Symbolic masks, cherubs and cupids are found in the fabric, metal and plaster decorations throughout the room. Two large chandeliers carrying cherubs with trumpets resemble those of the Chateau Maisons-Lafitte near Paris. In the four corners of the rooms are candelabra held by sea urchins seated on pedestals of Fleur de Pèche marble.

An eclectic display of furnishings are found in the Marble House's Gothic Room, the rococo library, the elaborate dining room and the patios. The Gothic Room, a fine example of Alva's eclecticism, was designed in the French Gothic decorative style; with characteristic arches, ribbing, figurative carving, fireplace and stained glass windows. The grand staircase to upper floors is a centerpiece. Rising in a hall that is forty-feet high, it is composed of the same yellow marble as that in the paving and walls of the hall. Its wrought-iron and bronze railing and gilt bronze trophies in the eighteenth century style were made in Paris by Jules Allard (1831-1907) from designs produced by Hunt in collaboration with Alva Vanderbilt.

Hanging above the mezzanie is a chandelier from the Allard workshop, a marble bust of Louis XIV and several portraits. A mural on the ceiling, created in the Venetian manner of Gianbattista Tiepolo (1696-1770), depicts a woman clad in red and blue garments with a star above her head. Cherubs lay at her feet while a winged woman is blowing a trumpet.

Bedrooms, sitting rooms and landings are similarly decorated and furnished. Alva's bedroom is ornate. On the walls are cherubs with shields bearing her initial; the room is in the ebullient style of Louis XV. Wood and stucco arabesques as well as figures from the ceiling and overdoors are repeated in the design of her elaborate custom-made bed inspired by a Daniel Maro (1663-1752) drawing. The recently restored wall fabrics by the designer Roux contain rich tones of lavender. They have been rewoven for this room by the original maker, the French firm of Prelle in Lyon. Mr. Vanderbilt's bedroom is simply decorated in the sober style of Louis XVI. The mantelpiece is of purple breccia marble.

The grounds of the mansion are populated by fine stands of beech, linden, maple, elm, oak and horse chesnut trees. Located on the Bellevue Avenue side of the property is a high wall of Tuckahoe marble and a wrought-iron gate.

On the edge of the cliff overlooking the ocean is a Chinese Teahouse that Alva Belmont had built in 1913 when she had returned to the mansion following the death of Mr. Belmont. Craftsmen were brought from China to complete the structure, which served mainly a decorative purpose. Built for small receptions and tea parties, the interior decoration includes wooden panels painted in the style of the Ming Dynasty, a green-tiled roof with typically upswept eaves, half-round red pillars, and two dozen mahogany-framed glass doors. Moved to a new location on the estate in 1977, conservation work on the Teahouse was completed in 1982. That fall, the Chinese Teahouse was officially reopened by Ambassador Chai Zemin of the People's Republic of China.

Following Alva's death in 1932, the Marble House was purchased by Frederick H. Prince of Boston, owner of one of New England's leading brokerage firms and president of the Chicago Junction Railways & Union Stock Yards Company. The Prince family summered in the residence for thirty years. In 1963, the Preservation Society of Newport County purchased the home as a museum for the public to visit in perpetuity. The purchase of the mansion was made possible by gifts from Harold S. Vanderbilt, a son of the original owners and a noted yachtsman and contract-bridge authority, and the Frederick H. Prince Trust. In 1976, a Memorial Room was created to celebrate Harold S. Vanderbilt's distinguished yachting career. Vanderbilt's trophies, which include seven silver-gilt King's Cups and the Astor Cup, are depicted among drawings and photographs of Vanderbilt boats. An oil portrait of Harold Vanderbilt in New York Yacht Club commodore's dress by Bernard Boutet de Monvel (1884-1949) is also displayed.

• • • • •

The Marble House is located on Bellevue Avenue near downtown Newport, Rhode Island. It is open daily from 10:00 a.m. to 5:00 p.m. from March 31 through October 31. Admission is charged. For further information contact The Preservation Society of Newport County at: (401) 847-1000, or visit the Preservation Society website at http://www.Newportmansions.org.

Photos courtesy of the Preservation Society of Newport County.

The Model T Mansion

Henry Ford's Fair Lane

DEARBORN • MICHIGAN

THE SUCCESS OF the Ford Motor Company brought a stream of uninvited callers to the doors of Henry and Clara Ford's Edison Avenue Detroit mansion. Reporters, salesmen, and job seekers deprived the family of the privacy they desired. The couple soon wished to build a new home, one removed from the rapidly expanding city, where they could satisfy their love of nature, gardening and bird-watching. Never comfortable with the boisterous life of Detroit society, the Fords abandoned plans to follow the migration of the city's wealthy to the eastern suburbs, and instead chose to settle in the town of Dearborn, about two miles from the farm where Mr. Ford was born. The world-famous automaker had been buying property in the area for several years.

Fair Lane 87

A fireplace in the dining room is made from the same Ohio limestone as the exterior of the house.

So in February 1914, work began on what would be the couple's fifteenth and final home - Fair Lane.

Fair Lane is located two miles downstream from the Rouge River, near the Ford Motor Company. In this area Ford spent his childhood, went to school, then courted and married Clara Bryant. Although Mr. Ford chose to leave his father's farm to start his career as an apprentice machinist, he remained attached to his childhood home throughout his life.

Fair Lane would be a private place, close enough to Mr. Ford's work, but sufficiently secluded so that the automaker could spend his spare time tinkering with new ideas in his private laboratory, surrounded by acres of woods lush with the birds and wildlife he cherished. Between 500 and 800 masons, woodcarvers, and artisans worked year round to complete the estate as quickly as possible. Reflecting the Fords' love for nature, the residence was built with rough-hewn Ohio limestone to harmonize with the surrounding countryside. The goal was to make the house appear to be a natural part of the land. Designed by noted landscape architect Jens Jenson (1860-1951), the grounds were transformed from farmland into a natural, native landscape. Jensen was chiefly responsible for the establishment of the Cook County Forest Preserve, the most extensive system of nature parks instituted by any U.S. city or metropolitan area.

Fair Lane is neither the largest nor the most opulent house of its era. Mr. Ford was proud of his simple tastes and felt no need to flaunt his substantial wealth. He cautioned the architects against building lavishly; the residence's total cost was not to exceed $250,000. Despite this directive, building costs totaled $1,875,000 at the time of the mansion's completion. Interior decorating cost an additional $175,000 with property development and landscaping adding another $370,000 to the final bill. By January, 1916, the Fords were completely settled into their new home; the estate was named Fair Lane after the area in County Cork, Ireland, where Mr. Ford's ancestors had once lived.

More than most mansions, Fair Lane has the personality of its owner embedded into its 31, 770 square feet of living space, ten-car garage, secluded laboratory and vast gardens. Thus, 100 yards from his new home, Henry constructed a powerhouse that required three men to operate. The powerhouse was connected to his new home by an underground tunnel and contained two generators and several separate systems. Water power provided the estate with electricity; Mr. Ford was an avid promoter of water as a clean, abundant energy source. He dammed the river to divert a portion through two turbines built sixteen feet below the floor. In another room, two massive coke-running boilers provided heat for the residence. Mr. Ford also installed a steam engine and a unique bank of batteries to be used as backups should the water level in the river fall. The powerhouse contains many touches which make it decorative as well as functional. Gleaming dials, gauges, and circuit breakers stand encased in polished two-inch-thick marble panels. The copper-crafted air vent covers depict the birdlife which could be found in abundance on the estate. Such care was lavished on the building that President Herbert Hoover, once caught in a rainstorm during his visit to Fair Lane, was able to dry his hat by placing it on a spotlessly clean boiler steam pipe.

During the Fords' residency, the 1,300 acres of Fair Lane bustled with activity. In addition to the residence and its powerhouse, the estate included a summer house, a man-made lake complete with skating house for the winter, staff cottages, a gatehouse, pony barn, greenhouse, root cellar, vegetable garden, a "Santa's Workshop" for Christmas celebrations, a maple sugar shack, a working farm for the Ford grandchildren built to their scale, agricultural research facilities, and 500 bird houses to satisfy Mr. Ford's interest in ornithology.

The gardens were the scene of Mr. Ford's frequent strolls and long meetings with such notables as Thomas A. Edison, who laid the cornerstone of the mansion, and John Burroughs, the naturalist. Mr. Edison had a permanent room in the house. A Burroughs grotto and garden are located behind the house. When Burroughs died in 1921, Mr. Ford ordered a vigil lantern be kept lit in the grotto for ten years. The main rose garden of three acres contains 10,000 hybrid tea roses, 1,000 climbers and 500 pillar roses. The grounds also contain a flower garden with over 1,000 specimens of peonies. A continuous flow of water reaches pools and lily ponds.

An avid reader, Mr. Ford maintained a library of 10,000 books at Fair Lane and occasionally spent $4,000 a month on limited editions. Many titles were left unread and still crack when opened. His favorites included Dickens' novels, the McGuffey

The upper level of Fair Lane's staircase features elaborate carvings and a window etched with one of Ford's favorite quotes.

readers, *Gray's Anatomy* and scientific articles. He often jotted on the pages of these his thoughts, such as:

"The man who cuts his own wood warms himself twice."

" I don't read newspapers, they confuse me."

"The man who smokes in the dining room needs his mother again."

"Any fool can save a dollar. It takes a smart man to spend it wisely."

In like manner, Mr. Ford's philosophy is etched and carved on the mansion.

Inscribed in a lead-glass window of the main staircase is his famous "don't waste time" admonition, which reads:

"To no one is given
right of delay.
Noted in heaven pas-
seth each day.
Be not thou fruitless,
work while ye may.
Trifling were bootless,
watch thou and pray."

Mr. Ford frequently entertained at Fair Lane, including scientists, businessmen, royalty, various presidents of the United States and other notables on his list. The Fords, who did not drink, kept ample supplies of liquor on hand for guests. They also maintained an indoor swimming pool (now filled in and serving as a restaurant), a bowling alley and a ballroom. The house has walls that are

Fair Lane's dining room, where Thomas A. Edison and other notables were entertained, has mahogany paneling and sterling silver fixtures.

two-feet thick, some 200 feet long, and which conform to the contour of the land in a manner common to more modern structures - even those of Frank Lloyd Wright. Because the Fords designed Fair Lane to be highly private and self-contained, it is uncertain how large a staff was retained to run the estate. About a half-dozen people worked in the residence itself while technicians, stokers, and electricians were always on duty in the estate's powerhouses. A considerably larger staff was needed to maintain the extensive gardens of Fair Lane. Up to twenty-five men tended the grounds on a seasonal basis, but exact numbers are difficult to determine due to Mr. Ford's practice of augmenting the staff with workers temporarily pulled from his assembly lines.

On April 6, 1947, a spring flood sent the Rouge River cascading over its bank; smashing walls, toppling trees and crippling the generators. Although eighty-three years old, Mr. Ford inspected the damage and planned repairs for the next day. Ford went to bed at 9:00 p.m. by candlelight, after power went on long enough for him to listen to two of his favorite radio shows. Two hours later he notified his wife that he felt ill. She was instantly at his side, as she had been for fifty-nine years. The telephone

The master bedroom at Fair Lane, where Henry Ford died in 1947.

lines were out of order so she sent a chauffeur for medical assistance. When a physician arrived on the scene, Mr. Ford was already dead. On a wall of the powerhouse workmen have chalked the high-water mark, with a notation concerning "the boss:" *As he was born, he died by candlelight.*

Mrs. Ford remained in the residence for three more years until her own death in 1950. Upon her death, her grandchildren commissioned the Parke-Bernet Galleries of New York to conduct an auction of the home's furnishings; other sales occurred to disperse less valuable furnishings.

In 1952, the Ford Motor Company purchased the estate from the heirs and, after renovating parts of the interior, established its corporate archives in the office. Ford Archives remained until 1957, when the company donated the residence, powerhouse, 210 acres, and $6.5 million to the University of Michigan for the creation of a Dearborn campus. In 1963 a local group, the "Women of Fair Lane", persuaded university officials to allow tours of the home. These lasted for three years, until Ford Motor Company and the University of Michigan reacquired much of the house for administrative purposes. The Henry Ford Estate, including seventy-two of the original 1,300 acres, was designated a National Historic Landmark in 1966. Public tours of the historic home were reintroduced in the 1970s. Since then, a limited staff, generous contributors, and approximately 250 volunteers successfully continue ongoing renovation of the estate.

Work has been undertaken to preserve and protect the site for future generations.

Interior rooms and five acres of gardens have been renewed and restored. Critical infrastructure repairs have been completed. Just recently, the 1915 powerhouse hydropower plant began generating electricity again. The strides that have been made are significant and, in large measure, are driven by the importance of the Henry Ford Estate as a National Historic Landmark to the local and world community.

• • • • •

Fair Lane is located ten miles west of Detroit and just north of Michigan Avenue. Tours are available Monday through Saturday from 10:00 a.m. to 3:00 p.m., and on Sundays from 1:00 p.m. to 4:30 p.m. Tours are restricted during the months of January-March. The estate is closed on Thanksgiving, Christmas Eve, Christmas, New Years Day and Easter. Admission is charged. Children under five are admitted free. For further information call: (313)593-5590, or visit the mansion website at http://www.umd.umich.edu/fairlane.

All photos by: Balthazar-Korab, Ltd., courtesy of the collections of the Henry Ford Estate-Fair Lane.

The Steamboat Gothic

San Francisco on the Mississippi

Reserve • Louisiana

THE PACKETS ON THE Mississippi River never pretended to have the grace of the prima-donna yachts of Newport or the big sharp-prowed ocean liners of the Atlantic and the Pacific. Although ornate and often elegant, they were clearly the work horses of the river trade and not the high-stepping trotters of the race tracks. Ghostlike, the great cumbersome boats churned their way slowly up and down the Mississippi through misty moonlight, fog, rain and sleet, as well as sunshine. Their steam-stained copper throats bellowed deep notes of warning as they crept around blind curves in the river. And as these white, tall-chimneyed monsters hove into sight at wharves, river-front folk hurried to the shore to watch and wave.

Of an exterior design that became known as Steamboat Gothic, San Francisco is the most famous of several mansions that Southerners, infatuated with the picturesque packets, built on the shores as homes for their families.

Francis Parkinson Keyes immortalized San Francisco in her novel *Steamboat Gothic* and currently the seventeen-room mansion is a select attraction among plantation tours sponsored by the State of Louisiana, oil companies and educational groups. Officially called the San Francisco Plantation House, this recently restored landmark is located on the east bank of the Mississippi in St. John the Baptist Parish, less than an hour's drive from New Orleans.

The house resembles a floating packet as much as a stationary structure can and still be useful as a dwelling. Its broad double galleries resemble the spacious double decks of a ship. Twin stairways rise to the front door as stairways on a luxurious packet rose to the entrance of the main saloon. Even the belvedere of the mansion has a glitter of glass that suggests a pilot house. As on a ship, the main hallway bisects the entire structure, with rooms opening onto it.

The entryway is lit by a chandelier installed by former resident Clark Thompson.Electricity was not added to the mansion until 1954.

Edmund Marmillion, who built the mansion, was a wealthy planter who lived across the river on a plantation of cane fields, slaves and sugar mills. The family acquired 240 acres for the property from Elise Rilleaux, a free man of color, in 1830. A small white residence on the property became the core of San Francisco, not visible from outside the mansion but a vital part of the framework. The main crop at the plantation was sugar cane; thus, Edmund followed his good business sense and built his sugar mill first, then his dream home.

The house, which took three years to build, was completed in 1856. In plan and design the interior of the house is Louisiana Creole: rooms open *en suite,* with the main living quarters located on the second floor and secondary rooms on the ground floor. The style of the interior is juxtaposed with the Victorian style of the exterior, which features Corinthian columns and Gothic revival dormer windows. It is believed that the mansion was built with the assistance of slave labor. Through inventories which were meticulously recorded throughout the original owners lives, it has been revealed that Edmund Marmillion owned 143 slaves and his son Valsin, who was in charge of the plantation's initial renovation, owned 180.

The Downriver Parlor, showing a portion of the of the ceilings by Italian artist Dominique Canova.

Marmillon was his own architect and builder, and he was good at both professions - later it was discovered that much millwork was marked with his initials, "EBM." He imported iron grillwork from France for the balustrades, used fluted Corinthian columns abundantly on the exterior and interior of the house, bought costly cast-iron capitals from northern foundries, used triple dentil moldings where one would have sufficed and added rococo grillwork, fretwork and gingerbread to achieve the architectural likeness he had found in packets.

After Edmund's death in 1856, his two surviving sons, Valsin Bozonier Marmillion and Charles Bozonier Marmillion, lived in the mansion until their deaths. Valsin was educated in Europe and while touring there he met Louise Von Seybold from Bavaria, Germany. They married in Europe soon after meeting. The couple had originally planned to visit Valsin's family in Louisiana and then return to Europe to manage a vineyard and produce wine for sale/shipment to the United States. They arrived at the Plantation in 1856 to discover that their father had suddenly died of a stroke; immediately Valsin was overburdened with family responsibilities. Charles, then sixteen years old, was still too young to effectively oversee maintenance of the estate.

Valsin and Louise decided to remain at the plantation, temporarily at first, but were soon overburdened themselves with Louise's first pregnancy and the approach of the Civil War. Despite the couple's change in plans, Louise would feel comfortable in her new home; there were so many German families living on the east and west banks of the Mississippi that it was known as the German Coast. Valsin and Louise had five children, all girls. Only three would survive to adulthood; one died at birth and the fifth died after falling down the stairs of the mansion.

A series of good sugar crops triggered Valsin and Louise's decision to undertake a renovation of the plantation in 1858. Louise Von Seybold Marmillion, who would later be credited for her considerable architectural influence upon the house, was responsible for the selection of the brilliant exterior colors of the mansion as well as the faux marbling and five hand-painted ceilings of the interior. It is said that Louise enlisted the aid of a young artist by the name of Dominique Canova, a young Italian artist working in New Orleans at the time on the St. Louis Cathedral and St. Louis Hotel. He was hired to paint the five hand-painted ceilings and the faux marbling throughout the house. Two 8,000-gallon cisterns, built of cypress and copper, were installed beside the mansion. Rain water drained into them from the roofs and then flowed into the house's plumbing system.

After the work was completed, Valsin wrote on the expense ledger he had drawn up with his wife to refurbish the house, "I am Sans Fruscins," meaning "I am without a penny in my pocket."At that point, Marmillion chose a name for the mansion, deciding to call it Saint Son-Fruscins, the loose translation of which meant that he had spent everything on the home and was broke. The name would be retained until the plantation passed into new ownership in later years.

Charles, the youngest of eight children, shared the mansion with his brother Valsin, Louise and their growing family from 1856-1875. Charles served during the Civil War as a Captain for the Confederacy. He fought in almost every major battle including Gettysburg and Harper's Ferry. Charles was wounded in the Antietam campaign of 1862, and in Chancellorsville, VA in 1863. He never completely recovered from these wounds, nor from his experience as a prisoner of war. While quite handsome and gallant, Charles died a bachelor in 1875 after a long illness at the age of thirty-five.

Valsin Marmillion died of yellow fever and consumption in 1871. His widow and three daughters returned to Munich in 1879 shortly after she sold the plantation to Achilles Bougère, a retired army colonel. Louise Von Seybold died and was buried in Munich in 1904. Her gravestone reads "widow of a Louisiana planter."

Bougère and his family did not want to be associated with the name given the plantation by Valsin Marmillon, which might indicate to others that they were without a penny. Thus, they changed it's name to San Francisco. They bought the home complete with its furniture (which was later destroyed by fire) and would perform further remodeling, including the addition of two bedrooms on the first floor. They also added gaslights. The Bougères maintained the property until 1904, when they sold the property to the Ory/Levet families, who were particularly interested in growing and manufacturing sugar in the immediate area. Incorporated as the San Francisco Plantation and Manufacturing Company in 1909, the Ory-Levet sugar concern gradually acquired 3,000 acres and became an economic boon to the area. Every Christmas between 1904-75 the neighbors received gifts of hundreds of pounds of sugar. Yet largely as a result of modernization, the mansion's prosperity was placed continuously under siege. During the Ory/Levet ownership the mansion was nearly destroyed by the local Army Corps of Engineers, and as a result of dwindling financial means in the World War II years, lost to decay and neglect.

The existence of San Francisco Plantation was threatened in 1926 when recurring floods motivated the state government to try and erect a high levee directly through the mansion, to protect the nearby area extending from Baton Rouge to New Orleans.

Fortunately, the Ory/Levet families protected the San Francisco Plantation from being destroyed. Sidney Levet, Sr., an educated engineer as well as a non-practicing lawyer, petitioned the Levee Board - United States Engineers, and convinced them that they were choosing the wrong side of the Mississippi to establish a levee. Although Mr. Levet's efforts were successful, the state eventually destroyed over 1,200 feet of formal gardens in front of the mansion.

After World War II, there was little money to maintain the property and the Ory family feared they would lose it to decay. Mr. and Mrs. Clark Thompson, originally of Louisville, Kentucky, wrote to the family in 1952, requesting to rent the mansion. The family indicated that the house needed many repairs and had no indoor privy facilities or electricity. Mr. and Mrs. Thompson would not be swayed and proceeded to lease the house from the Ory family in 1954. Mr. Thompson, a retired electrical engineer, wired the entire building for electricity, replaced the roof and installed bathroom facilities. To further defray costs, the couple opened the mansion to the public. Mrs. Thompson gave tours charging $1.00 for adults and $.50 for children. A gracious hostess, she welcomed thousands of visitors annually, serving watercress sandwiches and café-au-lait with a jigger of Irish whiskey for those who so indulged. In addition, she convinced several antique dealers to put items in the house for sale, which aided her in furnishing the large rooms of the mansion. In 1974 Mrs. Thompson, by then widowed, moved out of San Francisco Plantation so that structural restoration could begin.

In 1973 the Energy Corporation of Louisiana, Limited (ECOL) purchased the San Francisco Plantation as the site for an oil refinery. Through the philanthropic intervention of Frederick B. Ingram, a New Orleans businessman and philanthropist, the decision was made to preserve and restore the plantation. During the years 1974 to 1977, a thoroughly researched $2.5 million restoration of San Francisco was conducted, the results being a faithful rendition of the plantation as it originally was. In 1974 the National Park Service declared the house a National Historic Landmark.

• • • • •

The San Francisco Plantation House is located on River Road, otherwise known as State Highway 44, on the east side of Mississippi, two miles up the river from Reserve, Louisiana. It is open from 10:00 a.m. to 4:30 p.m. daily. The mansion is closed Christmas, New Years Day, Thanksgiving, Easter Sunday and during Mardi Gras Day. Admission is charged. For further information call toll free at: (888) 322-1756, or visit the San Francisco Plantation website at http://www. sanfranciscoplantation.org

Photos courtesy of San Francisco Plantation.

The Rough Rider's Favorite Haunt

Theodore Roosevelt's Sagamore Hill

OYSTER BAY, LONG ISLAND • NEW YORK

NOBODY EVER EXPECTED Theodore Roosevelt to settle down contentedly in just one home after his exploits as a Dakota ranchman, South African explorer, hunter of Western grizzlies, and President of the United States. It seemed just as unlikely that the pale, thin, nearsighted and asthmatic youngster from mid-Manhattan might become a rugged Rough Rider on San Juan Hill and one of the most vigorous public leaders in history. But from 1885 until his death in 1919, Mr. Roosevelt's Sagamore home at Oyster Bay on Long Island, New York, was his personal castle. It also served as the summer White House - a focal point of World Affairs between 1902 and 1908.

"After all, fond as I am of the White House and much though I have appreciated these years in it," he said upon leaving the Presidency, "there isn't any place in the world like home - like Sagamore Hill, where things are our own, with our own associations."

Theodore's affection for Oyster Bay began as a child when his father, Theodore, Sr. had rented a summer home there. As a youth he roamed Cove Neck, where Sagamore Hill now stands, and six months after graduating from Harvard University young Roosevelt bought the nucleus of what was to become his estate. For the first acreage he paid $10,000 cash and assumed a $20,000 mortgage. Adding more tracts, he finally owned 155 acres, and at his death still held ninety-five acres.

"I began my education after leaving Harvard," he said of his real estate deals. Always devoted to that institution, he later explained that a person's education expands when he comes face to face with the facts of life.

While the young Mr. Roosevelt was in the planning stages of his mansion in early 1884, a double tragedy beset him. His first wife Alice Hathaway Lee, the-love-of-his-life, and his mother, Mittie Roosevelt; died coincidentally of unrelated illnesses on the same day, February 14th. The builders were ready to begin construction of the mansion, designed by the New York architectural firm of Lamb & Rich. Devastated by his double tragedy, Mr. Roosevelt signed the building contract and then went to the Bad-Lands of North Dakota for two years to refresh his mind and his health. Throwing himself into the dangerous lifestyle there, the twenty-five year old widower was able to dispel much of his grief. He would later celebrate the area in lyrical prose in *The Winning of the West*.

In 1886, Roosevelt remarried and took his new bride, Edith - a former childhood friend - to live at Sagamore Hill directly after their honeymoon. Four sons and a daughter of the second marriage grew up in the house. Originally, Mr. Roosevelt had intended to name the estate Leeholm for his first wife, whose surname had been Lee. But immediately after her death he changed the name of his new home to Sagamore Hill, after an old Indian chief named Sagamore Mohannis who had once ruled this part of Long Island.

"At Sagamore Hill," Mr. Roosevelt later wrote, "we loved a great many things - birds and trees and books and all things beautiful, and horses and rifles and children and hard work and the joy of life."

There too, he wrote most of his thirty-nine books. Teddy often thought of himself as a writer first and a public official second. When he felt like writing and family turmoil was too great on the lower floors of the house, he took his writing materials to a private study on the third floor also known as the gun room, and closed the door.

After two years of literary pursuits and playing host to distinguished guests at the mansion, Mr. Roosevelt returned to public life in New York and Washington; however Sagamore Hill remained the home he constantly returned to. It was on the wide piazza of the mansion that he was notified of his nomination for Governor of New York state and later Vice President of the United States. After the assassination of President William McKinley(1843-1901) catapulted Mr. Roosevelt into the White House at age forty-two, it was also at Sagamore Hill that he obtained news of his nomination to run for a full term

Visitors to the dining room at Sagamore Hill are greeted by a few of Roosevelt's numerous hunting trophies.

as President. Roosevelt wrote his acceptance speech within the first-floor library.

For over two decades Sagamore Hill was one of the most conspicuous houses in America. Representatives of other countries came to heated meetings in the library, and Mr. Roosevelt enunciated his national philosophy: "speak softly and carry a big stick." Roosevelt mediated a settlement of the war between Japan and Russia at Sagamore Hill during the summer of 1905, for which he later received the Nobel Peace Prize, the first awarded to an American.

People everywhere talked about "the President who is never too busy to be a devoted husband and a good father." Teddy was photographed at Sagamore Hill romping with his children, hiking, swimming, riding horseback and chopping wood.

The North Room of Sagamore Hill contains two enormous elephant tusks that were presented to Roosevelt by the Emperor of Abysinnia, a nation now known as Ethiopia.

Sometimes he was shown leading a procession of children to a fresh grave in the animal cemetery of the estate.

The Sagamore Hill home is a twenty-three room, three-story Queen Anne structure of frame and stone, with rambling extensions and an irregular roof line. Mr. Roosevelt stated early on that he had "perfectly definite views" of what he wanted in the house. The role of the architects was merely "to put on the outside cover with but little help from me."

"I wished," he went on, "a big piazza where we could sit in rocking chairs and look at the sunset, a library with a shallow bay window looking south, the parlor or drawing room occupying all the western end of the lower floor and big fireplaces for logs. I had to live inside and not outside the house, and while I should have liked to express myself in both, I had to choose, and I chose the former."

On the first floor are a large center hall, a library that became Mr. Roosevelt's office, a dining room, Mrs. Roosevelt's drawing room and a pantry and kitchen. In 1905, a spacious first-floor room was added to the building to accommodate Mr. Roosevelt's hunting trophies.

The second floor has family bedrooms, a nursery and two guest rooms. The gun room, containing Mr. Roosevelt's personal artillery from big-game expeditions, is on the third floor. There too, Mr. Roosevelt sought quiet to write. All of the rooms contain original Roosevelt furniture and family memorabilia. The spacious piazza Mr. Roosevelt ordered is on the west side of the home, overlooking Oyster Bay, Long Island Sound and the estate's landscaped lawns.

Visitors to Sagamore Hill today may be startled at the masculine decor of the mansion. There is a profusion of elephant tusks, bearskin rugs - including snarling heads - and uncountable mounted heads of American and African buffalo, white-tailed deer, elk, bison and antelopes. Edith's drawing room provides the one possible exception - where softer colors, French tapestries, elegant rugs and Sèvres porcelain dominate. According to his biographer Hermann Hagedorn, "Theodore took more pride in those game- heads than in any of the books he had written or political accomplishments that he had achieved."

After leaving the Presidency, Mr. Roosevelt hunted in Africa, visited Europe and later explored the jungles of Brazil. He wrote constantly upon his return. By July, 1913,

Representatives of other countries came to heated meetings in the library at Sagamore Hill. Roosevelt wrote his presidential acceptance speech here.

he had spent more time living continuously at Sagamore Hill than he had spent living in any one house since he was a child. Declining health and the loss of one son to World War I preceded Roosevelt's death in the gate room there in 1919. His widow died in the south bedroom in 1948.

Sagamore Hill, with eighty-three acres, was bought in 1950 by the Theodore Roosevelt Association. Many of the original contents of the mansion were included in the acquisition. The association is a nonprofit corporation founded in 1919 to make people aware of "Mr. Roosevelt's personality and achievements and the ideals of individual and national life that he preached and practiced."

Many years earlier the association also rebuilt the five-story brownstone town house at 28 East Twentieth Street in New York City where Mr. Roosevelt was born. The son of a wealthy glass manufacturer, he lived there until he was fifteen years old. The house had been built for Theodore's father in 1848. It was there that he strengthened his body and pursued early intellectual interests. The old brownstone has eighteen rooms, five of them now restored and furnished with Roosevelt possessions. The building had no elevator until its restoration following Mr. Roosevelt's death.

In 1963 the Theodore Roosevelt Association presented Sagamore Hill and the New York City town house to the United States government. The properties are now administered by the National Park Service.

• • • • •

Sagamore Hill is located on 20 Sagamore Hill Road; off Cove Neck Road, 3 miles east of Oyster Bay, New York. The park is open daily except on Thanksgiving Day, Christmas and New Year's Day. Tours are conducted from 9:30 a.m. to 4:00 p.m. Admission prices are $5.00 for adults seventeen and above. Persons under sixteen are admitted free of charge. For further information call: (516)922-4788, or visit the Sagamore Hill website at http://www.nps.gov/sahi.

The Roosevelt home at 28 East Twentieth Street in New York City is open Wednesday through Sunday throughout the year, with tours conducted every half hour from 9:00 a.m. to 5:00 p.m. Admission prices are the same as Sagamore Hill. For further information, call:(212)260-1616, or visit the website at http://www. nps.gov/thrb.

Photos courtesy of Sagamore Hill: Oyster Bay, New York.

Coke, Bloodshed and Grandeur

Henry Clay Frick's Sanctuary

NEW YORK CITY • NEW YORK

HENRY CLAY FRICK, who lit the coke ovens of Pennsylvania for the age of steel, emerged from the murky smoke and bloody labor strife of mill towns to build one of the finest private homes on New York City's fashionable Fifth Avenue. It is one of the few in the metropolis that will remain indefinitely as evidence of an era when millionaires did not have to share their wealth with the government, but could freely indulge their own set of living standards.

Indulge is just what Mr. Frick did on a plot of land between Seventieth and Seventy-first Streets on Fifth Avenue, across the avenue from Central Park. To assure perpetuity of his block-long creation he would eventually bequeath it to the public for

the display of fine arts, and set up a $15 million trust fund to pay the bills.

Visitors commonly refer to the building as a "mansion" being used as a "museum." These two words are shunned by the Frick family and associates, who refer to the building as a "former residence" that now is the home of "The Frick Collection." This terminology seems appropriate for a legacy from the cool, taciturn and strong-willed Mr. Frick, who spent money freely but spoke modestly.

Mr. Frick built the residence in 1913-14, a goal he never would have accomplished if the marksmanship of a Russian assassin had been better in 1892. The

Built of five varieties of imported and domestic marble, the grand staircase of the Frick residence features a large landing for an organ.

building, however, bears no evidence of the violent life he once led. As it stands today, the big stone structure typifies a man of culture and generosity - which Mr. Frick was - not the tough manufacturer and unrelenting labor-union smasher, which he was more widely reputed for.

The first floor of the house is open to visitors. Several of the rooms - including a gallery 100 feet long - are arranged much as Mr. Frick had left them. In forty years of collecting, Mr. Frick left 126 paintings as the core of the future Frick collection, but also hundreds of other items, including sculpture, decorative arts, drawings, prints, and various enamels. The number of rooms in the entire house, which has two floors above and two below the main floor, is not publicly discussed. The structure is larger in some respects than the Georgian mansion that Andrew Carnegie built twenty blocks further north on the avenue, which has sixty-four rooms and its own miniature railroad in the basement to move supplies.

Henry Clay Frick was born in Pennsylvania's Westmoreland County in 1849, the

year of the California gold rush. His father, of Swiss ancestry, was a farmer. His mother, of a Mennonite family, inherited an interest in the profitable Old Overholt whisky distillery. With only thirty months of formal schooling, Mr. Frick went to work at the age of seventeen in an uncle's store and later became a bookkeeper at the Overholt Company at a

The West Gallery is one hundred feet long. The room features much of the art that Mr. Frick collected in his lifetime.

salary of $1,000 a year. In the financial debacle of 1873 he bought coke ovens and coal mines at panic prices. Known as the King of Coke, he was a millionaire when Andrew Carnegie later made him a manager and partner in the Carnegie Steel Corporation.

In 1892 Mr. Carnegie posted notices in his factories which threatened the wages and jobs of members of the Amalgamated Association of Iron and Steel Workers. Then he departed on a luxury liner for his castle in Scotland for a long vacation, leaving Mr. Frick to fight what was to become the bloody Battle of Homestead, Pennsylvania, on July 6, 1892.

Mr. Frick, married at the age of thirty-two to Adelaide Howard Childs, had begun planning his castle as well as traveling to Europe to begin his art collection. As the labor disputes intensified, his lack of tolerance matched Mr. Carnegie's. In 1892 Frick reminded the workers that their contracts would terminate in early July; after this point salary scales and working hours would be those he chose to establish. The workers not only refused to accept this but some of them fortified themselves behind fences that Mr. Frick had installed to protect the mills. He hired 300 Pinkerton detectives, who tried to enter the river-front plant secretly by armored barges to maintain order.

When the workers detected the advance of hired forces, they opened fire with rifles. The Pinkertons returned the fire, and a savage battle ensued. At the end of the day fourteen men had been killed and 163 had been seriously injured. As federal troops moved in to restore order, Mr. Frick's business future and his dreams of a castle seemed to be in eclipse. Seventeen days later, Frick's very life was threatened when a Russian anarchist by the name of Alexander Berkman entered Mr. Frick's office in downtown Pittsburgh, shot him twice with a revolver, and stabbed him several times with a knife. Remarkably, Frick survived. Public sentiment, which had been violently

The living hall of the Frick residence features intricate cornices, paintings by El Greco and Hans Holbien and sculpture by Giovanni Bologna.

against him, now turned strongly in his favor. Editorials, sermons, and political speeches lauded his "courageous fight." The union left Homestead, and Mr. Frick resumed his art collecting and the planning of a residence to house it.

A bitter quarrel soon ensued between Frick and Mr. Carnegie over the value of Mr. Frick's interest in the company, but was settled after long litigation. Although both built large houses on Fifth Avenue, they stopped communicating with each other after the quarrel - even when they mixed with the same business leaders and searched for treasures within the same art galleries.

Mr. Frick had seen some of the Vanderbilt mansions in New York City and had estimated that the upkeep of one of them was about $300,000 a year, or nearly $1,000 a day. That, he thought, would be just about right for him. He proceeded to buy the old Lenox Library in the block above Seventieth Street, tore it down, then picked the brains of architects and friends to determine what style house he should build.

Georgian mansions, Tudor castles, Venetian palazzi and Spanish villas were rising wherever millionaires lived. Mr. Frick decided on a style reminiscent externally of an eighteenth-century French town house with interiors based on seventeenth-century English models. Mr. Frick chose American architect Thomas Hastings (1860-1929) of the former New York firm Carrère and Hastings, to do the planning. Educated at the famous École des Beaux Arts in Paris, Hastings previous commissions included The New York Public Library, The Century Theater, and the Carnegie Institution of Washington. His planning for Frick resulted in a sculptured masterpiece, with every cornice, balustrade and wrought-iron fence designed carefully to harmonize with all other parts of the home.

The exterior of the museum is of Indiana limestone. The adornments, which visitors are immediately aware of in the fences and walled gardens, were produced by Piccirilli Brothers. Ceilings and woodwork of some of the rooms are of walnut and mahogany, and many of the walls, even in upper-floor corridors, are of marble. Among the marbles used in harmonious contrast are three from France - Tavernelle Fleuri, Tavernelle Rose and Rouge de Rance. Others include a veined red Italian marble and St. Geneviève Rose Marble from Missouri.

A grand staircase composed of five marbles is located directly near the entrance hall. A modern organ console was installed near the landing, and the actual organ pipes are located behind the wall of the staircase. Frick hired a professional organist to play for him, and often staged organ and chamber concerts in his home throughout the year.

Near "The Living Hall" and gardens Mr. Frick built a west gallery that is 100 feet long. This room houses much of the art that Mr. Frick collected, displayed as it was when he was alive. Prominent among these works of art is his favorite and one of the finest pieces in the collection, a self-portrait by Rembrandt made late in the artist's life.

A classical garden fountain of. St. Geniève rose marble is a focal point of the Garden Court.

Frick Museum, Fifth Avenue façade

Throughout the remaining downstairs rooms are paintings by Ingres, Goya, Van Dyck, Velazquez, Turner, Whistler, Gainsborough, El Greco, Renoir, Vermeer, Holbein and Constable, as well as statues by Houdon and others. Some of the Persian carpets are over 300 years old.

The Boucher Room has eight panels painted by the eighteenth-century artist François Boucher for Madame de Pompadour. The Fragonard Room contains fourteen panels by the eighteenth-century painter of that name, bought by Mr. Frick from the J.P. Morgan family for $1,250,000. The panels were installed in the Frick home under the supervision of the highly respected English art dealer, Sir Joseph Duveen. In the Enamel Room are forty Limoges, also bought from the Morgans, for $1,500,000.

Some of the art works in the house have figured in history. A Holbein portrait of Sir Thomas More was believed to have once been in the possession of Ann Boleyn, the ill-fated second wife of Henry VIII. After her execution, the painting was rumored to have been found by a servant and taken to Rome, where it was exhibited for many years before reaching the Frick home.

A classical garden fountain of St. Geniviève rose marble forms a focal point of the room called the Garden Court. Records show that eighteen blocks of marble were quarried and carefully examined before one was found with the exact tonalities desired.

Mr. and Mrs. Frick had four children, two of whom lived to maturity. A picture of his deceased daughter, Martha, appeared on many of the checks that Mr. Frick gave to children's charities. He contributed generously to hospitals for children as well as to various charities which benefited them in the New York area.

Mr. Frick died in 1919 and left the Fifth Avenue home to his wife. Within the same year, a self-perpetuating Board of Trustees was established which included the Frick's surviving son and daughter, Childs and Helen Clay Frick. After Mrs. Frick's death in 1931, the mansion became a public shrine for display of The Frick Collection.

Following the death of Mrs. Frick, John Russell Pope, principally known for the design of Washington D.C.'s National Gallery, was retained as architect to alter the residence for public use. Pope's renovations included the addition of an entrance hall, a cloakroom, a garden court, a music room and two galleries. The numerous bedrooms were converted into administrative offices, study rooms, and galleries for future use.

The public opening of the collection in 1935 was attended by 1,600 leading citizens, with thirty-five special detectives supplementing regular guards to make certain that none of the art objects would disappear. Attendance now averages about 800 visitors per day, 250,000 per year.

Ms. Helen Frick, the surviving daughter, built a reference library as an adjunct of the collection before her resignation from the Board of Trustees in 1961. It is alleged that her departure was the result of differences in acquisition policy with the Board of Trustees.

The Frick Collection continues to grow through acquisitions made by the Trustees and contributions of art. Since Ms. Frick's death in 1984, the latter category has included some major paintings by Algardi, Bernini, Corot, Greuze, Ingrès, Liotard, Severo da Ravenna and Watteau. Illustrated lectures are given from October through May, and a variety of musical recitals are also regularly presented.

• • • • •

The entrance to The Frick Collection is at 1 East Seventieth Street, just off Fifth Avenue. The collection is open from 10:00 a.m. to 6:00 p.m., Tuesdays through Saturdays, and from 1:00 p.m. to 6:00 Sundays. The museum is closed on Mondays, January 1st, July 4th, Thanksgiving, Christmas Eve and Christmas Day. Admission is $7 (students and seniors: $5). For further information, contact the museum at: (212)288-0700, or visit the museum website at http://www.frick.org.

Photos courtesy of the Frick Collection, New York.

Long Island's Flowering Wonderland

Old Westbury Gardens

OLD WESTBURY • LONG ISLAND, NEW YORK

THE FORMERLY PRIVATE HOME and gardens of John S. Phipps, a multimillionaire financier whose father was a partner of Andrew Carnegie in the steel business, was opened to the public in 1959. The estate's 150 acres have eight distinctive gardens, some formal and others informal, grand allées of European linden and beech trees, lawns that roll down to shores of lakes, lily ponds, a swimming pool and woodlands, and a sixty-room mansion furnished with fine English antiques and decorative arts from the Phipps' fifty years of residence.

Known as Old Westbury Gardens, the estate is located in Old Westbury, on Long Island. It has few equals in the United States as a handsomely designed and furnished mansion combined with scrupulously maintained gardens of exceptional size and variety. The estate seems to be constantly ready for a white-tie party; a splendid example of how wealthy families of the twentieth century have lived in the elegant style of their ancestral forebears. The visitors are numerous, since the estate is within forty-five minutes of Manhattan by car or train.

John S. Phipps' father, Henry, was a co-founder of the United States Steel Corporation. His wife, Margarita, was a daughter of Michael Grace, founder of the Grace Steamship Lines. Mr. Phipps established a career in the field of real estate, as a sportsman, and as a manager of the family fortune. In 1906 he built Westbury House as a home for his growing family, which ultimately included three sons and a daughter. The children shared his interest in polo, so three polo fields were developed. One of the sons, Michael, became a noted star of the sport. Mr. Phipps kept adding to the estate and embellishing the mansion.

Westbury House was designed by George Crawley, a London designer. It is a typical English manor house of eighteenth-century tradition. When visitors pass through wrought-iron gates thirty feet in height and approach the house on a long winding driveway, the pale-gold roof of the structure suddenly comes into view. The roof is of stone slabs imported from Rutlandshire, England. The walls of the mansion are of cherry-red brick, with limestone trim and green shutters. Inside the mansion are distinguished objets d'art of past centuries, including English furniture, Oriental curios, and paintings by Joshua Reynolds, Henry Raeburn, Thomas Gainsborough, John Singer Sargent, William Orpen, and others.

Allées of majestic beech and linden trees reach half a mile from the north and south of the house. Off these allées, winding paths branch off to boxwood gardens and reflecting pools with Grecian columns, a wrought-iron domed gazebo called the Temple of Love, a split-level Walled Garden, the Ghost Walk of groomed hemlocks, an English Rose garden, a pinetum of coniferous trees, a Cottage Garden with a playhouse once used by the Phipps' daughter and log cabins for three sons. There are also terraced gardens, lily ponds, a swimming pool with a tunnel to the mansion, pergolas of wisteria and grape vines, twelve-foot-high ledges, and bowers of climbing roses, azaleas, and hybrid rhododendrons.

Fourteen servants originally maintained the mansion and twenty kept the grounds. The servants are now gone, but the grounds have nine gardeners constantly at work. Flowers are rotated so that all the gardens offer blooms during the growing season; from tulips in the spring, to delphinium and Canterbury bells in the summer and chrysanthemums in the fall. As the Phipps family grew, so did Westbury House. In 1911 a wing was added, which was designed by Horace Trumbauer, the noted Philadelphia architect. As was customary in those days, large sculleries, storerooms and servants' work areas were constructed underground. During World War II, civil defense officials found the underground rooms and passageways so large and so protected that they designated the cellar as a bomb shelter with a capacity of 1,800 people.

George Crawley designed the large state dining room for Mr. And Mrs. Henry

The large foyer was designed by Frank Derwent Wood, a professor in England who spoke for the Empire on questions concerning sculpture.

The family drawing room, decorated in white and light colors, features a Carrara marble fireplace and paintings by English, Swiss and American artists.

Phipps' Manhattan townhouse. It was relocated to their son's estate in 1915. A glass-enclosed porch was added in 1924. The house became large enough for several dozen occupants, and when England was threatened with invasion by the German army in World War II, the Phipps family became hosts to several refugee children from London. Another bright event took place at the mansion in 1953 when Mr. and Mrs. Phipps celebrated their golden wedding anniversary.

The Phipps no longer reside at the mansion, but the John S. Phipps family Foundation supports thirty percent of the operating costs, with visitors contributing ten percent; fund-raising and earned income supply the rest.

The saying Pax Introentibus - Salus Exeuntibus is inscribed over the front door of the mansion, wishing peace to those who enter and good health to those who exit. The foyer, larger than most modern living rooms, has wall panels of carved oak and a ceiling painting of a blue sky and white clouds, offset by brilliantly colored parrots and flowers balanced on an enframing balustrade painted by A. Duncan Carse. The mantelpiece in the foyer, like several others in the mansion, was designed by Frank Derwent Wood, a professor in England who spoke for the Empire on questions concerning sculpture. It depicts the legend of Atalanta's suitors in a race for her favor, with cupids symbolizing time and love. A basalt bust of Milton looks down on the scene.

In the center of the foyer is a William and Mary library table dated 1680. It is of walnut, with inlaid panels of seaweed marquetry. On the table is a large Japanese Imari porcelain platter. Near the fireplace are an Irish Chippendale table of 1775 with a carved frieze, cabriole legs and a green marble top; a Georgian carved-wood eagle console of 1760; and high-backed English chairs of the seventeenth century in the style of Daniel Marot. Nearby is a mounted tiger that was shot by Mr. Phipps on his honeymoon in India three years before the mansion was built.

All the rooms are furnished with rare antiques and family treasures, including many family portraits and other paintings by world-famous artists. Mrs. Phipps' study has pale-green walls, Chippendale and Heppelwhite furniture, an ornamented Benjamin Gray clock and brass wall sconces. Mr. Phipps' study has dark-green paneled walls and antique furniture of several centuries.

The mansion's west porch

The Red Ballroom was often a setting for gala family parties. It is now used for public concerts, art shows and lectures.

The Boxwood Garden, viewed from the West Pond.

contains massive oak beams, a marble floor and an elevator for servants to bring tea from a cellar kitchen. The large glass windows of the porch are hydraulically lowered into the cellar in warm weather. Porch ornaments include Chinese Ming jardinières of bronze, playful French cupids of terra-cotta and continuing displays of the cut flowers such as those made famous by Mrs. Phipps at Westbury House and her Palm Beach home.

The family drawing room, decorated in white and light colors, contains a treasure trove of Waterford-style crystal chandeliers, Chinese Chippendale furniture, English clocks, French tapestries, a Carrara marble mantelpiece and paintings by English, Swiss, and American artists.

The Red Ballroom was often a setting for gala family parties. It is now used for public concerts, art shows and lectures. The walls are covered with red damask and the floor in teak parquet. Another Carrara mantelpiece adorns the room, along with cut-glass crystal chandeliers and candelabra, eighteenth-century English mirrors, Chinese K'ang His porcelain, Foo Dogs mounted on Louis XV bronze dore candalebra and a Louis XV ormolu clock. Museums have exhibited the fireplace's cast-iron fireback and cast-bronze andirons made in 1649 and 1655, respectively.

The state dining room is a showplace of the mansion. It features oak paneling, a marble mantelpiece with bare-breasted caryatids, swags carved in the manner of Grinling Gibbons and an elaborately molded plaster ceiling monogrammed "JSP." Some of the finest wood carvings in the room were imported from England by Henry Phipps and used in his home at 1063 Fifth Avenue in New York City before he gave them to his son for display at Westbury House.

Children's Cottage Garden at Old Westbury Gardens.

The second-floor hallway is large enough to host a grand party. It contains yet another marble mantelpiece, and it is furnished with antiques, some of them 300 years old, many with curious inlays. In the master bedroom is a tester Chippendale bed, circa 1750, a mahogany secretaire made in England in 1770 and a Louis XV commode. The master bathroom, largest of six on this floor, could accommodate six apartment-size bathrooms. It features silver-plated fixtures and Oriental porcelains. Stairs from the bathroom lead to a nursery directly overhead on the third floor. Mr. Phipps had his own dressing room elaborately furnished with Chippendale furniture and oil paintings, while Mrs. Phipps had a boudoir decorated in beige and white, with a magnificent view of the grand beech allée.

The second floor features an Adam-style bedroom, a blue room with hand-decorated antique Chinese wallpaper in blue offset by bright-colored birds and flowers, and a Chippendale room, with similar Chinese wallpaper but with birds and butterflies set against a white background. These extraordinary wallpapers had been sent by Chinese hongs to their favorite customers in London; often laying unused until persons of wealth offered to buy them. The Chippendale room features K'ang Hsi ornaments, Oriental curios and ornate mirrors. This room was generally occupied by Mr. Grace, the father of Mrs. Phipps, when he visited Westbury House. The third floor contains six bedrooms, five bathrooms, a studio and a nursery.

Mrs. Phipps died in 1957, and her husband a year later. Their sons, John (who was known as Ben), Hubert and Michael, and a daughter Margaret, now known as Mrs. Etienne Boegner, set up the John S. Phipps Family Foundation as a nonprofit corporation to own and maintain the estate as an endowed museum and botanical garden for public benefit.

• • • • •

Old Westbury Gardens and the Westbury House are located on Old Westbury Road, near the Long Island Expressway (Exit 39S), Meadowbrook Parkway, Jericho Turnpike and Exit 32N, at Old Westbury on Long Island, New York. They are open to visitors from 10:00 a.m. to 5:00 p.m., Wednesday through Monday, from late April to mid-December; also on Memorial Day, July 4th and Labor Day. Admission fees are charged. Children under 6 are admitted free of charge. For further information, contact: (516)333-0048, or visit the Old Westbury Gardens website at: http://www.oldwestburygardens.org.

Photos courtesy of Old Westbury Gardens.

A Biographical Monument

Thomas Jefferson's Monticello

CHARLOTTESVILLE • VIRGINIA

THOMAS JEFFERSON'S MIND generated grand ideas about such things as the innate freedom and equality of all men, a theme he crystallized so effectively in the Declaration of Independence that he became one of the founders of American Democracy. He also pondered important ideas for new buildings - ideas so appealing that he became a leading force in American architecture.

One of the brightest stars in the constellation of Jefferson's buildings is Monticello, his home for fifty-seven years. A forty-three room structure on a 3,000-acre tract of property, it stands majestically atop an 867-foot lofty plateau in the Blue Ridge mountains of Virginia near Charlottesville. The repository of Jefferson's architectural ideas and also many of his former possessions, the mansion has been called the quintessential example of an autobiographical house.

Jefferson began building Monticello in 1769, when he was twenty-six years old; however the planning of the estate began to take shape in the future president's mind when he was just a boy. His father, Peter, had received a royal grant of land on the mountain and Jefferson roamed the grassy hillsides to dream of building a mansion. Before the first stone was turned he decided to call it Monticello, or "Little Mountain" in Italian. But it was not until 1767 when Jefferson was formally admitted to the Virginia bar that he began detailed plans for a house. He continued the job for forty years, interlacing the task with his work as a lawyer, revolutionist, diplomat, governor of Virginia, secretary of state, vice-president, and third president of the United States.

When Jefferson went to college, architecture was not included in the

Thomas Jefferson's library at Monticello.

curriculum. Deciding to teach himself, he assembled an extensive collection of books on the subject including Andrea Palladio's *Four Books of Architecture*, a standard guidebook, British sources and his own imagination. The future politician typically displayed a pragmatic, experimental, and flexible attitude toward his work. "Architecture is my delight," he is quoted as saying, "and putting up and pulling down is one of my favorite amusements." Before the end of the eighteenth century, Jefferson would renovate Monticello at great expense and inconvenience, redesigning and rebuilding until he had achieved the perfection of the Monticello Americans know today.

Jefferson was as much of an avant-gardist in his day as Frank Lloyd Wright was to become a generation later. He rebelled against Georgian architecture, as he did against Georgian tyranny. Monticello was his timber-and-brick "declaration of independence." Its original Classical Revival design became a favorite of many homeowners, while its dome inspired those later built on the United States Capitol as well as the Jefferson Memorial in Washington. A recognized expert, Jefferson would later be called upon to design the University of Virginia, the State Capitol and many private homes.

Jefferson's participation in the shifting political scene was a constant source of interruption in his plans for Monticello. Throughout the latter twenty years of the eighteenth century, positions in government both at home and abroad would draw him away from his home, including a role as Minister to France in 1784 and a four-year term as vice president in 1796. From 1801-1809 he would again be drawn away to serve as President. During one occasion in 1781 when Jefferson was home, a British dragoon under the leadership of Col. Banastre Tarleton made a raid on Charlottesville. Jefferson had been warned that they intended to imprison him and he fled successfully as they swarmed across the lawns and into the mountains.

To construct his mansion, Jefferson brought artisans from New York, Philadelphia and Europe, besides teaching slaves how to work as masons and carpenters. All intricate work was so closely supervised by him that he once commented that the workmen "could not proceed for more than an hour without me." Virtually all the materials for the house were obtained on the property. Stones for the foundation were quarried from the side of the mountain. The red bricks were baked in a kiln by slaves. During the first two years his slaves molded and fired thousands of bricks, blasted and dug great cellars in clay. The timbers were cut from his forests. Nails were made in his own nailery. Window glass came from Europe, while most of the window sashes were made in Philadelphia of imported mahogany.

Floor plans were drawn to exact scale by Jefferson. Using ink that permitted no erasures, he calculated all proportions in advance. So precise was he that he did not translate 26/63 of an inch to one-half an inch, or even five-twelfths, but made it .4127 of an inch. As architectural historian Jack McLaughlin puts it, Jefferson's drawings "were mathematical absolutes that recorded universal verities." Disregarding structural difficulties, he designed rooms of beauty and then decided how to build them. Some of the structural problems concerned Monticello's dome, from a design borrowed from a temple of Vesta, also a Corinthian frieze borrowed from a temple of Jupiter.

Most of the living quarters, including three bedrooms, are located on the first floor of Monticello. Six auxiliary bedrooms are located on the second floor and three on the third floor. Dependencies are in long wings projecting from the rear of the building on a lower level, with a "breezeway" linking the north and south terraces. A weather vane atop the house turns a large arrow on the ceiling of the porch, where it can be viewed through the windows of five rooms.

One thing that Monticello lacks is a grand staircase to bedrooms and the Dome Room over the main living quarters. Instead, the two stairwells that connect the basement to the third floor are so dark and narrow that persons who are feeble or heavy have difficulty navigating them. This is a result of Jefferson's own taste - he thought that grand staircases were a waste of space.

Creative ingenuity is apparent even as one enters Monticello. Floor-length windows, and the placement of mirrors opposite them to catch and amplify the light; reflect ideas Jefferson acquired while living in France. Over the front door of the entrance hall is Jefferson's clock, the winding of which requires a ladder and fifteen minutes of a houseman's time once a week. The clock has long cables extending to each side of the hall, with cannonball- like weights at the ends. The weight of the cannon balls, after being raised by the winding of the clock, powers the time-keeping mechanism. As the cannon balls creep lower on the wall each day they indicate the day of the week as marked on the walls.

Other devices in the house include a revolving chair, similar to a modern day recliner, a rotating pantry door, a chair resembling a modern posture chair, an octagonal table, octagonal rooms and a revolving bookstand. Jefferson was a known bibliophile throughout his life, acquiring enough books on one excursion to France to fill 250 running feet of shelves. About sixty percent of the furnishings on display in Monticello are or may be items original to Jefferson. Other items are period pieces or reproductions of original pieces.

Jefferson took great delight in horticulture. "There is not a sprig of grass that shoots uninteresting to me," he said. Flower and vegetable gardens, as well as two orchards, two vineyards, and an eighteen-acre ornamental grove, were included in his landscape plans. The gardens and orchards have been restored to their original appearance, and many of the trees, vegetables, and flowers that Jefferson once cultivated are grown at Monticello today.

Jefferson brought only one bride to Monticello in his lifetime. She had been Mrs. Martha Wayles Skelton, a twenty-two-year-old widow whom he had met while practicing law in Williamsburg. The life of the couple together at Monticello was happy but brief. Upon his marriage to her, Martha moved into Monticello in 1772. They had six children, then Mrs. Jefferson died in 1782. Jefferson never remarried; his daughter Martha, the only child who lived as long as he did, became his hostess at the mansion.

Retiring to Monticello in 1809, Jefferson had a continuous stream of visitors from many parts of the world. Some guests who had "just come for dinner" stayed for weeks. Visitors considered Monticello one of America's most interesting homes and their host one of the most gracious and fascinating of statesmen. Entertaining, with the cost of almost 200 slaves and foods, placed a heavy burden on Jefferson. As a lawyer he seldom earned more than $3,000 a year and after many years of public service, he had no savings at his disposal. As his plight worsened, Jefferson sold his library of nearly sixty-five hundred books to the Library of Congress for $23,950 in 1814. After the last wagonload of books departed from Monticello, Jefferson wrote to his friend John Adams, "I cannot live without books." Immediately he began to buy more.

Jefferson died in his bedroom at Monticello on July 4, 1826, the fiftieth anniversary of the Declaration of Independence that he had drafted. He was buried near his home. Monticello had to be sold to pay his debts, as did the remaining furnishings that had been his choicest possessions. Thomas Jefferson Randolph, Jefferson's grandson, was placed in charge of this unwelcome task.

In 1831, James T. Barclay, a local apothecary, purchased the home and 552 acres for $4,500, less the value of his own home. Unsuccessful in his attempts to cultivate silkworms there, he offered Monticello for sale barely two years later. It was bought in 1834 by Commodore Uriah Phillips Levy of New York, a retired Navy officer. He paid only $2,500, just about what the place was worth, with its sagging roofs, rotted tim-

'The bed in which Thomas Jefferson died at Monticello

bers, mutilated walls and neglected gardens.

Mr. Levy, an admirer of Jefferson, undertook to restore the property and retrieve some of the furnishings. When he died, he willed Monticello "to all the people of the United States" if certain conditions were met. Levy's executors felt Monticello should remain in the family and contested ownership. Not until years of litigation had passed did Jefferson Monroe Levy, Uriah P. Levy's nephew, take possession of the home in 1879. Both uncle and nephew strove to preserve Monticello as a memorial to Jefferson. In 1923, Jefferson Monroe Levy sold Monticello to the newly created Thomas Jefferson Memorial Foundation, which owns Monticello today.

The mansion, its gardens and its 360-degree views across the valleys of the Blue Ridge Mountains now are seen by over 500,000 visitors a year. Today, the architectural masterpiece is the only house in the United States on the United Nations' prestigious World Heritage List of International treasures.

• • • • •

Monticello is on State Route 53, three miles southeast of downtown Charlottesville. Roadside signs mark the route. The mansion is open from 8:00 a.m. to 5:00 p.m. daily from March 1 to October 31 and from 9 a.m. to 4:30 p.m. daily from November 1 to February 28th. For ticket information call: (804) 984-9844, or visit the Monticello website at http://www.monticello.org.

Photos by R. Lautman courtesy of Monticello/Thomas Jefferson Memorial Foundation, Inc.

The Courtyard in springtime. Photographer: John Kennard

A Venetian Palazzo in New England

Isabella Stewart Gardner's Fenway Court

BOSTON • MASSACHUSETTS

Mrs. Isabella Stewart Gardner suffered greatly after the death of her husband, John L. (Jack) Gardner from heart disease in 1898. For a year she slept badly and ate little. In thirty-eight years of married life the couple had cut a brilliant social and cultural swath in Boston to become the envy of Beacon Hill, the pride of the literati, and the target of villainous gossips.

Mrs. Gardner was a slim, vivacious coquette, with an easy manner and flirtatious eyes. She broke most of the rules in the books of etiquette. Her famous friendships with many noted men of her day sprang from mutual interests in the arts, rather than

The Dutch Room (second floor) facing the Courtyard. To the right of the door is an early self-portrait by Rembrandt (c. 1629).
Photographer: David Bohl

self-interest, which Boston never quite understood. Artists John Singer Sargent and Anders Zorn painted at her house museum, then called Fenway Court, while musicians such as Charles Loeffler premiered new work to audiences invited by Isabella. She became a well-known champion of the arts, both visual and performing, and at the end of her life, left the gift of her beautiful house full of art "for the education and enjoyment of the public forever."

In the aftermath of her tragedy, Belle Gardner devoted all her energies to the cultivation of music and art as avenues to completion of life. So brick walls rose on the Fenway as the nineteenth century ended, while all of Boston speculated about what Isabella Gardner was doing. Fenway Court, now the Isabella Stewart Gardner Museum, was built in the style of an Italian palazzo. Ever since she had visited Venice as a young woman, Gardner had wanted to build such a palace filled with fine things. Her friend Ida Agassiz Higginson would write to her in 1923, reminding her that "You said to me…that if you ever inherited any money that was yours to dispose of, you would have a house…like the one in Milan filled with beautiful pictures [the Poldi Pezzoli] and objects of art, for people to come and enjoy. And you have carried out the dream of your youth."

Isabella Stewart Gardner was born in New York City in 1840. Her maternal grandfather was a Brooklyn tavern keeper and her father, David Stewart, did so well in business as president of an iron company, that he took his family on frequent trips to Europe. One of Isabella's schoolmates, Julia Gardner, invited her to Boston and there she met Julia's brother, John. Five years later they would be married. John L. Gardner was a wealthy owner of shipping lines, and they moved into a house on Beacon Hill. Their beloved son "Jackie", born in 1863, would die at twenty-two months, and during the two years that followed Isabella endured depression and illness. At a doctor's suggestion, Jack Gardner took his wife to Europe, her condition so poor that she had to be carried aboard ship on a mattress. Later, the couple would become parents to three orphaned nephews.

Throughout her life, Belle expressed a growing interest in art and literary life. The friends of Isabella Gardner included F. Marion Crawford, a young writer who was received into Gardner's boudoir to read Dante; Henry James, Sarah Bernhardt, opera singer Nellie Melba, and scores of others. Walter T. Rosen, a Harvard student who later built the palazzo Caramoor at Katonah, New York, visited her. Gardner engaged the world-renowned Polish pianist Paderewski to play a private concert for her- later she paid him for a recital in the museum's music hall, sending all the tickets to Boston musicians. This creative entourage, with more added and some dropped, followed Gardner throughout her days.

Long before Jack died, Mr. and Mrs. Gardner had made tentative plans to erect a museum somewhere in Boston, thus Isabella's work fulfilled a dream the two of them had shared. All of the artwork that ultimately would appear in the museum was donated from Mrs. Gardner's own collection. With her husband's support, she had formed most of the collection herself, independently acquiring works such as Vermeer's *The Concert*. Members of

Isabella Stewart Gardner (1888) by John Singer Sargent. Photographer: David Bohl

her creative inner circle would be influential in decision making; especially John Singer Sargent, Henry Adams, and Bernard Berenson, a graduate of Harvard College and an authority on Renaissance paintings, who would become her most influential advisor and agent concerning the acquisition of European paintings and Oriental art.

To bring her vision to fruition, Gardner hired Willard T. Sears of Boston as her architect and, working together, they designed a building containing three floors of galleries that opened onto a large inner courtyard filled with flowering plants and trees. The land that Gardner bought on the Fenway faces one of the parks in Frederick Law Olmsted's famous Emerald Necklace, a series of parks in Boston. The museum is also near Massachusetts College of Art, Simmons College, the Museum of Fine Arts, Northeastern University and Wentworth Institute of Technology. Isabella's mission was twofold: her museum was to reveal masterpieces of art and horticulture to delight visitors, but the building itself would provide surprises and delights on its

The Spanish Cloister (first floor) showcases John Singer Sargent's early masterpiece, El Jaleo (1882), which features a flamenco dancer with musicians accompanying her in the background. Gardner redesigned this space specifically to house this painting. Photographer: David Bohl

own. Isabella's use of theatrical effect is evident everywhere in the overall design - a few steps through darkened cloisters and then the sudden blaze of light and color of the interior courtyard. She set the stage for the monumental work by John Singer Sargent; *El Jaleo*, located directly across from the entrance, by framing it with a Moorish arch with footlights below, playing their light up upon the painting's central figure - a dancer caught in the passion of dance and the sound of castanets.

While the foundations were being laid, Mrs. Gardner traveled to Venice to purchase hooded fireplaces, arches, doors, marble columns, capitals, wrought iron, marble fountains and staircases, paintings, statues, and furniture for the mansion. When she returned to Boston, Mr. Sears was making great progress on the palazzo; it turned its back on the gray New England landscape to have the brilliance of Venice inside. Mrs. Gardner, who visited the site daily, wanted eight balconies of the four-story building to look down upon a mosaic courtyard in the early Venetian style. She insisted that every detail of the galleries resemble those of the fifteenth and sixteenth centuries along the Grand Canal.

She made a chief aide of a stone mason whose name was Bolgi, an assistant who would remain with her for many years. Once, while at the Worthington Street dump, Bolgi spied two capitals, discarded from a demolished Masonic Temple. He called them to Gardner's attention and they were brought to Fenway Court and placed together, as a footstool before a throne in the central courtyard.

Mrs. Gardner's plans included a break from the rigidities of convention that often defined the public display of art. Disliking the windowless galleries of many public art museums, she created a glass roof to allow natural light to fill the center of the building. To foster the love of art for its own sake, she left many art treasures unlabeled, a practice that continues to this day. As construction was completed, Isabella Gardner designed a seal for the building bearing a phoenix as a symbol of immortality. It bore the motto, *C'est Mon Plasir*, and can be seen outside today, above the original front entrance of the museum.

As work on the palace progressed, Mrs. Gardner took great pleasure in keeping its design a secret from the media, even as the project reached completion. Newspaper

The Titian Room (third floor) includes one of the museum's most important works, Europa (1559-62) by Titian. Photographer: David Bohl

reporters were turned away from the construction site and when they went to City Hall to inspect the building plans they found that none had been filed. Information that ultimately was leaked to the press was kept deliberately vague.

A two-story music room was built on the east side of the building. Fearing the wood might cause bad acoustics, Gardner supervised the carving of plaster panels with folds like those of linen drapes. She had a double staircase built to the balcony and a private door for her to enter after the public had arrived for a concert.

The first event held in Fenway Court was an Anglican midnight mass in its chapel on Christmas Eve of 1901. Only six persons, all members of the Gardner family, attended. In the following years, while furniture and pictures were being arranged, only close friends of Gardner saw the rooms while, outside, the curiosity of the public mounted.

On New Year's night of 1903, the official opening took place. Hundreds of guests attended and the Boston Symphony Orchestra played under the baton of Wilhelm Gericke. While a blizzard raged outside, Bostonians stepped into the inner courtyard to find the balconies decorated with flame-colored lanterns. Candles flickered under the arches, mimosa trees spread their perfume, water danced from a fountain, and the orchestra played Bach, Mozart, and Schumman.

Portraits of Isabella Gardner were painted by William Orpen, James Abbott McNeill Whistler, Anders Zorn, and John Singer Sargent. One by Sargent portrayed her in a dress cut so low that stories circulated in Boston that he had painted her "down to Crawford's Notch." Angered by this story, Jack Gardner promised physical harm to anyone telling the story, and he withdrew the Sargent portrait from public display. Only after his - and her - deaths was it shown again, and today it is among the pictures hanging in the Gothic Room of the museum.

Gardner developed the rooms of Fenway Court in specific styles. Besides the Gothic Room there are the Titian, Veronese, Raphael, and other such rooms containing more than 2,500 objects of art. In 1914 she converted the two-story music-room on the east side of the museum into two galleries - the one on the first floor to showcase the painting *El Jaleo* by Sargent with a music room above to display tapestries, textiles, ceramics, furniture, and carvings. Her collection emphasizes Italian paintings of the fourteenth, fifteenth, and sixteenth centuries. There are also French, German, Dutch, and Flemish paintings. Courbet, Holbein, Corot, Bonheur, Manet, Degas, Matisse, and Van Dyck are represented.

The collection gathered by Isabella Stewart Gardner is one of the most important art treasures of the world. The installation is a tribute to Gardner's talent for combining art, music, and flowers in ways that engage the senses and delight the imagination. Some of the art objects are stories by themselves. A Botticelli painting was smuggled out of Italy by a prince who wanted American cash. He went to jail for the offense, since Italy had a law against such departures of its art works, but Gardner secured the picture.

Other smuggled art that she obtained without being a co-conspirator was shipped from England by an acquaintance. It was listed at United States Customs as having a value of $8,000, but an inspector noticed that it was insured for $60,000. The inspector opened the crates and found works of art that were ultimately appraised at $82,500. Penalties of $70,000 were imposed, but Gardner paid the entire bill anyway in order to take possession of the art.

Gardner limited the number of visitors to the museum on open days, and she charged one dollar a person to pay for special guards until the government ruled that the charge could not be made if the property was to be a tax-exempt museum. She solved the problem by inducing Harvard students to keep an eye on the visitors.

In 1919 Isabella Gardner suffered a stroke. She never walked again. Continuing to live in Fenway Court, she wrote in 1922 to her old friend, Count Hans Coudenhove: "I'm quite an invalid but cheerful to the last degree. I think my mind is all right and I live on it. This house is very nice, very comfortable, and rather jolly. It is in the outskirts of Boston, not in the country. I have filled it with pictures and works of art, and if there are any clever people I see them. I really lead an interesting life."

Mrs. Gardner died in 1924 at the age of eighty-four. By her will, the Isabella Stewart Gardner Museum is now maintained as it was on the day of her death. Nothing can be changed or altered in any way. An endowment provides a significant portion of operating funds; a membership program, grants, and generous gifts contribute the remainder. She wanted her art treasures perpetually maintained in congenial and charming surroundings. Most visitors at the museum feel her goal has been achieved. A new audio tour offers interesting commentary on the museum and its founder, as well as on many of the objects on view.

• • • • •

The Isabella Stewart Gardner Museum, located at 280 The Fenway in Boston, Massachusetts, is open to visitors from 11:00 a.m.-5:00 p.m., Tuesday through Sunday, as well as on the following holidays: New Year's Day; Martin Luther King, Jr., Day; Presidents' Day; Memorial Day; Independence Day; Labor Day; Columbus Day; and Veteran's Day. Admission is charged. Members and children under 18 are admitted free at all times. For further information call: (617) 566-1401 or visit the Isabella Stewart Gardner Museum website at http://www.boston.com/gardner.

The Cottage that Grew and Grew

Henry Davis Sleeper's Beauport

BEAUPORT, THE FORMER HOME of Henry Davis Sleeper (1878-1934), is a pioneer showcase of American architecture. Once a twelve-room shingle cottage on the rocky shore of Gloucester Harbor, it has slowly evolved into a forty-room, crazy-quilt mansion. Every room has been developed differently to recapture some specific mood or era of American culture, from the time of the Plymouth Colony to the early years of the Republic. Sometimes the theme is historical, sometimes literary. The mingled skeins, often incongruous and confusing, have been merged into a glowing tapestry of bricks, timbers and antiques. It has been called the "House of Mystery" and is surrounded by apocryphal tales. It could be labeled more precisely "The mansion of a thousand dreams."

The China Trade Room features a marble fireplace and hand-painted Chinese wallpaper which are both from the 18th century.

Passing through the little cupolated gatehouse, visitors to the mansion today are struck by the flowing mixture of styles including Norman, Gothic, Tudor and Chinese, which characterize the exterior of the home. The exterior describes an exotic blend of shadowed recesses, a round tower, bay windows, manorial chimneys, a spiral belfry, and peaked roofs above latticed and Palladian windows; all winding about granite outcroppings and stepped terraces at the harbor's rocky edge.

Henry Davis Sleeper, known as Harry to close friends, was an architect, interior designer and antique collector. He was a grandson of Jacob Sleeper, a founder of Boston University, and the son of Major J. Henry Sleeper, who earned fame on Civil War battlegrounds. As a youth, forays for antiques with his mother encouraged a taste for collecting objects of an eclectic nature while inheritances from the family also enabled Mr. Sleeper to journey to Europe. Sleeper's primary residence - his family home in Boston - became a virtual warehouse for hundreds of pieces of furniture, prints and decorative objects that he would collect throughout his early life. A confirmed bachelor, the future decorator finally created a home to meet the discriminating taste of one strong-willed person - himself.

In 1604, French explorer Samuel de Champlain (1567-1635) had explored the Gloucester area and called it "le Beau Port," or Handsome Harbor. Sleeper remembered this historical detail in 1907 when he began construction of his summer "cottage" near the tip of Eastern Point on Cape Ann, naming it Beauport. Sleeper's dream house resembled scores of other vacation retreats in this fishing region, but at one acre, its small size allowed it to become overshadowed by larger estates that soon dominated the area. It was, in fact, an architectural wallflower.

Beauport was distinguished, however, by a 180-degree view of the harbor, of Five-Pound and Ten-Pound Islands, and the Reef of Norman's Woes, a treacherous 200-

The Colonial Kitchen or Pembroke Room is the largest room at Beauport. It features pine paneling believed to have been taken from a 17th century Massachusetts home.

foot ledge of rock immortalized by Longfellow in the "Wreck of the Hesperus." Inspired by doting friends and neighbors - including famed art doyennes Isabella Stewart Gardner, John Singer Sargent and Paul Manship - Mr. Sleeper soon decided to make Beauport a showplace, a task that he would devote the next twenty-seven years of his life to completing. It soon took shape as one of the landmarks of aesthetic rediscovery of America since known as "Americana."

The metamorphosis of his new home began one day when Mr. Sleeper was driving through the nearby shopping village of Essex and noticed the dilapidated William Cogswell home was for sale. Select pieces of the 200-year-old colonial home became interior pieces of Mr. Sleeper's new home. A pine-paneled room became the front hall of Beauport, with the roofs and ground rearranged to accommodate it. Other pieces of that home would later become central to the interior design of the Green Dining Room and Central Hall. The success Mr. Sleeper had in his dealings with Cogswell house would set a precedent for collection of architectural elements and antiques. A visit to important historic sites in Virginia and Massachusetts in 1911-12 would determine Mr. Sleeper's focus towards American themes and memorabilia, and the character of Beauport began to change.

Other rooms were soon added - each bearing Mr. Sleeper's peculiar stamp of originality. Traveling through a Boston junkshop one day on an antique foray with friends, Sleeper purchased, to their amazement, three carved wooden curtains thought to come from an old hearse. The curtains had previously been installed on curved windows and were semi-elliptical. Mr. Sleeper soon designed three snug, Gothic-arched, diamond-latticed windows to fit them. He then decided that curved curtains called for a round room, which in turn would call for a Norman tower, which Sleeper added in 1911. So the Tower Room was conceived, which is today a small library; a scholar's nook with historic accents.

In 1909 Beauport had thirteen rooms. By the outbreak of World War I it contained twenty-two. Then an interruption in its growth occurred when Mr. Sleeper became a founder of the American Field Service. He operated ambulances behind the battle lines in France for four years and was decorated with a medal of the French Legion of Honor. After the war he returned to Beauport. Although he was experiencing financial difficulty, Sleeper's skills as an architect and decorator soon brought in more funds to resume the expansion of Beauport, which continued until his death in 1934.

The fame of Beauport gradually spread while Mr. Sleeper's trend-setting influence became the subject of numerous book and magazine articles. He played a major role in decorating and furnishing homes of Hollywood motion-picture stars of the jazz age. Some people credit him with fathering the art of merging antique items in ultra-modern settings to generate dynamic interest. He was particularly famous for his genius with interior colors. Mr. Sleeper had demonstrated that white did not have to predominate in colonial color schemes. Hues he "discovered" popular among colonial Americans through his own restoration work included chocolate brown, rust red, and robin's egg blue, all of which appear at Beauport.

Those who admired Mr. Sleeper's work and would later commission him as an interior designer for their own home included Henry James, Helen Hayes, Joan Crawford, Isabella Stewart Gardner, Frederic March, and R.T. Vanderbilt. Widely quoted for his knowledge of historic paint colors, visitors also included museum directors and other famous collectors of Americana. Notably, Beauport's interior would become the inspiration of Henry DuPont's house in Winterthur, Delaware (now a renowned museum), a project Mr. Sleeper served as design consultant for until 1931.

Standing at the front gate of Beauport is a sheet-iron Indian beckoning to visitors and pointing the way along short garden paths to the front door. Terraces, low walls and quaint shrines flank the paths. The entrance hall is the Cogswell Room, with old paneling painted a dull ivory. The floor is of red brick with a glossy wax finish, as are many other floors in the mansion. Visitors find themselves amidst a maze of antiques - colonial, English, Chinese, French and Portuguese. In rooms off the hall are ledges laden with copper and pewter antiques, collections of early glass in kaleidoscope colors, bull's-eye windows artificially illuminated, and quantities of old furniture.

Central Hall, otherwise known as Stair Hall, lies at the very heart of the mansion. In this room stands a life-size, cast-iron stove in the shape of George Washington wrapped in an iron sheet, as a Roman emperor might wear a toga. Hooked rugs, curly maple furniture and a spectacular amber glass collection of over 130 pieces delight and enthrall the incoming visitor.

The Franklin Room, one of Sleeper's earliest additions, contains a variety of Franklin memorabilia, including a bronze bust of his head, a Franklin stove, and painted chairs from Pennsylvania, the statesman's native state. The Paul Revere Room once held Sleeper's large collection of Revere silver, which is now on display at

A marvelous secret bower, the Belfry Chamber represents one of Sleeper's most masterful decorative schemes.

The Museum of Fine Arts in Boston.

The largest room in a house of small rooms is the Pembroke Room or Pine Kitchen. The most widely imitated of Sleeper's creations, it is ensconced by a large central fireplace surrounded by oversized eighteenth-century style wooden wing chairs, the creation of Gloucester's venerable cabinetmaker, Frederick Poole (1849-1930). The walls are lined with unpainted pine paneling believed to be originally from the seventeenth-century home of Robert Barker - Sleeper's ancestor -of Pembroke, Massachusetts. Everywhere are embellishments typical to colonial kitchens including an authentic cranberry rake, a cheese press, jugs, plates and other cutlery.

The Golden Step Room, one of Beauport's many dining rooms, contains a rare Chinese funeral bier that supports a large model of a Chinese Trade vessel. It is one of five rooms for dining, arranged like a satellite around a working kitchen. A huge, diamond-shaped central window may be lowered into the wall, opening the porch to the air and sea. Another dining room is octagonal; twenty-feet wide, it is decorated strikingly in aubergine, amethyst and crimson. Numerous pieces of authentic nineteenth-century French toleware, custom-made tiger-maple furniture, morocco - bound, gilt-edged books, and a brass-bordered fireplace are gathered together under a slightly-peaked octagonal ceiling.

The China Trade Room is thirty-five feet long. It includes a pagoda-type ceiling twenty-five feet high, a serpentine chandelier of Waterford crystal and cluttered Oriental antiques. The hand-painted Chinese wallpaper was imported in the 1780s

The Indian Room commands the most spectacular view in the house.

but remained unused until Mr. Sleeper found it stored in the attic of its original owner, the patriot and banker Robert Morris (1734-1806). The room also features an elaborate eighteenth-century marble fireplace, a pagoda containing seats and a magnificent chandelier.

The second floor includes six bedrooms, four bathrooms, and three sitting rooms, also in a variety of thematic styles. The Indian Room and Porch, which Sleeper used as his bedroom, is built directly over the water and features the most spectacular view in the house. A central feature of the room, an antique Indian Door from an old house in Deerfield, Massachusetts, contains layers of wood with vertical and diagonal running grains and a sheet of leather in between, so no hatchet could pierce it. Unpainted pine walls, native American decorations, German colored prints, and a large double rocking chair create a theme of simple life in early America.

Nautical themes predominate in the adjacent Mariner's room, whose name refers to master mariners of the past. The room features a massive doorway, probably taken from a house in Newport, as well as a variety of objects - including sextants, telescopes, compasses, charts, ship's logs, and other seafaring items. The creation of the Mariner's Room in the 1920s coincides with the rediscovery of Herman Melville (1819-1921) as a major American writer.

A secret staircase leads from the Jacobean Room. Three guest bedrooms created in the English style are located nearby. The Strawberry Hill Room, named after the home of English statesman Horace Walpole (1676-1745), wins the heart of many visitors. Sleeper often liked to compare Beauport to Strawberry Hill, a fantasy home created by Walpole in Twickenham, just outside London. Although there are no direct links to Strawberry Hill in this room, it was often rumored that the wallpaper had been taken from the walls of Walpole's home. Directly across from the room, Sleeper dedicated two smaller bedrooms to English heroes Lord Nelson and Lord Byron. Sleeper believed the bed in the Byron room once belonged to the poet, and he planned the color scheme of the room around it.

The future of Beauport was in doubt following Mr. Sleeper's death but a Woolworth chain-store fortune finally came to its rescue. Mrs. Helena Woolworth McCann, a daughter of F.W. Woolworth, bought the home intact in 1935 after seeing the house on a yachting trip and falling in love with it. Following Helena's death in 1937, her children: Constance, Frazier and Helena, transferred Beauport to the Society for the Preservation of New England Antiquities. Mrs. McCann's children provided a grant for maintenance of the estate through the Winfield Foundation, directing that Beauport remain permanently available to the public as a memorial to their mother. As a result of the McCann's continued commitment to Beauport, SPNEA continues to welcome the public to tour the house, a practice Sleeper himself established.

• • • • •

Beauport is located on 75 Eastern Point Boulevard in Gloucester. To arrive there take Route 1-25/128 North to the end. Follow East Main St. 1.5 miles to the stone gate at the entrance to Eastern Point Boulevard. Continue along Eastern Point Blvd. to Beauport. The estate is open to the public Monday through Friday from 10:00 a.m. to 4:00 p.m. from May 15th to October 15th, and closed on all holidays. Admission is $6.00 for adults, $5.50 for seniors, and $3.00 for students and children ages 6-12. For further information contact: (978)283-0800 or visit the Beauport website at http://www.spnea.org.

Photos courtesy of the Society for the Preservation of New England Antiquities. Photographs by David Bohl.

Photo by David Wright

The Mecca of American Horsemen

Belle Meade Plantation

NASHVILLE • TENNESSEE

"LUKE BLACKBURN, SOLD FOR $20!" The bang of the auctioneer's gavel signaled the demise of the famous Belle Meade Thoroughbred Stud. The last stallion sold that day in November, 1904, was Luke Blackburn, son of the great Bonnie Scotland and twenty-seven year old sire of Proctor Knott, who once brought $30,000 at auction. This was the final sale of the stock and household furnishings of one of America's premiere thoroughbred stud nurseries, Belle Meade, proclaimed by Frank Leslie's *Illustrated Newspaper* in 1882 to be: "The Mecca of American Horsemen."

The mansion, an imposing gray stucco structure, serves as the centerpiece for tales of hardy pioneers and dashing Confederate Generals, the romance and tragedy of the

The dining room, restored to its 1890s splendor, was the setting for gracious dining with Southern hospitality. Photo by David Wright

Old South, and the stark clarity of the New. But it's legacy is found in the surrounding pastures and barns - home to the most magnificent thoroughbred horses on the American scene in the nineteenth century, as well as four generations of one family who lived for over one hundred years in the beautiful mansion on a hill.

Tennessee was on the Western frontier in 1807 when Virginian John Harding (1777-1865) purchased a log cabin and 250 acres of land on the Old Natchez Trace in pursuit of the American Dream. Inspired by the meadow surrounding his new home, he later named the property Belle Meade, which means "beautiful meadow." Over the years his small farm grew to a 5,400 acre plantation, and along the way he acquired two other plantations in Nashville: one in Louisiana, and a 10,000 acre cotton plantation in Arkansas. The thoroughbred horse, however, was his first love and in 1816, Imp. Boaster, whose racing career spanned at least seven decades, was standing at Belle Meade. This marked Belle Meade's beginning as a stud farm.

By 1843, Belle Meade's reputation as a stud farm had spread beyond the state. In those early days, Harding's close friends included such notables as President James K. Polk, Sam Houston and President Jackson, who often paid visits. On one occasion, the honored guest was David Crockett, famous bear hunter and Tennessee congressman. Dessert was a particularly light concoction and Crockett asked what it was. Harding replied, "The ladies call it syllabub. Do you like it?" The witty Crockett responded, "Well, I don't know. I took a snap or two at it, but I reckon I missed it."

John Harding moved his family from the log cabin to a nearby Federal-style, two-story house in 1820. A simple brick home, it still exists at the core of the present-day Belle Meade mansion. General William Giles Harding, John Harding's only son, made two additions to this structure. In 1840, he added a nursery over the adjoining plantation office and a two-story kitchen wing, which he connected to the house by an open two-story breezeway.

Nursery, Belle Meade Plantation. Photo by Bill Lafevor

Belle Meade was constructed in accordance with the Greek Revival style of the mid-nineteenth century, and was "bold in silhouette, broad in proportions, and simplified in detail." There were six limestone columns located to the front of the house at this time, a trait typical to many plantation homes of this period. The identity of the person who designed Belle Meade remains a mystery, although the most likely explanation is that William Giles Harding himself worked out the plan for the mansion with the help of skilled carpenters and bricklayers. An additional garden to the rear of the house included roses, clematis, coral honeysuckle and jasmine as well as perennials and virtually every shrub known at the time.

By 1840, William Giles Harding was running Belle Meade with his bride Elizabeth McGavock (1818-67). Daily life included picnics in Deer Park, a 450-acre piece of property adjacent to the plantation grounds. There were also fox hunts and parties in the garden which was meticulously groomed by their Swiss gardener. With war looming, General Harding organized the Harding Light Artillery, which he armed and equipped with his own money. As president of Tennessee's Military and Financial Board, he was reported to have donated $500,000 in cash to arm the South. Absolutely devoted to the Cause, Harding grew a beard and vowed that he would wear it until the South prevailed. True to his word, he still wore a beard when he died many years later in 1886.

When Nashville was occupied by Union troops early in 1862, General Harding was arrested for treason and sent to a Michigan prison, leaving his wife to manage the plantation. One of Dixie's legendary heroines, Elizabeth struggled to feed on a daily basis the 150 slaves and relatives in her care while Union and Confederate soldiers routinely requisitioned foodstuff and livestock. During one such encounter, Elizabeth confronted the marauders, standing on the front porch with a gun in her hand. Upon sighting her, the officer of the troops bowed, tipped his hat, and directed his men to leave, saying, "Boys, we don't want to bother no lady (as) game as that!"

Belle Meade became the center of one Civil War skirmish during the Battle of Nashville on December 15, 1864. A Confederate soldier named Bleeker and his men saw about 250 Federal soldiers in the Harding's yard when an attack was decided. Bleeker's men charged from behind a barn, but they were faced with some resistance when they reached the front yard close to the house. As Bleeker retreated, he saw Selene Harding, William's daughter, standing on the front porch waving her hand-kerchief. Bleeker passed by and caught the handkerchief while urging her to go into the house, but she refused until the soldiers were safely away. The bullet holes remain in the massive stone columns of the porch.

Throughout The Civil War, few of Harding's slaves ran away even though many were conscripted by the Union to dig fortifications in Nashville. It was the slaves who hid the thoroughbred horses in the hills of the High Pasture and the family silver . . . where? The Hardings so trusted these loyal servants that they never asked.

Although saddled with war-time debt, Belle Meade survived the cataclysm of war with a bright future. Selene was wooed and won by Confederate General William Hicks Jackson, a graduate of West Point and a distinguished cavalryman. Following the war, Jackson was stripped of all rights to American citizenship, a particular form of punishment endured by a small, select group of ex-Confederate soldiers. He was never pardoned by the United States government. He and Selene were married on December 15th, 1868. Upon their engagement, he presented his belle with a large dia-mond ring. The ring was so large, in fact, that Selene questioned if the diamond was real. To be certain, she inscribed her name on a windowpane in the plantation office. If the stone cut the glass, it was a true diamond. Her signature can still be seen on that windowpane. General Jackson retired from the military and assumed success as a horse breeder and plantation manager after his marriage. He and General Harding soon established Belle Meade as one of the world's premier studs. Six years later on April 30, 1874, Selene's sister Mary married William's brother Howell, a local lawyer who would rise to become U.S. Senator from Tennessee and a judge on the U.S. Supreme Court. A new generation would lead Belle Meade through the post-war years.

Within a year of the surrender at Appomatox, 700 guests were invited to a party at Belle Meade, with fifteen former Confederate Generals present. In 1867, the first thoroughbred yearling sale was held, followed by a barbecue on the plantation grounds, a routine that continued for many years to come. General Harding's repu-tation brought large crowds to the sale. By this time, Harding had won more purses with the horses he had owned and bred than any man living in the United States. Yet the former general never bet on a horse race in his life.

The hallway, with its graceful cantilevered stairway, displays portraits of notable Belle Meade Thoroughbreds. Photo by Ralph A. Meacham

Ironically, Harding retired from racing the same week that the first Kentucky Derby ran in 1875, a year in which six of the fifteen horses running in the horse race had direct ties to Belle Meade. Harding and Jackson would concentrate on breeding thoroughbreds, and fame and fortune came through two outstanding studs. Bonnie Scotland stood at stud for eight years at Belle Meade, and in 1880, he was acclaimed America's leading sire. Forty-six of fifty-three thoroughbred horses alive between 1937 and 1989 are descendants of this horse, and his blood-line includes the great Secretariat, Northern Dancer and Seattle Slew. His offspring won 137 races and over $135,000, surpassing the record set by Kentucky's great Lexington.

In 1886, another great stallion joined Belle Meade to head the stud. Iroquois, one of the most famous American Thoroughbreds of the nineteenth century, was the first American bred and owned horse to win the prestigious English Derby and Doncaster St. Leger Stakes; a feat not equaled until 1954. Hearing that a foreign stable was interested in the stallion, General Jackson purchased Iroquois at a cost of $20,000 to keep him on American soil. Others were soon willing to pay even more, and at one time General Jackson refused an offer of $150,000 for him. Nashville's Iroquois Steeplechase is run every May in his honor. A street in the city of Belle Meade also carries his name, while two of his portraits remain on exhibit at the National Museum of Racing in Saratoga Springs, New York.

All important visitors to Nashville were entertained at Belle Meade, including President and Mrs. Grover Cleveland on their honeymoon in 1887. In all, seven Presidents have been guests at Belle Meade, with a visit by President Taft in 1908 causing some commotion when he got caught in an upstairs bathtub. Taft was a very portly gentleman and this was not the first nor the last such occurrence of its kind for him at Belle Meade. In honor of his second visit to the plantation, a unique shower was installed for his use. The shower is spacious with bands of water jets set in its walls, a forerunner of today's Jacuzzi.

In 1853, Harding made the last major renovation to Belle Meade; a two-story addition to the front of the plantation resulting in the traditional four-square design of the home. The changes to the house were likely the result of a fire which had recently occurred on the property, causing significant damage to the house. The two-story addition included a full basement, raised ceilings, an attic, as well as a second parlor and a library on the main floor. Harding also added an imposing Greek portico and two enclosed gable-end chimneys, corresponding to the chimneys of the earlier structure. This style was in turn divided by spacious hallways with a cantilevered stairway winding to the third floor. This addition abuts the original structure, with a stucco

Carriage house and stables, Belle Meade Plantation.

exterior to tie together the two houses. The Greek portico was supported by massive limestone columns quarried on the plantation and had his initials and the Harding's date carved on the entablature.

Thirty years passed before William and Selene Jackson added their touch to the mansion. Since little had been done since 1853, the renovations of 1883 were extensive, or as Selene wrote, "new from garret to cellar." The stucco was painted a stone color with shutters of a darker shade. The interior was replastered and repainted. Chandeliers were hung from cream-colored ceilings in the library and the sitting rooms. Pantries were replaced by bathrooms both on the upper and lower floor, and an elaborate hot water system was installed.

The hall was painted a smoke color, which the family portrait painter John Wood Dodge recommended as being particularly effective as a background for paintings in the plantation. In other homes, portraits of distinguished ancestors were hung; but at Belle Meade, the walls were covered with portraits of the most valuable thoroughbreds. Seven of the twenty horse paintings on display were undertaken by Henry Stull (1851-1913), a leading Canadian artist who was one of the most outstanding painters of thoroughbred race horses in the U.S. and England during the late nineteenth century. Paintings also include works by Edward Troye, Harry Hall and Stewart Treviranus.

Almost ten years later, General Jackson enlarged the master bedroom and a downstairs sitting room to be used as the formal dining room. He also added a portecochère to the rear of the mansion. America was in the midst of an economic downturn, but General Jackson proceeded to build a state-of-the-art dairy, a colossal carriage house and stables for the family's carriages and riding horses. His eldest daughter had recently had one of the largest weddings in Nashville's history. As the bridal couple left the church, the organist played "There'll Be A Hot Time in the Old Town Tonight." It was the Gay Nineties, but the turn of the century did not bode well for Belle Meade.

Depressed by the death of his wife Selene, who had passed away in late 1892, Jackson relinquished control of his responsibility for the plantation and left for England in October, 1896. Before leaving, he had entrusted ownership of Belle Meade to his children, not realizing at the time that they would soon mortgage the plantation. The true state of Belle Meade's financial difficulties did not surface until the tragic suicide of General Jackson's son-in-law, Albert Marks, in 1902. The death of Marks, who had involved himself with a number of questionable financial transactions, created considerable embarrassment for the Jackson family as front-page stories about his death appeared for days in the Nashville newspapers. Within the year, both General Jackson and his son William Harding Jackson would also pass away. Thus it was that William's young widow was left to struggle with insurmountable debt. Belle Meade, one of America's greatest Studs, went on the auction block in November, 1904. Over the next five decades, the plantation and its surrounding property would belong to five different owners. During this time, some renovations were made to the mansion's interior and a brief, unsuccessful attempt was made to revive Belle Meade as a stud facility. The Belle Meade Land Company, created by one investor in 1916, began the process of land division which resulted in public ownership of much of the property. In 1938 the city of Belle Meade was created when residents of Belle Meade Park voted to incorporate. Since its inception, it has remained Nashville's most exclusive residential area.

In 1952, the State of Tennessee purchased the mansion, eight out-buildings, including a carriage house, stables, smokehouse, garden house, mausoleum, dairy, cabin and play house, and twenty-four acres of land. Within the year, the state deeded the property to the newly created Association for the Preservation of Tennessee Antiquities (APTA), which has faithfully maintained the property to the present day. Belle Meade has been restored to the 1883 era and over one-third of the original furnishings have been returned, including the original bed in which President Grover Cleveland slept on his visit to the mansion in 1887. The outbuildings and some of the gardens have also been renovated. The site was placed on the National Register of Historic Places in 1969 and is visited by approximately 120,000 people a year.

• • • • •

Belle Meade Plantation is located on 5025 Harding Road, seven miles from downtown Nashville. Visiting Hours are between 9:00 a.m. to 5:00 p.m Sunday through Wednesday and Thursday through Saturday from 9 a.m. to 9 p.m. The mansion is closed Thanksgiving, Christmas and New Year's Day. Admission fees are charged. For further information call: (615) 356-0501/ (800)270-3991, or visit the Belle Meade website at http://www.citysearch.com/nas/plantation.

Photos courtesy of Belle Meade Plantation.

A Plantation Owner's Bridal Gift

The Daniel Turnbull's' Rosedown

ST. FRANCISVILLE • LOUISIANA

WHEN ASKED TO PINPOINT a plantation that may be considered among the most adequately and appropriately restored in Louisiana, experts at the State Department of Commerce and Industry unhesitatingly suggest Rosedown. A virtual time capsule, it is filled with all of its original contents in room settings authentically reflecting their 1835 appearance. The plantation includes over 8,000 original historic documents supporting the acquisition of almost every object in the mansion; one of the best documented decorative arts collections in the nation.

When Daniel Turnbull, a prosperous, middle-aged planter of cotton, indigo and sugar, married eighteen-year old Martha Hilliard Barrow, he promised to build for

The dining room at Rosedown features portraits of Martha and Daniel Turnbull, Rosedown's original owners, by artist Thomas Sully (1783-1872).

her one of the most splendid mansions in the plantation country of St. Francisville. He chose a tract on the east side of the Mississippi River about midway between New Orleans and Natchez. The plans were drawn and some of Mr. Turnbull's 450 slaves went to work on the construction.

Martha Turnbull had some of the slaves dig shallow slit-trenches in straight lines along both sides of the main road leading up to the site of the mansion. With an apron full of acorns from her favorite oak trees, she then planted the seeds into the soft earth in hope of some day having a great alleé of oaks on the approach to her home. Her hope was fulfilled: today the alleé of moss-hung oaks leading to the patrician white mansion is a dramatic sight.

After planting the trees and seeing the start of the construction, the Turnbulls sailed for Europe to buy crystal chandeliers, rugs, paintings, tapestries, furniture, china, and bric-a-brac for their home. On their return, they moved into the nineteen-room dwelling with a shipload of European furnishings.

Somewhat similar to the early manor houses of Georgia and Virginia, the structure was built of cedar and cypress, with double galleries across the front, plastered-brick wings on each side, classic Doric columns, richly ornamented cornices, and Georgian fanlights of leaded glass. It also had servants' buildings, pigeon houses, stables and thirty acres of gardens, with occasional gazebos beside the walks.

Martha Turnbull was delighted when she first saw the mansion, just as visitors are today when they see it in the splendor that has been restored by Milton R. Underwood, a

New York and Texas stock-broker, and his wife.

Romance played a part in giving Rosedown its name. While the mansion was still nameless, Martha Turnbull remarked to her husband that it seemed so gay and delightful that it reminded her of a romantic play entitled "Rosedown" they had seen in New York. The luxurious setting of roses in this production impressed Mrs. Turnbull greatly. Her husband agreed, so the mansion became Rosedown.

Although the original floor plans of Rosedown remain, there is no clue as to whom the original architect was. A typical "hill plantation," the architectural features of Rosedown include columns, elaborate stairs, and stylish trim; depicting the owner's association with affluent Tidewater culture. Mr. Turnbull already owned three adjoining plantations in the state of Louisiana - the 900-acre *Inheritance*, the 2,250-Acre *De Soto* and the 2,400-acre *Stypoa*. The last two plantations were located on Red River Island near Simmesport and Fort Adams.

The Henry Clay Room: Rosedown. The furniture in this room was created by Crawford-Riddle of Philadelphia for Henry Clay's occupancy at the White House. It is considered the premiere suit of Gothic furniture in America.

The gardens at Rosedown would become the most ambitious undertaking of Martha Turnbull and ultimately the most significant feature of the plantation. Some of the Rosedown gardens were patterned after those the Turnbulls had seen at Versailles and in other post-Renaissance gardens. The Turnbulls also planted an abundance of camellias of exceptional size, hip gardenias with bright red seed pods that show all winter, Japanese trees of the cypress family, and decorative Oriental shrubs and princess trees

Rosedown's famous Oak Alley is surrounded by twenty-eight acres of historical gardens containing century-old camellias, azaleas and crepe myrtles.

with lavender trumpet flowers. At the time of the Turnbulls' first tour of Europe, there was no existing model for gardens of the scale and scope that the family would develop at Rosedown.

The Turnbulls had three children. Two of them were sons, one of whom died when he was seven years old; the other drowned at the age of twenty-seven. In a gesture of mourning, the Turnbulls painted a heavy black band around the outside of the house just below the eaves. The band is still visible on the two wings of the mansion.

The third child of the Turnbulls was a daughter, Sarah. Slim, vivacious and beautiful, she was the queen of St. Francisville and had so many ardent suitors that the talk of the parish often centered around her romances. She reportedly received one hundred proposals of marriage and said "maybe" to many. To maintain suspenseful speculation, she always wore jewelry and handkerchiefs that swains other than her immediate escort had given to her.

Finally she married James Pirrie Bowman, the son of a minister who lived next door. They had two sons and eight daughters. Sarah inherited Rosedown, and even while managing the plantation and a family of ten children, continued to cut a wide social swath in St. Francisville.

Each of Sarah's daughters went on to become an accomplished musician, either with a violin, piano, mandolin, harp or other instrument. John James Audubon (1780-1851), the naturalist, would be a close neighbor. An original set of his *Birds of America* paintings, as well as other artwork he was commissioned to do by the Turnbulls, are still on display on the walls of Rosedown.

Sarah Turnbull Bowman died in 1914, and upon her death she left her plantation and other assets to her children. She willed Rosedown as a joint inheritance to her four unmarried daughters: Corrie, Isabel, Sarah, and Nina. These were not easy times for the Bowmans and their neighbors. The mansion fell victim to worsening economic conditions throughout the South as a whole, specifically the complete downfall of the cotton culture. To help pay expenses on the house, the sisters potted small plants from the now famous garden and sold them to tourists, who began flocking to the

South in the late 1930s. The sisters did most of the garden and housework themselves; so proud of Rosedown they would endure any sacrifice to keep the plantation in the family.

After the death of the last sister, Miss Nina Benoist Bowman, in 1955, her heirs offered Rosedown with its 2,500 remaining acres for sale. At that time, Mrs. Underwood, who was president of the River Oaks Garden Club of Houston, Texas, was vacationing in nearby Natchez, Mississippi. When she heard Rosedown was available, she rushed to see it. A woman associated with Texas oil wealth, her interest would be of great future significance to the mansion's outcome. After inducing her husband to see Rosedown, the couple purchased the property in 1956, complete with fringe lands that increased the tract to 2,600 acres.

Eight years of restoration work soon followed. Early in the planning stages, Mrs. Underwood made it clear that authenticity and perfection were her goals. The technicians would be given all the time they needed for their work. Architect George Leake of New Orleans was placed in charge of the restoration in 1960, while McMillen, Inc. of New York City assisted Mrs. Underwood with the interiors. The architect and other specialists followed the directive: "If there is a better way to do it, than do it that way. If you can't find what you need, have it made." The work resulted in one of the most extensive, and ultimately authentic, historic restorations ever undertaken in the United States. The results attained in this eight-year project represent the highest perfection of preservation standards.

Since the death of Catherine Underwood in 1970, the operation of Rosedown as one of the South's most distinguished homes has continued, as well as the preservation of the outside property. Rosedown's twenty-eight acres of gardens - the earliest of the major nineteenth-century historic gardens in the nation - have been completely restored to their original form. They have been recently recognized as one of the nation's five most important historical gardens. Virtually all of the original contents of the mansion are on display, as they were in the years when the Bowmans lived there. Rosedown now stands as a legacy to the grace and grandeur of the Old South.

• • • • •

Rosedown is located just east of St. Francisville at the junction of State Highway 10 and U.S. Route 61. It is open from 9:00 a.m. to 5:00 p.m. daily. The admission fee is $10.00 per person. For further information, please contact Rosedown Plantation at: (225) 635-3332.

Photos courtesy of Rosedown Plantation, St. Francisville, Louisiana.

Entrance façade of the Elms with sculpture of "Cherub astride a Sphinx" after Sarrazin.

The entrance hall and grand staircase of the Elms features white marble and veined breccia molding.

They Paid Half the Taxes

"Cottages" of the Elite
The Elms • Hunter House • Rosecliff • Château-sur-Mer

NEWPORT • RHODE ISLAND

SINCE THE WITHERING of the big fortunes in the Depression of the 1930s, the Newport "cottages" that begin at the top of the hill on Bellevue Avenue have undergone drastic changes. Most of these have been to the benefit of ordinary citizens who have more and more leisure time to go touring.

Many of the original mansions still standing in monumental dignity are open to the public. Others have been converted into clubs, condominiums, luxury apartment houses, museums and motels. Still others remain as private homes, their original splendor somewhat tarnished. The giant parties and other social extravaganzas are only memories, as are the tax-

Hunter House is an architectural treasure of early Newport.

free lifestyles and cast-iron social codes which underscored the existence of Newport's former "elite."

In 1962, The Preservation Society of Newport County rescued from total destruction a fifty-six room mansion on Bellevue Avenue known as The Elms. It had been a house of mystery for two generations, protected from the outside world by a palace guard. High stone walls punctuated with occasional iron grills permitted strangers to get only glimpses of the elegance inside.

E.J. Berwind, a coal baron from Pennsylvania, was at the peak of his career when work was completed on The Elms in 1901. His firm, a family operation known as the Berwind-White Coal Company, operated more than 260,000 acres of coal lands in Pennsylvania, West Virginia and Kentucky; the country's largest individual owned coal company. Berwind-White was chief supplier of coal to the U.S. Navy and Merchant Marine, and had outlets in New York, the Caribbean, France and Italy.

The site of The Elms was purchased by Berwind in 1888, shortly after his marriage to Sarah Vesta Herminie Torrey, a daughter of a U.S consular agent to Italy. The architect, Horace Trumbauer of Philadelphia, modeled the structure after the Château d'Asnières, a distinguished eighteenth-century country house located near Paris. Like its French counterpart, The Elms has a rounded central section flanked by wings of equal size - a simple classical plan of balanced proportions. Statues, fountains, and marble gazebos line the walks to the gardens, terraces and balustraded stone stables.

All of the original turn-of-the-century architectural decorations of The Elms, designed by Allard et Fils of Paris, remain intact. The interior is distinguished by fine parquet floors, ceiling paintings, reliefs, and elaborate moldings in the eighteenth-century tradition. Highlights of the interior include a grand staircase of white marble and veined breccia molding, an opulent drawing room in early Louis XVI style, and a gazebo-like conservatory in the south-wing filled with plants, marble sculptures, and a fountain of rouge royal marble. Throughout the house a sense of symmetry prevails. Windows are positioned to balance windows, mirrors oppose mirrors, and doors correspond to other doors, creating vistas through up to four rooms at once. In architectural terms, this effect is known as *enfilade*.

The mansion is distinguished by its exceptionally beautiful grounds, carefully clipped maple and linden trees, and enormous weeping beeches. Ironically, the species of tree for which the property acquired its name have disappeared. Located on the western edge of the property are two small marble teahouses with copper roofs in the eighteenth-century French style. They form the entrance to a sunken garden filled with hundreds of pink and white begonias and ornamental parterre patterns composed of miniature boxwood hedges. Behind the mansion, a carriage and garage built in 1911 stand as replicas to an 1898 pavilion by architect Henry Goury (b. 1850) on the grounds of the château of Madame Du Barry at Louveciennes.

Edward Berwind's work kept him in Manhattan much of the time, but like many of his counterparts in Newport, he often spent his weekends traveling from Manhattan to Newport by steamer or aboard his yacht, the *Truant*. After Mr. Berwind and his wife died, his sister, Miss Julia Berwind, lived at The Elms until her death in 1961. In 1962, a nephew of Miss Berwind auctioned the property to a real estate syndicate that planned to raze the mansion and subdivide the land. A subsequent decline in the syndicate's financial concerns led it to accept an offer by the Newport Preservation Society to buy the estate for public display.

Unfortunately, many of the Elms' original art and antique furnishings were sold at auction before the Preservation Society purchased the home. Television and motion-picture producers purchased much of the ornate furniture for future spectaculars. However, by borrowing from museums and rummaging through attics and warehouses of its own, the society quickly furnished the mansion with items such as those the Berwinds collected, and the estate was opened to the public. Some items have since been returned to the Elms through gifts and loans.

When James B. Duke; Robert R. Young; Mrs. Perle Mesta; Oliver H.P. Belmont; Mrs. Stuyvesant Fish; the Vanderbilts; the Firestones; the Jelkes; the Van Rensselaers; the Havemeyers and others in the social whirl spoke of their "cottages" they meant just the reverse. Similar "logic" seems to have governed the choice of names for some of their estates. Champ Soleil is in the shade of huge trees. Land Fall was built by an admiral. Château-sur-Mer is not on the sea. Exceptions are the Waves, at the edge of the surf, the Marble House, built largely of marble, and Shamrock Cliff, rising in an escarpment reminiscent of the Irish coast.

The Cliff Walk, which skirts the seashore near Bellevue and Ochre Point Avenues, provides a good opportunity for visitors to observe the fronts of many of the mansions. Estate owners were once so irked by the curious tourists that they built stone walks across the cliffs. Newport residents who did not have ocean views tore down the walls and flung the rocks into the sea. The walls were rebuilt, but again were torn down. After long litigation the courts decided that the public had a right to use the Cliff Walk, so today it is open. Part of it passes through a tunnel, and it twists and has many steps, but the views from it are rewarding.

Newport was settled in 1639 by former members of the Massachusetts Bay Colony seeking greater religious freedom. One of the finest surviving houses from Newport's era of great prosperity before the American Revolution is the Hunter House, in the center of the city. Built in 1748 and far from being a mansion, it is considered one of the finest colonial structures remaining in America and is included in this discussion because of its sharp contrast with the architectural styles of the comparatively recent social era of Newport. The early cottages, which really were timber framed cottages, explain why Newport once attracted such residents as Edgar Allen Poe, Oliver Wendell Holmes, Henry James and Henry Wadsworth Longfellow.

The Hunter House was built at a time when Newport was a greater seaport than either New York or Charleston. Washington Street, where it stands, was lined with the homes of merchant princes. The house was occupied successively by Jonathan

The Hunter House's parlor features authentic period furnishings from the 18th century.

Nichols, deputy governor of Rhode Island and the owner of a fleet of ships; Colonel Joseph Wanton, a son of Governor Joseph Wanton; and William Hunter, a U.S. Senator from Rhode Island and Minister to Brazil. His purchase of the home in 1805 saved it from devastation enabling the Hunter family to occupy it for more than fifty years. After the house was again sold in 1863,

The ballroom of Rosecliff is the largest in Newport.

it would pass through many hands before becoming the first site in Newport County to be operated as a house museum by The Preservation Society. Completely restored to its eighteenth-century appearance, Hunter House is prized for the quantity and quality of its faithfully restored interior decorations, including one of the country's most characteristic collections of eighteenth-century period furniture. The exterior of the home has been restored to its original appearance and features decorative symbols of colonial hospitality including an eighteenth-century style garden and pergola; similar to the formal design of period Newport landscaping.

Known as an architectural landmark of the high Victorian Age, Château-Sur-Mer stands out as a bridge between the earlier human-scale "retreat" homes of Newport and the palatial Marble House and its Gilded Age successors. It combines the work of Newport contractor Seth Bradford (1801-1878) with later modifications by noted architect Richard Morris Hunt (1827-1895) and interior designer Ogden Codman (1868-1951). A scene of memorable

Rosecliff Heart staircase and entrance hall.

Château-sur-Mer today. West Elevation.

social galas, including a picnic for two thousand in 1857, Château-sur-Mer was the most palatial residence in Newport between the time of its construction until the appearance of the Vanderbilt houses in the 1890s.

Château-sur-Mer was constructed between 1851 and 1852 for William Shepard Wetmore, a China trade merchant whose trading company: Alsop, Wetmore & Cryder, was an exclusive agent for British and American trade in China in the early nineteenth century. After retirement in 1840, Wetmore began to purchase land in Newport, but did not begin construction of Château-sur-Mer until 1852. There he would live until his death in 1862 with his wife Antice Derby Rogers and children: William Shepard Jr., George Peabody, and Annie Derby. William Wetmore's son George Peabody, then only sixteen, would become master of the house - "the most substantial and expensive residence in Newport"(William P. Clark, 1877).

The commission of Richard Morris Hunt in 1873 would produce a significant trans-formation upon the fortress-like character of the original house. Changes were espe-cially apparent in the interior which included the most fashionable French, British and Italian design concepts of the time. Hunt's innovations included the addition of a galleried three-story entrance hall, a morning room, a stairway enhanced by stained-glass landing window, a painted-glass ceiling and French bronze figures of Japanese influence. Thrilled with Hunt's work, Wetmore would re-engage him in 1876 to perform additional changes to the house.

Wetmore also employed the services of Ogden Codman in 1897 to redecorate the drawing room, now known as the French Salon. Codman, a cousin of Wetmore, applied to this room design concepts outlined in his *The Decoration of Houses*, written with Edith Wharton and published that year. During the years 1915-18, the firm of Olmstead Brothers was hired to make improvements in the grounds - already famed for its original greenhouses, palm houses and wineries. Successive changes to Château-sur-Mer fused major design trends of the last half of the nineteenth century. Today the house has been preserved as one of the country's finest examples of high Victorian architecture. Following the auction of its original contents, it was purchased by the Newport Preservation Society in 1969.

Before it attained its nickname, the "Queen of Resorts," Rosecliff, former home of undisputed high society matron Theresa Fair Oelrichs, was a bargain-basement steal. The Oelrichs purchased the Bellevue Avenue estate from historian and diplomat George Bancroft in 1891 for $140,000 and spent a reported $2.5 million transforming it into a showcase for some of Newport's most lavish summer events. Featured amusements at this top social draw included ballet and opera and even an entire circus - until Newport's Gilded Age ended with the advent of World War I. The splendor of Rosecliff's past would later be recreated when the mansion was used as a setting for scenes from the films *The Betsy* (1978) with Sir Laurence Olivier, *The Great Gatsby* (1974) starring Robert Redford, and *Amistad* (1997).

Born in Virginia City, Nevada to a family of ordinary means, Theresa Alice Fair was one of the four daughters of James Graham Fair, a mining engineer who would make his fortune during the Comstock Silver Lode in Nevada; one of the richest silver finds in history. An Irishman, Mr. Fair had emigrated to the U.S. and followed the Gold Rush's call to California in 1849. Mr. Fair's wife, Theresa Rooney, would divorce him on grounds of adultery in 1883, inheriting the richest divorce settlement the country had ever witnessed. Seven years later, the couple's daughter Theresa married Lloyd line shipping agent Hermann Oelrich, in a spectacular San Francisco wedding ceremony. With a $1,000,000 wedding gift from her father, Theresa purchased Rosecliff the same year.

Rosecliff bears the firm imprint of Boston architect Stanford White (1853-1906), whose achievements would also include New York's Century Club, the neoclassical arch in Washington Square, and the original Madison Square Garden, where he was tragically assasinated in 1906. Rosecliff was modeled after the Grand Trianon, a baroque pleasure pavilion built in the great park of Versailles for Louis XIV, by Jules Hardouin Mansart (1648-1708) between 1687 and 1691. The floor plan is greatly modified and takes the form of an "H," with a horizontal central section flanked by two vertical wings of equal size. Sheltered courtyards fill the spaces between the wings while a terrace on the east-side of the house overlooks an ocean; on the west entrance an eighteenth-century courtyard.

The house features Newport's largest ballroom, and is connected to each court area by five sets of gracefully arched French doors. Highlights of White's work also include an elegant rococo staircase with delicate black wrought-iron railing, a Palladian-style entrance hall, and a neo-Renaissance style chimney piece copied from

Exterior view of Rosecliff, former home of undisputed high society matron Theresa Fair Oelrichs.

a sixteenth-century original at the château d'Écouen, France. Steel beam construction was utilized and plumbing and electricity were also added.

Following her death in 1926, Theresa's son Hermann continued to occupy Rosecliff during the summers until 1941. The house, purchased that year for only $21,000 as a gift, passed through the hands of three subsequent owners before being donated to The Newport Preservation Society in 1971. Surrounded by magnificent lawns, nearly 200 hybrid tea rose bushes and ever-blooming climbers now flower there every summer.

• • • • •

The Elms, Hunter House, Rosecliff, and Château-sur-Mer are located on Bellevue Ave. and Washington Streets near downtown Newport. Rosecliff is open daily from March 31-October 31. The Elms, Hunter House and Château-sur-Mer are open only on weekends from March 21-April 30, and daily until the end of September. Hours of operation at all sites are 10:00 a.m. to 5:00 p.m. Admission is charged. For further information call: (401) 847-1000, or visit the Newport Preservation Society website at http:// www.newportmansions.org.

Photos courtesy of the Preservation Society of Newport County.

Thomas Edison's Glenmont Estate in New Jersey. Photo by K. Daley.

The "Thought Benches" of A Wizard

Thomas A. Edison's Glenmont and Seminole Homes

WEST ORANGE • NEW JERSEY
FORT MYERS • FLORIDA

AT THE AGE OF ONLY THIRTY-NINE, Thomas Edison was a widower, his hearing was almost gone and he was so ill that doctors shook their heads and despaired of him. Professional educators had long been doing likewise because of his lack of formal schooling. However, the stubborn Edison resolved to prove all the pessimists wrong. He recovered, married for the second time and acquired two new homes in sylvan settings - one in New Jersey and one in Florida - where he could perform scientific experiments.

He had given his bride-to-be, the former Mina Miller, a choice of living space in New York City or fashionable Llewellyn Park at West Orange, New Jersey. She preferred the convenience of a town house but chose the suburban one because she knew that her husband would be freer and happier there. Edison moved into Glenmont in 1886, soon after marrying Miss Miller, the 20-year-old daughter of a wealthy mid-western manufacturer.

The Florida home on the Caloosahatchee River at Fort Myers Edison chose for him-self in 1885, purchasing the property within twenty-four hours of viewing it. As had the blue waters of the frigid St. Clair in Edison's youth in Port Huron, this very dif-ferent Southern river exerted the same powerful allure, symbolizing a natural force pulsing with steam transport, freight, and commerce -- a combination Edison found irresistible.

Both homes - Glenmont and Seminole - are now publicly-owned shrines enabling the public to see how the wizard of the electric light, the phonograph, the motion pic-ture, the storage battery, the electric locomotive and a thousand other innovations lived and worked and sometimes played. They were also the homes of his six chil-dren, three each by two different wives. Both homes typify the philosophy that Edison expressed one day when a visitor at Glenmont called him a genius. "Genius," Edison retorted, "is one percent inspiration and ninety-nine percent perspiration!"

To prove his philosophy, Edison worked in the homes and nearby laboratories from eight in the morning to sundown, often returning after dinner to continue with his experients until midnight or later. Chairs and lounges where Edison rested are still where he left them after using the two houses as bases for the forty-four most pro-ductive years of his life. He died at Glenmont in 1931, and his widow sixteen years later.

Glenmont is a many-gabled house of brick and timber with a slate roof. It has twen-ty-nine rooms on its four floors. It has a greenhouse and other subsidiary buildings, broad lawns and a garden on thirteen-and-a-half acres. Its architect was H. Hudson Holly of New York, who designed it for a business executive of Arnold Constable & Company.

Here was "the natural building style for America…an architecture of our own…worked out in an artistic and natural form…expressing real domestic needs of which it is the out-come," he announced.

Entrance to the house is through a massive porte-cochère, which has rooms above it. The foyer features an ornamental tile floor, walls paneled with quartered oak and a grand staircase of South American mahogany. The adjacent library, which the designer insisted should reflect "the mastermind of the household," is made entirely of mahogany bookcases, their doors lined with box-pleated silk, while its walls and ceilings are stenciled decoratively. "A house without books is like a room without windows," the architect wrote.

The drawing room is furnished entirely in rosewood and adorned with popular oil paintings of the period. The conservatory, approached via French doors from the drawing room, is lush with tropical and subtropical plants, arching palms, and ferns, and furnished simply in willow and wicker. It was frequently used for bird-watching,

Thomas Edison with his second wife Mina and their children at his home in Glenmont, New Jersey.

a favorite pastime of Mina Edison's.

The spacious dining room, equipped with Venetian-glass cabinets, a grandfather clock and other antiques of the Edisons, seems to echo the lively conversations Edison had there with such luminaries as John Burroughs, Henry Ford, Harvey Firestone and many other colleagues and acquaintances.

On the second floor is a living room, with more books. This room was used as a retreat by the Edisons when children and guests were on the first floor. This was Thomas Edison's favorite room in the evening, his "place of quiet repose" where he

The living room at Seminole Lodge was Edison's place of "quiet repose."

Edison's laboratory at Fort Myers. When working on a difficult project, Edison would lock himself and his staff inside for up to three days at a time.

sat at his "thought bench"; it was more comfortably used for game-playing, needlework, and letter writing. It has large windows facing the lawns and a valley. An adjoining den also served as a place of family relaxation. Filled with medals, certificates, gifts, souvenirs, and memorabilia from around the world, the room reflects Edison's fame and international renown. Five large bedrooms on the second floor include one in which Edison's last three children were born. In a canopied bed of another room Edison died after murmuring to his doctor: "It is very beautiful over there…"

The laboratory Edison developed nearby his Glenmont home in West Orange would be the most productive of all those he owned: more than half of his 1,093 U.S. patents were for inventions developed there. West Orange set the standard for all research labs. It was here that Edison perfected work on the phonograph, the first movie projector, the storage battery, the fluoroscope, and other inventions. This lab included Edison's library, a stock room, two machine shops, and approximately thirty experiment rooms on the second and third floor. Edison owned over 10,000 books as well as 3,400 notebooks and 5,000,000 miscellaneous papers. A driven perfectionist, the scientist is known to have locked himself and his staff in his laboratory for up to three days in order to complete a project.

In 1962, Congress designated Glenmont and the Edison laboratory a National Historic Site. The entire property has been given to the government by Edison's family and by his corporate enterprises. The government expanded the property to sixteen acres and opened six laboratory buildings to the public, in addition to the mansion.

When Edison visited Fort Myers in 1885 he had been impressed by the jungles of bamboo along the Calloosahatchee River. After over 6,000 failed experiments creating incandescent bulbs he wanted to explore new possibilities with bamboo. Besides, he enjoyed the semitropical climate which was good for his health. After purchasing fourteen acres on the river, Edison built Seminole Lodge, one of the first precut homes in America. Designed, cut, and assembled in Fairfield, Maine, it was ship-

The reception hall at Glenmont. Here Edison would greet notable friends, including Henry Ford and Harvey Firestone. Photo by K. Daley.

ped to Fort Myers on two schooners just as almost everything was in the era before extensive and easily accessible transportation was available.

The Edison estate in Florida is composed of two, two-story, mirror-image homes connected by a pergola. The main part of the home contains a library, living room and dressing room with bath on the first floor and three bedrooms and one bath on the sec-

Edison's winter home, Seminole Lodge, at Fort Myers, Florida.

ond floor. The second or "guest" house contains an attached kitchen with servants' quarters above and a dining room and living room area on the first floor, with three bedrooms and a bath upstairs. Edison disliked the odor of food in rooms where he read, worked, slept, or met with friends, so in one wing he placed his living quarters; in the other, the kitchen, dining area and servants' quarters. Edison also had an electrical laboratory built on the estate grounds at the same time the home was constructed.

Seminole Lodge is spacious but simple. The main living areas on the first floor of both buildings have no windows, relying instead on many French doors placed to draw in breezes from the river. Edison called it the first air-conditioned house. The doors open onto a 14-foot wide verandah whose roof keeps off all but the most aggressive rainfall.

Many of the rooms contain electroliers. These chandeliers, built by the Bergman Company (owned by Thomas Edison), were the first to be designed exclusively for electricity, not just reworked gas fixtures. The electrolier's picturesque lightbulbs are reproductions of the earliest lamps Edison created.

On the grounds is a 50-foot swimming pool, one of the first constructed in Florida. Edison had it made with steel reinforced concrete which became a popular form of building material. The pool is supplied by an artesian well that keeps the water clean by its continuous flow. Edison didn't actually enjoy swimming, or any other form of physical exertion for that matter, believing that the body's function was merely to carry the head, not to waste one's time exercising. Despite his philosophy on health, however, the inventor lived to the age of eighty-four.

Edison developed the botanical gardens surrounding his home and laboratory into one of the most extensive in the South, containing over 1,800 varieties of flowers and 300 varieties of trees and shrubs, ninety percent of them foreign to the United States. There are trees with leaves like chamois skin, trees with pods resembling human ears and Strangler Fig trees with roots that can choke other vegetation to death.

Other exotic plants abound, such as great masses of flowering bougainvillea, African "sausage trees," with pods resembling huge sausages planted conveniently near the "fried egg tree" from Brazil, and "dynamite trees" whose tomato-size pods explode with the startling sound of a firecracker to scatter seeds for hundreds of feet. Edison also cultivated huge specimens of goldenrods for experiments, seeking an alternate, botanical source of rubber. The gardens also contain wild orchids, papayas and pineapples from Hawaii. Next to the Mexican sapodilla are mango trees from India, plus sweet Asiatic orange trees and plants from Java and Ceylon. Seventy varieties of palms are also located on the grounds.

The most spectacular gift of greenery to Fort Myers was the stand of stately Royal Palms that Edison had planted along both sides of McGregor Boulevard, where a cow trail formerly ran beside his home. He imported shiploads of the tall palms from Cuba, although they grew locally in the Everglades. It was much easier to transport the trees the ninety miles by sea then to try to pull them out of the trackless swamp only a short distance away. A mile of the trees were planted, which has since been extended to fourteen, helping to confer on Fort Myers the nickname "City of Palms."

Winding from the street to the main house is the Friendship Walk. Mina Edison found the idea of a "Walk of Fame," developed by Rollins College in Florida, so charming that she wanted a similar design at Seminole Lodge. Requesting that friends and family imprint large stepping stones with their names, Mrs. Edison created a path that is still visible while touring the grounds. One prominent block of rough stone sits on the path with no name on it. As the story goes, billionaire industrialist and next door neighbor Henry Ford donated this rock, saying that he was just a poor country boy who couldn't "afford" the cost of imprinting it!

Across McGregor Boulevard is the museum for the Edison estate which houses many of Mr. Edison's inventions and personal treasures. Among the cars displayed is a Model-T Ford given to the inventor by Henry Ford. This car was "upgraded" annually by Ford and his designers because Edison refused the new car Ford offered him each year. A special place is reserved for a phonograph model Edison used that bears his teeth marks. Edison was almost totally deaf, with one hundred percent hearing loss in his left ear and ninety percent in his right. In order to "hear" the sound made by one of his most original inventions, the phonograph, he had to bite into the frame to make the sound vibrations reach his inner ear. It is believed, however, that Edison actually felt his deafness was a blessing rather than a curse, for without the interference of outside noises he felt free to "concentrate on worthwhile things."

Thomas Edison died in 1931. Just before her death in 1947, his widow, Mina Edison, gave the home and grounds to the City of Fort Myers as a living memorial to her famous inventor-husband. Thomas Edison has been named the number one "Man of the Millennium" according to the *Life* magazine's October, 1997 issue, which lists the hundred most influential persons of the past 1,000 years. The citation reads, in part, "Because of him, the millennium will end in a wash of brilliant light rather than in torchlit darkness as it began."

• • • • •

The Glenmont Estate, Edison's home in West Orange, New Jersey, is located at Main and Lakeside Ave. near Exit 145, Garden State Parkway. Tickets are available at the Visitor Center, which is open from 9:00 a.m. to 5:00 p.m. daily. Glenmont tours are available Wednesday through Sunday from 11:00 a.m. to 4:00 p.m. except Thanksgiving, Christmas and New Year's Day. Laboratory tours are available from 10:30 a.m. to 3:30 p.m. daily.

The entrance fee is $2.00 per person, ages 17 and over. For more information please call: (973)736-0550. The Glenmont Estate will be closed for extensive renovations from June 6, 1999 through Spring, 2001. For further information, contact the museum website at http://www.nps.gov/edis.

Seminole Lodge, the Edison winter estate in Fort Myers, Florida, is located at 2350 McGregor Boulevard. It is open every day except Thanksgiving and Christmas, from 9:00 a.m. to 5:30 p.m., Monday through Saturday, and Sundays from 12:00 noon to 5:30 p.m. The last guided tour starts at 4:00 p.m. daily. For more information please call (941)334-3614 or (941)334-7419, or visit the Seminole website at http://www.edison-ford-estate.com.

Photos courtesy of the U.S. Department of the Interior, National Park Service, Edison National Historic Site and the Edison and Ford winter estates, Fort Myers, Florida.

The Gilded Age Estate

Henry Morrison Flagler's Whitehall

PALM BEACH • FLORIDA

IN 1902 THE NEW YORK HERALD proclaimed Whitehall, the Palm Beach home of Henry Flagler, "the Taj Mahal of North America" and published an extensive article illustrating the home. Flagler built the 55-room Gilded Age estate as a wedding present for his wife, Mary Lily Kenan Flagler, occupying the home as a winter retreat from 1902 until his death in 1913. Construction of the mansion was just one of many projects Mr. Flagler would undertake in Florida throughout his life, in a tireless quest to transform the Florida coastline into an American Riviera.

The achievements that inspired the incarnation of Whitehall included Flagler's own canny realization that great things were in store for Florida. This is the state with the old-

The fireplace and mantel in Whitehall's dining room are designed in the French Renaissance style. Like the Library, the dining room ceiling is cast plaster made to look like wood.

est history and the newest population, where Spanish conquistadors landed long before the pilgrims reached Massachusetts. It remained for one man with vision and money to stabilize the state's resources and initiate a process which would transform Florida into a mecca that currently attracts millions of people annually.

Henry Flagler, one of America's most prominent Gilded Age figures, was born January 2, 1830 in Hopewell, New York. His father, the Reverend Isaac Flagler, was an impoverished Presbyterian clergyman and farmer. In 1844, after finishing the eighth grade, Flagler left home and moved to Bellevue, Ohio, to become a clerk in the store of L.G. Harkness and Co., earning $5 per month plus room and board. It was as an employee for this firm that Flagler met his first wife, Mary Harkness, the third daughter of the owner.

After gaining and losing fortunes in the salt business and other ventures throughout the 1850s, Flagler became acquainted with John D. Rockefeller, who was looking to expand his own small oil company. In 1870, Flagler and a young Englishman named Samuel Andrews became Rockefeller's founding partners in the Standard Oil Company, with Flagler as Secretary and Treasurer. As the legal mind behind Standard Oil, Flagler helped determine the modern industrial corporation by establishing the business trust, making interstate commerce a reality. Within ten years he attained a position of great prestige in the nation's loftiest industrial and financial circles.

In 1877, Standard Oil moved its location to New York. At this time, Mr. Flagler had been in the oil business for ten years. Unfortunately, Mary Harkness Flagler's health, which had never been good, had deteriorated since the birth of their son in 1870. Concerned over his wife's condition and upon the advice of her doctor, Flagler took his wife to Jacksonville, Florida, hoping that the warm sunshine and brisk sea air would provide a cure. Her condition never fully improved and on May 18, 1881, Mary Flagler died. Although the outcome of this trip was tragic, it provided Flagler with his first glimpse of Florida. Amazed by the lack of adequate rail and hotel facilities, he decided to withdraw from the oil business and take a close look at the Sunshine State.

In 1883, at the age of fifty-three, Henry Flagler married Ida Alice Shourds and later that year, they traveled to St. Augustine for a delayed honeymoon trip. Flagler was captivated by the city, and even more impressed with its obvious potential as a winter resort. Flagler retained his enthusiasm for this area and proceeded to build the 540-room Ponce de Leon hotel, now Flagler College, which opened in St. Augustine in 1888. The next year Flagler purchased one hotel and remodeled another, both in close proximity to the Hotel Ponce de Leon. The opening of these luxurious hotels attracted the wealthy and the famous of the day. St. Augustine enjoyed remarkable popularity and bolstered Flagler's determination to help develop the eastern coast of Florida.

The success of resort hotels, however, depended largely on convenient transportation, which Mr. Flagler was determined to provide for his hotels' guests. He began purchasing existing short-line railroads in northeastern Florida, converting them to a standard gauge, then connecting

Henry Morrison Flagler (1830-1913).

them, eventually reaching Daytona. In 1892 Flagler obtained a Florida State charter to extend his tracks as far south as Miami. By 1894, the railroad reached Palm Beach where Flagler constructed the 1,150-room Hotel Royal Poinciana. The largest wooden structure in the world at the time, the Royal Poinciana quickly became the country's most fashionable winter gathering place. By 1896, Flagler's railroad reached Miami, where two years later the tycoon began construction of the city's first hotel, The Hotel Royal Palm. Along the Florida coast, Flagler continued to develop and improve the quality of life for communities along the FEC Railway's tracks, including donating land for Miami's first public school, financing the area's first hospitals and financially supporting many churches in West Palm Beach and St. Augustine. Upon Miami's incorporation, local residents wanted to name the new town "Flagler" in appreciation of the sponsor's many contributions to the city, but Flagler urged the city to be called "Miami," the Indian name for the city's river.

In addition to building cities and establishing the tourism industry in Florida, Flagler encouraged the development of Florida land for farming and agriculture through the creation of the Model Land Company in 1896. His biggest accomplishment, however, would be to link Key West to the Florida mainland through a 156-mile extension of the Florida East Coast Railway. During the seven-year project, five hurricanes threatened to halt construction. Completed in 1912, the massive undertaking employed up to four thousand men. Nearly half of the railroad was raised over water or marshland on steel and concrete viaducts and bridges.

During the period of Florida's development, Flagler faced challenges and changes in his personal life. His wife, Ida Alice, who became increasingly erratic and delusional, was institutionalized for mental illness in 1895. Ida Alice and Henry Flagler were divorced six years later but Flagler contributed financial resources which provided for her care until her death in 1930.

On August 24, 1901, Flagler married Mary Lily Kenan at her family's home in North Carolina. He was seventy-one and she was thirty-four. A woman of grace and charm, she played the piano, sang, and enjoyed a wide variety of cultural interests. Mr. Flagler had met her at a party in 1891 and subsequently lavished gifts on her, stirring much gossip in the society world. Flagler built Whitehall for his new bride as a wedding gift, sparing no expense as the bills rolled in. He succeeded in building the home in the incredibly short time of eighteen months.

Flagler commissioned John Carrère and Thomas Hastings, the architects who had previously built Flagler's Ponce de Leon hotel in St. Augustine. Carrère and Hastings, graduates of the premier architectural school, the École des Beaux-Arts in Paris, also

The music room at Whitehall features a 1,249-pipe organ, the largest ever made for a private home up until that time.

Seven different types of marble were used for the 4,400 square foot entrance to Whitehall.

designed other Gilded Age landmarks such as the New York Public Library, the Senate and House of Representatives Office Buildings in Washington, D.C., and the Standard Oil office building in New York.

For Whitehall, Carrère and Hastings had originally designed a Spanish-style dwelling, but in early 1901, Flagler wrote to his architects from Palm Beach: "This afternoon I have noticed for the first time, the elevation of the gables of my house here. I don't like them. I much prefer something more on the Colonial order, and less of the Spanish." The reasoning behind Flagler's shift in tastes is unknown, but perhaps Mary Lily's southern heritage led her to desire a more neoclassical home typical to the style of southern plantations.

Whitehall occupies an eight-acre tract facing Lake Worth, which is part of the inland waterway separating islands such as Palm Beach from the mainland. The selection of this site rather than one facing the outer ocean was used to protect the mansion from the damaging effects of area hurricanes, setting a new trend in area construction. The grounds of the mansion are rimmed by a high, ornate wrought-iron fence, the most elaborate and extensive fence of the period anywhere in America. Designed by Carrère and Hastings, it measures over 900 feet in length and nine feet in height. On the grounds are royal palms, hibiscus, orange trees and other native Florida vegetation mingled with rare plants from around the world.

Whitehall was designed around a central courtyard to take advantage of the Atlantic's ocean breezes and cross-ventilation. Visitors enter Whitehall through the Marble Hall, which at 4, 400 square feet, is the largest room in any home built during the Gilded Age.

The colonnaded entrance, which opens directly into the Marble Hall - 110 feet wide and 40 feet deep - faces a marble staircase that divides into two parts as it rises to the second floor. There are seven varieties of marble in the hall's walls and floors. A painting molded into the ceiling's twenty-foot central dome represents the "Crowning of Knowledge," while painted panels on the walls symbolize prosperity and happiness.

The New York design firm of Pottier and Stymus was selected to create the look of the interior rooms of Whitehall. There were fifty-five rooms in the original estate, including the servants rooms. Many of the these, such as the Salon and the Billiard Room, were designed as distinct masculine or feminine spaces, for use primarily by one gender or the other. The first floor of Whitehall was reserved for entertaining, consisting mostly of very large public rooms. The second floor was made up of private living spaces for the Flaglers' guests and domestic staff. In typical Gilded Age fashion, the furnishings the designers chose for Whitehall were largely reproductions of the periods the rooms reflect.

Adjacent to the Marble Hall is the library, which is decorated with furnishings typical to the Italian Renaissance period, including carved panels, a massive fireplace and rich red tapestries. Portraits of the Flagler family are mounted on the walls, including a painting of Flagler above the fireplace. Artisans molded and painted this room's cast plaster and fabric ceiling in an attempt to replicate wooden beams with leather insets. Across the Marble Hall, the French Grand Salon is decorated in the style of Louis XVI and has an elaborately carved marble fireplace, a domed ceiling, and the finest paintings and sculpture in the mansion.

A broad doorway connects the library with the music room, which is fashioned in Louis XV style. The room contains a 1,249-pipe organ that was, when Mr. Flagler bought it, the largest ever made for a private home. The domed ceiling of the room has a painting of the Aurora, with great crystal chandeliers casting a glow in lounges. Near the music room is a Billiard Room of Swiss design.

A ballroom ninety-one feet by thirty-seven feet, with glittering chandeliers, mirrored walls, soft Boucher and Watteau-style panels, and Louis XV gold-and-white decorations, is a room of splendor. It opens into an interior courtyard, which has in the center a large marble fountain designed after the original "Venus" fountain by Renaissance sculptor Giovanni da Bologna (1524-1608).

Mr. Flagler's favorite part of the house was the "stone area" facing Lake Worth and his yachts. This part of the house, atop which the hotel annex was built, had an office, a great marble terrace and a rose garden. A wing for domestic space and another garden adjoin it.

Whitehall was used by the Flaglers as a winter retreat primarily during the months of January and February. While in Palm Beach, the Flaglers entertained frequently and Whitehall reflects this use. Within the confines of the music room, guests were frequently entertained by a resident organist. One of the most lavish events at Whitehall, the Bal Poudré, was held in honor of George Washington's birthday and became the highlight of the season. The *New York Herald* described the event as "one of the most sumptuous social affairs ever attempted south of Washington."

When Henry Flagler died in 1913, Whitehall and the bulk of his estate were left to Mary Lily. The house remained closed until the season of 1916. Mary Lily visited the estate once more, in 1917, shortly before her own death that same year. Whitehall was then left to Mary Lily's niece, Louise Clisby Wise, who later sold the estate to a group of investors in 1925. They proceeded to add a ten-story, 300-room tower on the west side of the structure, thereby converting the property into The Whitehall Hotel, which remained in operation from 1925-1959. The addition that was built provided 300 bed-rooms while the mansion itself provided space for a lobby, lounges, card rooms and guest suites.

By 1959, the hotel was in financial distress and the entire complex was in danger of being razed. Henry Flagler's granddaughter, Jean Flagler Matthews, learned of the estate's fate and formed a non-profit corporation, the Henry Morrison Flagler Museum, Inc., to purchase the property. The following year, Whitehall was opened to the public as the Henry Morrison Flagler Museum. Most of the ten-story addition was successfully razed in 1963, leaving one floor for administrative and curatorial use.

Today, nearly 100,000 people from around the world visit the Flagler Museum annually. They come to experience not only the splendor of this great Gilded Age estate, but to learn more about the man whose vision helped to create Standard Oil and develop Florida as a leader in tourism and agriculture.

• • • • •

The Flagler Museum is located on Whitehall Way, Palm Beach. It is open to the public Tuesday through Saturday, from 10:00 a.m. until 5:00 p.m. and Sunday, from noon until 5:00 p.m. The museum is closed Mondays, Thanksgiving, Christmas and New Year's Day. Price of admission is $7.00 for adults; children aged 6-12, $3.00. Group tours and rates are available. For more information, please call: (561)655-2833, or visit Whitehall's website at http://www.flagler.org.

Photos courtesy of the Henry Morrison Flagler Museum

Washington Irving's Sunnyside estate

The Sleepy Hollow Triptych

Washington Irving's Sunnyside, Frederick Philipse's Manor and Stephanus Van Cortlandt's Manor House

TARRYTOWN, SLEEPY HOLLOW AND CROTON-ON-HUDSON • NEW YORK

THE RIP VAN WINKLE countryside of the Lower Hudson Valley has a folklore of romantic legends. It also has a political history that mirrors the birth of the nation and strong cultural overtones which reflect the rise of the Romantic Movement in American art and landscape design.

The legends and the history of this region date back to a warm September afternoon in 1609 when Henry Hudson sailed the *Half Moon* up the river in search of the

The parlor at Sunnyside served as the heart of Irving's home. A portrait of the author by John Wesley Jarvis (1781-1839) hangs above the sofa.

Northwest Passage and dropped anchor in the Tappan Zee, a stretch of the river that is three miles wide, off Tarrytown. He had discovered a great harbor and a fertile countryside that were to play major roles in the development of America. The Dutch sailors called the paradise *Die Slapering Hafen*, which became known as The Sleeping Haven and, later, Sleepy Hollow.

Three historic sites that rose in Sleepy Hollow in the seventeenth, eighteenth and nineteenth centuries were considered so interesting and significant in the twentieth century by philanthropist John D. Rockefeller, Jr. that he donated an estimated $3,000,000 to their restoration as well as a long-term commitment to providing endowments that would guarantee their perpetual maintenance.

Although the houses are not exceptionally large in size, they are mansions in their literary, historical and architectural importance. Thousands of visitors every year find as much fascination in them as Mr. Rockefeller, who lived nearby at Kykuit, in Pocantico Hills. He cared deeply for land and historic places, and had a particular affection for "Sleepy Hollow," portions of which were on his estate. He demanded of his researchers and carpenters total authenticity in its redevelopment. The result is a small northern counterpart of Colonial Williamsburg.

The Sleepy Hollow homes that Mr. Rockefeller restored are those of Washington Irving- diplomat, folklorist, bon vivant, and the most famous American author of his time; Frederick Philipse, who owned all the land from the Harlem River in New York City to the Croton River in northern Westchester County; and Stephanus Van Cortlandt, whose land reached twenty miles northward from the Croton River and eastward across Connecticut.

Washington Irving's home, Sunnyside, is located on the site of a former Indian village beside the Hudson at Tarrytown. The fifteen-room structure began life as a simple four-room colonial saltbox in 1656. Part of the domain of Peter Stuyvesant, governor of New Netherlands, and later part of the manor of Philipsburg, it was first occupied by Wolfert Aker, a farmer and his family, until 1750.

Soon after it fell into the possession of another farmer, Jacobus Van Tassel, who made the mistake of firing a rifle at a British warship in the river during the Revolutionary War. British sailors climbed the hill and burned most of Mr. Van Tassel's house. It was rebuilt, however, and Washington Irving bought the "Old Cottage," with twelve acres of land, in 1835.

Purchase of the house occurred fifteen years after publication of *The Legend of Sleepy Hollow*. Irving purchased the home in his fifties, after twenty years of life in Europe. As a pragmatist, the author was well aware of the inseparable link he had to the area and hoped to use the move to increase his fame. People today still confuse Sunnyside and Sleepy Hollow, just as Irving would have wanted it.

Washington Irving called the new abode his "snuggery" and said "I would not exchange it for any château in Christendom." Irving's literary friends shared his view and often visited the author at his new home. Among the persons who trod the paths and joined in discussion groups there were William M. Thackery, William Cullen Bryant and C.P. Putnam. Sunnyside's notoriety increased with Irving's growing reputation as a writer, particularly with publication of his best-selling novel, *Wolfert's*

Irving's bedroom at Sunnyside. The Federal style high-post bedstead dates circa 1810.

Roost (1855), a fictionalized account of "a little old-fashioned stone mansion." Soon the home came to symbolize American home-life during the mid-nineteenth century.

Irving never married. There are a variety of reasons suggested for his lifelong bachelordom. Many believe he never stopped mourning the loss of his fiancée, Matilda Hoffman, who died suddenly from tuberculosis during their engagement in 1809. Other historians suggest that he was not comfortable with the financial and emotional commitment associated with marriage as suggested in some of his earlier publications, notably *The Sketch Book*. Irving did succeed, however, to create a familial environment at Sunnyside by inviting his widowed brother Ebenezer and his five daughters to live with him.

Irving's vision for his home at Sleepy Hollow was shaped by fond visits to the valley and of the Dutch legends that he had heard while first vacationing there at the age of fifteen. He sketched on paper the odd shape that he wanted his home to take. In executing his plans, he had the assistance of at least one professional architect, as well as George Harvey (1800-78), a friend and artist who had created his own Romantic cottage in nearby Hastings.

Exercising his extraordinary imagination, Irving immediately added rooms and changed the entire appearance of the house. He added stepped parapet gables, cluster-columned chimney stacks, steeply pitched roofs, and a Moorish tower in 1847. He bought and sold neighboring property, enlarging the estate to twenty-seven acres. He also added a service wing across the rear of the house and created a working farm. Overall, the variety of architectural influences at Sunnyside tangibly express the author's strong ties to Dutch New York, Scotland and Spain; areas of the world Irving had lived as a writer and diplomat.

Off-white concrete and red bricks were used for the exterior walls, with roofs of red tile. Ivy from Sir Walter Scott's home at Abbotsford, Scotland, was planted along the east side of the house. Ancient wisteria, trumpet creeper and honeysuckle that Washington Irving planted in the late 1840s now have grown to huge size and are carefully preserved. Irving also created winding paths and two ponds. The first pond, which he referred to as the "Little Mediterranean," was home to waterfowl. He also constructed an ice pond in a shaded glen.

The main corridor of the first floor has colorful Minton tiles. Off this corridor are Irving's study, with original books, papers and pens, a parlor, a dining room, a sitting room and a kitchen. The kitchen, considered modern for its time, features a cast-iron wood-burning stove, a cast-iron sink and hot and cold running water. An air of hospitality pervaded Sunnyside, and Irving's guests included Charles Louis Napoleon Bonaparte (later Napoleon III), Dr. Oliver Wendell Holmes and Martin Van Buren.

On the second floor are bedrooms, including the one in which Irving died. In this room are a Federal-style, high-posted bedstead dated circa 1810, as well as old medicine bottles - mute evidence of the famous author's illnesses. His shaving equipment is also there. Irving would occasionally arise in the middle of the night to shave; the soothing effect of the lather assuaged the attacks of asthma that often bothered him.

The furniture in the house is largely Washington Irving's. Among the porcelains on display are some given to him by Prince Louis Napoleon when he was a house guest. Much of the original furniture remains, including Irving's writing desk, several upholstered armchairs used by Irving and his family, "high end" painted furniture, a rosewood pianoforte which Irving bought for his nieces, and antique textiles and rugs. The house also features framed sketches by English satirical artist George Cruikshank, paintings and portraits by Sir Joshua Reynolds and John Wesley Jarvis, and drawings by Felix Darley.

In 1847 the tracks of the New York Central Railroad were laid beside Sunnyside. Irving bitterly nicknamed the trains "snorting monsters" that intruded on his solitude and interfered with boating on his "Little Mediterranean." His antipathy lessened somewhat when he became gravely ill one night and a train from New York allowed a doctor's visit.

Irving died of a heart attack in his bechamber on November, 28, 1859, at the age of seventy-six. Upon his death, the house and property were passed on to his nieces who lived there until 1875. Sunnyside's next owner, Alexander Duer Irving, added a baronial ballroom that would accommodate 200 persons. Sunnyside was thus transformed from a personal snuggery into a social mansion.

Historians induced John D. Rockefeller, Jr. to buy Sunnyside and twenty surrounding acres in 1945 from Louis du Pont Irving, another collateral descendent of the author. Determined to attain full authenticity, Mr. Rockefeller reduced the mansion's size by fifty percent, razing the wing that had been added in 1896. Reconstruction then began on rooms and structures destroyed by the wing, including the picture gallery, bathroom, pantries, laundry room, fenced-in kitchen yard and Gothic Revival icehouse. The restoration was guided by many letters, published and unpublished accounts of visitors to Sunnyside, as well as sketches and paintings and other memorabilia. The estate opened to the public in 1947 and is now a property of Historic Hudson Valley.

• • •

Three miles up the river in Sleepy Hollow is Philipsburg Manor, part of what was once considered the greatest commercial empire of colonial New York. Extant today are the restored stone manor house, seventeenth and eighteenth-century period furnishings, water-powered grist mills, and a reconstructed tenant house and church, where the original owner of the property, Frederick Philipse, is buried. Mr. Rockefeller barely saved the buildings from house wreckers in 1940 by buying them and twenty acres after the land was threatened with development.

Built in 1683, the stone-and-timber dwelling place has been the focal point of the 52,000 acre domain of Frederick Philipse, whose Dutch name had been Fredryck Flypson. The son of a carpenter, he became one of the wealthiest men in America. From the docks and warehouses beside his manor house he carried on an import-export business around the world which was operated by enslaved Africans.

Philipsburg Manor, dockside view. To the left is a gristmill, which has been restored to its original function.

The kitchen at Philipsburg Manor. The collection of 17th and 18th century furnishings in this household is one of the finest in the nation.

A gristmill was built on the Pocantico River, which empties into the Hudson near the manor house. From the late seventeenth century through the eighteenth century, tenant farmers brought their corn and their wheat to the Philipsburg Manor to be ground into flour. Sloops from the manor house then headed down the Hudson River to Manhattan. The gristmill has since been restored to its original function and visitors to the Manor today can watch the grindstones in action.

Frederick Philipse married the wealthy widow of Peter de Vries, who had inherited large shipping lines and other business interests. When she died, he married into the Van Cortlandt family, which had a manor almost as large as his own, further up the river. When the English took over the colony from the Dutch in 1664, Flypsen anglicized his name to Frederick Philipse. His subsequent skill at developing strong political liaisons and preferential treatment would soon legitimize his distinguished career as an entrepreneur, shipowner, landowner, and slave trader. In 1693, the year he was granted a charter to this property by King William III and Queen Mary, Frederick's 52,000 estate covered a third of what is now Westchester County and stretched along twenty-two miles of the Hudson River.

Following Frederic Philipse's death in 1702, his son Adolphe Philipse (1665-1750) inherited most of the property, which he doubled over the course of his lifetime. A descendant of Adolphe's, Colonel Frederick Philipse, inherited the property and its vast acreage at the outbreak of the Revolutionary War. He remained loyal to the British. George Washington had him imprisoned in Connecticut and near the conclusion of the war he fled to England. His manor was confiscated by New York State, broken up into parcels and sold at auction to repay the state's war debt.

Cornelia Van Cortlandt Beekman, sister of Philip Van Cortlandt, was the first owner of the manor house after the war. She lived there for the rest of her life. The house passed through many other owners, each time being altered with "modern improvements."

Elsie Janis, noted actress, mimic and dancer, who was known as the Sweetheart of the American Expeditionary Force in World War I, took a fancy to the manor in 1935 and bought it to use in the lavish entertaining of her stage friends. Soon after making improvements on the mansion, however, Miss Janis and her husband, Gilbert Wilson, were seriously injured in an automobile crash. The manor became vacant, dilapidated and in arrears on taxes. Reports spread that the property was threatened with destruction and subdivision into building lots.

Mr. Rockefeller was induced by the Historical Society of the Tarrytowns to buy the property when it was posted for sale at auction. He purchased the site in 1940, which today is part of Historic Hudson Valley, and largely financed the restoration of the manor house. To assist in this process, he brought in researchers from Colonial Williamsburg. Old drawings of the house, a picture made by Currier and Ives in 1880, and many documents, including a probate inventory of 1750, helped in planning the restoration and refurbishment of the manor house. The collection of seventeenth and eighteenth-century Dutch, English, and colonial American furnishings and household objects at Philipsburg Manor is currently one of the finest in the nation. The old grist mill, smokehouse and related buildings were also redeveloped. Today's mill, based on historical standards, can produce two tons of cornmeal or flour per day. The site is operated as a museum of living history and tours of the area are conducted by interpreters in eighteenth-century costume.

•••

Nine miles up the Hudson from the Philipsburg Manor, near the confluence of the Croton and Hudson Rivers, stands the manor house of the Van Cortlandts, one of New York's most prominent families. Established in 1680 on a parcel of land originally measuring 86,000 acres, it was occupied continuously for 260 years by seven generations of the same family - a remarkable record of lineal ownership. The last of the Van Cortlandts to live there was Miss Ann Stevenson Van Cortlandt, who died in 1940 at the age of ninety-three.

The Manor of Cortlandt was born in 1697. In that year, King William III granted a royal charter to the original owner, Stephanus Van Cortlandt, for lands he had purchased from the Kitchtawanc Indians and the European landowners. This charter, which bestowed favors and special privileges, was a recognition of political support, given in the same spirit as the royal charter Frederick Philipse had received at an earlier date. Stephanus did not capitalize on his good fortune however; truly successful exploitation of the Van Cortlandt property did not come until the mid-eighteenth century, when Pierre Van Cortlandt, Stephanus' grandson, inherited it. Pierre acquired an additional 1,225 acres of land and used it to gain his fortune as a land developer, landlord, commercial farmer, saw-and-gristmill proprietor, and tavern owner. He enjoyed a successful life at Van Cortlandt Manor with his wife, Joanna, whom he would remain married to for sixty years, along with eight children, and a number of African-American slaves that he depended on to run his house. In 1777 he was elected New York's first lieutenant governor.

Unlike the Philipses to the south, most of the Van Cortlandts fought with the American patriots. Son Philip fought at the battle of Saratoga, endured a harsh winter at Valley Forge, and took part in the siege of Yorktown, the battle that concluded the war. Overnight guests in the Manor House included General Washington, Benjamin Franklin, John Jay, Marshal Jean Baptiste de Rochambeau, Governor DeWitt Clinton and Bishop Francis Asbury. The Manor House also served as a center of religious life. Some of the most exciting revival meetings in the nation were conducted by preachers on the front steps.

The Manor shrank in size as ownership passed down through the family in the next two centuries. The property shrank to five acres by 1945, when it was sold outside the family for the first time in its history. It was reportedly about to become an office for a smoked-turkey concern when Mr. Rockefeller acquired it and an additional 120 acres in 1953. It was the last preservation project he would work on before his death in 1960.

The parlor at Van Cortlandt Manor features an outstanding collection of Chinese export porcelain. A portrait of Pierre Van Cortlandt by John Wesley Jarvis hangs above the sofa.

For the restoration Mr. Rockefeller again brought researchers from Colonial Williamsburg. It was decided to restore the house to appear as it had been maintained during Pierre Van Cortlandt's lifetime. Wings that had been added to the house in 1812 and 1847 were removed. This exposed some of the original window frames and unusual colonial stonework that set a pattern for the remaining restoration. Reconstruction work was also performed on the estate office, ice-house, privy, smoke-house, and tenant house. Although little information was handed down on the farm and gardens, they were also reconstructed on a conjectural basis. In 1959, Van Cortlandt Manor was opened to the public as a property of Sleepy Hollow Restorations, the forerunner of Historic Hudson Valley, and is now maintained as a museum of living history.

The three and one-half story Manor House, which has been restored to the New Nation period (1783-1815), is constructed mainly of irregularly shaped pieces of sandstone and granite. New shingles - copies of the original ones - are red and thick and have rounded butts. Slit openings preserved in the walls, formerly thought to have been used as firing posts during Indian attacks, now are believed to have been used merely for ventilation. The mansion had been used for the storage of raw furs bought from the Indians.

The kitchen contains a large Dutch oven as well as a variety of original eighteenth-century cooking equipment, a rare type of survival. The ground level also contains a dining room and a family sitting room. A handsome winding staircase leads to two upper floors. On the first floors are parlors, a formal dining room and bedrooms. A parlor located near the entrance hall, which contains an original portrait of Pierre Von Cortlandt by Wesley Jarvis (1781-1839), housed Benjamin Franklin on a return trip from Canada to Philadelphia in 1776.

Many of the items on display in the mansion are original. The furniture ranges from Queen Anne to Federal in style and much of it is over 200 years old. Possessions on display include a mahogany desk and bookcase, gaming and tripod tea tables from New York, an outstanding collection of Chinese export porcelain, a massive gateleg table used for dining, and original bedroom furniture. Woodwork found in the Northwest Chamber - a guestroom - includes an original paneled chimney breast that Revolutionary marauders covered with graffiti.

The grounds also contain a reconstructed eighteenth-century tavern and ferry house, original to the site, and a tenant house, which currently houses cooking and textile demonstrations. Demonstrations of colonial trades also include brickmaking and blacksmithing which occur on the outside grounds of the property. The gardens include the "Long Walk," planted with historic varieties of tulips, and a kitchen garden, planted with herbs commonly used during the eighteenth-century for both cooking and medicinal purposes.

• • • • •

All restorations associated with Historic Hudson Valley are located near the Albany Post Road (U.S. Route 9). The sites are open to the public from 10:00 a.m. to 5:00 p.m. daily except Tuesdays, Thanksgiving, Christmas and New Year's Day. Sunnyside and Philipsburg Manor are closed during the months of January and February and Van Cortlandt Manor is closed during the months of January - March. Admission fees for all sites are $8.00 for adults, $7.00 for senior citizens, and $4.00 for students. Children ages 5 and under are admitted free of charge. For further information call: (914) 631-8200, or visit the Historic Hudson Valley website at http://www.hudsonvalley.org.

Photos courtesy of Historic Hudson Valley.

A House of Heroes, Politics, and Lust

Stratford Hall, The Birthplace of Robert E. Lee

Westmoreland County • Virginia

If houses could talk, few would have more to say than Stratford Hall. It could even tell about the birth of a nation…

Stratford Hall has led as many lives as an apple has seeds, any one of which could furnish the basis for an exciting novel of love, hatred, loyalty and intrigue. It has witnessed:

…the evolution of the American colonies.

…the boyhood lives of the only two brothers who signed the Declaration of Independence - Richard Henry Lee and Francis Lightfoot Lee.

…the personal life of Henry "Light Horse Harry" Lee, Robert E. Lee's father, when he was a brilliant officer of Washington's military staff in the Revolutionary War, followed by his incarceration in a debtors' prison for not paying the bills of Stratford Hall.

...the birth and boyhood of General Robert E. Lee, commander of the Confederate Army in the Civil War and later the revered president of Washington College, now Washington and Lee University.

...the philandering of Henry "Black Horse Harry" Lee IV, Robert E. Lee's half-brother, including an alleged affair with his young and attractive sister-in-law.

...the sister-in-law's ultimate marriage to a man of wealth, followed by her return to Stratford Hall for fifty years of strange but contented life.

...the formation of the Robert E. Lee Memorial Association, with an enthusiastic Board Member in almost every state.

For over 250 years, the massive brick structure has stood on a plantation overlooking the broad reaches of the Potomac River, ninety-six miles south of Washington, D.C. The site chosen for the house is a mile back from the Potomac river. Steep cliffs, deep ravines and woodlands separate it from the water. However, the main highway - the river - was used for travel to other parts of the colonies and to Europe. The construction of Stratford Hall began in the late 1730s and was completed several years later. Slaves and indentured servants made the bricks for Stratford Hall from clay found on the property. They obtained lime for the mortar by burning oyster shells from the Potomac River.

The original owner was Thomas Lee, whose English grandfather had settled in Virginia in the late 1630s. Thomas Lee was a judge, president of his Majesty's Council and commander of the Virginia Colony. Rascals had burned an earlier home of his, causing the death of a young servant and forcing Lee's pregnant wife to jump from a window. The plantation once consisted of 6,500 acres, many of them planted with barley, oats, corn and tobacco. Only the tobacco is gone today; it robbed the soil of nitrogen. Prize cattle and thoroughbred horses still roam the pastures. A past director of a historic restoration in New York State once declared: "Stratford Hall is my favorite house in all the world!" Not many visitors at the plantation are inclined to share this enthusiasm when they get their first glimpse of the stark, harsh, and rather monotonous exterior of the house. However, they soon find that it has a dual personality; the interior is warm, inviting, and spacious, with architectural features and antique furnishings of exceptional interest. Adjacent out-buildings, including the kitchen, slave quarters, smokehouse, coach house and stables, as well as the gardens and boxwood hedges, add to that interest.

The Great House was built in the form of an H, a style of architecture popular in Tudor England. In America, the style was first used in the construction of Virginia's former capitol at Williamsburg. Stratford Hall has eighteen rooms, sixteen of them on corners of the building because of the H design. At the edge of the lawn to the south is a Ha-Ha wall - an eighteenth-century landscape feature, usually in the form of a ditch or trough, which kept farm animals from invading the lawn of the great house.

The chamber in which many members of the Lee family, including Robert E. Lee, were born.
Photo by Chris Cunningham

The lawn is on the same level as the top of the wall, which permits an unobstructed panoramic view of the countryside from the house.

The house was heated with sixteen wood-burning fireplaces in winter, and high ceilings on the upper level helped to cool the rooms in summer. Twelve outside doors aided ventilation. There is no furniture remaining from the time of Stratford's original occupancy. Furniture that was once used by the Lees, or is of the same time period, is being acquired gradually through gifts and purchases. A collection of books, manuscripts, letters, and other items identified with the Lees is currently kept in the Jessie Ball DuPont Memorial Library located on the site.

The second, or main, floor is accessed by an interior staircase or by exterior stairs on the south, east, and west sides of the house. The great hall of the main floor is thirty-five feet long and has a tray ceiling like those of English castles. The floor also has a library, a chamber, parlor and dining room and the most famous room of the house - the chamber- in which many of the Lees, including Robert E. Lee, were born. All the meals were cooked in the adjacent kitchen building, which has a fireplace large enough to roast an ox, and then were carried up the steps by the servants to the dining room.

A number of Lees of several generations served in high governmental posts under the British Crown. Then two brothers, Richard Henry and Francis Lightfoot Lee, rebelled. Richard, working with Patrick Henry, helped to inspire the break with England. Francis was associated with Benjamin Franklin in the cause. Matilda Lee, their niece, inherited Statford Hall. She married her cousin, Henry "Light Horse Harry" Lee and their son was Henry Lee IV. After the death of Matilda, "Light Horse

Harry" married Ann Hill Carter and Robert E. Lee (1807-70) was born. Unable to pay his bills at Statford Hall, "Light Horse Harry" was jailed twice for debt. Soon after, he moved to a more affordable dwelling in Alexandria, VA, with his wife and son Robert.

Although he left Stratford when he was only four years old, Robert E. Lee returned to visit his half-brother, who eventually became the owner. At some time during the Civil War, General Lee wrote that he hoped someday to buy Stratford Hall because it "would inspire me with feelings of pleasure and local love." He told his wife that it would be a poor place to earn a living but they could have cornbread and bacon and their clothes could be made in the weaving house.

Henry Lee IV, Robert E. Lee's half-brother, was twenty-one years old when he inherited Stratford Hall in 1808. He was not as handsome as the future Civil War general but he was a storyteller par excellence and a bon vivant of Washington and Philadelphia. He amused men and held women spellbound. Three times elected to the Virginia House of Delegates, he later served in the War of 1812.

Near Stratford Hall was the 2,000-acre plantation of the McCartys, a well-to-do family from Ireland. Anne and Elizabeth McCarty, sisters, were among the wealthiest girls in Westmoreland County; they had attended finishing schools and traveled extensively. Henry married Anne in 1817 and the union meant new wealth for his impoverished home. Anne brought servants and table silver made in 1620 with the McCarty coat-of-arms. She also brought to Stratford Hall her sixteen-year-old sister Elizabeth; soon after Henry Lee IV was appointed her guardian.

The dining room at Stratford Hall is located on the second floor of the mansion. Photo by Chris Cunningham

The entrance of Stratford Hall. Photo by Richard Cheek.

In 1818 Anne gave birth to a daughter, Margaret, who met a tragic death at two when she plunged down the steep stairs of Stratford Hall - exactly as another child of the Lee clan had done years earlier. In the gloom that began settling over the house soon after, Anne began using morphine while Henry spent money so fast that he dissipated Anne's wealth as well as his own.

Friends also reported that Henry developed a deep affection for Elizabeth, and he himself wrote that they were "thrown into a state of the most unguarded intimacy." Tongues wagged in Westmoreland. Henry was blamed for "seduction" and "crimes of the blackest dye."

Grim times settled upon Stratford Hall. Anne soon left and retreated alone to the area of Nashville, Tennessee. In desperation, Henry sold Stratford Hall in 1822 to an old friend, William C. Somerville, an author and diplomat. The sale, for an unknown price, was subject to a mortgage that had been given to Elizabeth. Henry went to Fredericksburg, but former friends slammed doors in his face. Soon after he obtained a menial job in the Post Office Department where he had the opportunity to meet President Andrew Jackson, who hired him to write speeches and edit personal papers.

Accompanying President Jackson to the Hermitage, the Jackson home near Nashville, Henry met Anne and they were reunited. Henry and Anne later went to Paris, where they lived in virtual poverty. Henry assumed the life of a writer, and died in 1837, soon after the publication of his first book - a biography of Napoleon Bonaparte. Anne would die soon after in 1840. Both are buried in unmarked graves in Paris's Montmartre Cemetary.

In 1826 Elizabeth McCarty married Henry Storke, of the respectable Storke family of Westmoreland County. Three years later she attained ownership of Stratford Hall through foreclosure of the mortgage and lived in the house for the next fifty years. In a state of penitence, she rarely left the plantation. She studied the medicinal properties of herbs and developed an outstanding herb garden. Deeply religious, she also taught the catechism to slaves on Sunday mornings. Elizabeth died in 1879 and is buried in a corner of the garden. The subsequent ownership of Stratford Hall went by inheritance to her two great-nephews, Charles E. and Richard H. Stuart, then to Charles E. Stuart, Jr.

In 1929, Stratford Hall was purchased by a group of dedicated ladies under the leadership of Mrs. Charles D. Lanier of Greenwich, Connecticut. Soon after, the Robert E. Lee Memorial Association was established to preserve this historic site as a permanent memorial to General Lee.

The importance of the Lee legacy can hardly be overestimated. President John Adams once wrote: "The complaint against the family of Lees is a very extraordinary thing indeed. I am no idolater of that family or any other, but I believe that their greatest fault is having more men of merit than in any other family." President Franklin D. Roosevelt said that he had "stumbled upon" Stratford Hall late in life and had been thrilled. He spoke of the "amazing dignity" of the mansion and declared that the shrine was a memorial to "a brave young civilization for which modern America will always be grateful."

• • • • •

Stratford Hall is located on State Route 214, just off State Route 3, east of U.S. Route 301. It is open from 9:00 a.m. to 5:00 p.m., all year, except New Year's Day, Thanksgiving, and Christmas Day.

For ticket information, please call: (804) 493-8038, or visit the Stratford Hall website at http://www.stratfordhall.org.

Photos courtesy of the Robert E. Lee Memorial Association

A Wonderland of Americana

Henry F. du Pont's Winterthur

NEW CASTLE COUNTY • DELAWARE

NESTLED IN THE WOODED HILLS of the Brandywine Valley, where the picturesque counties of southeastern Pennsylvania and northern Delaware meet, lays Winterthur, former home to one of America's foremost families - the du Ponts. Now considered a Museum of Americana, each room of the house represents a specific period of early architecture with its own distinctive style.

The years represented by the rooms span two centuries, from 1640 to 1840. The woodwork, ceilings, walls, windows, fireplaces and floors of entire rooms of old houses from New Hampshire to North Carolina were purchased by Henry Francis du Pont, who between the years 1928 and 1932 doubled the size of the existing house at

Winterthur and slowly succeeded in reestablishing it as a museum. When a 1775 parlor from Wernersville, Pennsylvania once failed to fit into its allotted space, the walls of Winterthur were pushed out twelve inches.

Winterthur's collection houses more than 89,000 objects, including textiles, clocks, silver, needlework, porcelain, Oriental rugs and paintings. The antique furnishings have been so painstakingly collected and sorted that all objects and decorations in each room harmonize. Collectors and architects agree that the result is probably the largest assemblage of bona fide decorative arts and collectibles in this country.

The patriarch of the du Pont family in America was Pierre Samuel du Pont de Nemours, a noted French political economist, publicist and statesman. He was formerly a constitutional monarchist

A graceful spiral staircase at Winterthur is from Montmorenci, a showplace built in 1822 near Warrenton, N.C. by General William Williams.

forced into hiding during the French Revolution. Captured and sentenced to death on the guillotine, he was saved by the fall of Robespierre at the end of the Reign of Terror. He faced, however, such a perilously uncertain future in France that he chose to come to America to reestablish his family and start a new career with the help of his old friends: the Marquis de Lafayette, Thomas Jefferson and George Washington.

The du Pont family arrived at Newport, Rhode Island, in 1800, soon settled at Bergen Point, New Jersey, and in 1802 moved to Wilmington, where Pierre's son, Eleuthere Irénée du Pont, built a powder mill in Brandywine Creek. Each successive war and its demands for gunpowder added to the family fortune, which ultimately exceeded $5,000,000,000. Expanding their investments, the du Ponts became major owners of General Motors, United States Rubber, and companies that produced rayon; cellophane; "fabrikoid"; "pyralin"; shatterproof glass; paints; dyes; photographic film; artificial rubber; cutlery and pharmaceuticals. Some of the profits from these investments helped to develop Winterthur.

The first owner of Winterthur was James Antoine Bidermann, who came to America from Winterthur, Switzerland, in 1814 to study the du Pont powder mills. In 1816, he married Evelina Gabrielle du Pont, the daughter of Irénée. Their son James was born in 1817. Upon acquiring 445 acres in Christiana Hundred, the Bidermanns built in 1839 a

The Phyfe room at Winterthur was specially designed for furniture by the New York cabinetmaker Duncan Phyfe.

large house that was the beginning of what is now the Winterthur Museum.

Additions to the Greek Revival house were made in 1884, 1902, 1929, 1959 and 1969, with the addition of the Louise du Pont Crowninshield Research Building, named for Henry du Pont's sister. Galleries were added in 1992.

James Bidermann, Jr. became the owner of Winterthur at his father's death in 1865. Two years later he sold the estate to his mother's brother, Henry du Pont, who doubled the size of the tract by acquiring adjacent farms. In 1889 the estate was inherited by Henry's son, Colonel Henry A. du Pont, who had won a Congressional Medal of Honor in the Civil War and later became a senator. At the Colonel's death in 1926, the estate passed to his son, Henry Francis du Pont, founder of the museum.

Henry Francis du Pont, who converted the old family home of Winterthur into the museum it is today, is a great grandson of Irénée, the founder of the du Pont company. Born in 1880 at Winterthur, he was the only son of Colonel Henry A. du Pont, a United States Senator and du Pont executive. Educated at Harvard at the turn of the century, Henry was on the board of the family company from 1915-1958, but was never active as a full-time executive. Instead his interests lay in collecting antiques, developing Winterthur's farmland, and in the arts - especially the perpetuation of the culture that in his view Winterthur exemplified.

Inspired by the growing enthusiasm for American objects which swept the nation after World War I, Henry Francis began extensive collection of old rooms and furnishings in 1927. He allegedly began his collection with the acquisition of a Pennsylvania walnut chest, circa 1737, as well as some woodwork from a Philadelphia home. Throughout the following year he acquired over 700 antiques, which quickly led to his decision to turn Winterthur into a museum. For the next two decades, Henry lived in the mansion with his wife and two daughters, spending most of that time enlarging and converting the home for public display. In 1951, the estate was opened to the public and deeded to the Winterthur Corporation; a non-profit, educational organization. Henry moved out of the mansion and took a smaller home on the estate, yet additions continued in the years that followed, the most recent one in 1992.

The museum now houses two buildings, one containing 175 period rooms and the other three exhibition galleries. The building is largely of concrete, with decorative dormer windows and shutters, many chimneys, an Italian tile roof and pillared façades. When the galleries were constructed, the architect used the original building as his inspiration, utilizing similar materials and design elements. He who regards antiques as outmoded or impractical cannot escape the impact here of the soundness of American craftsmanship, its functionalism and its enduring common sense. Two centuries of domestic architecture, furniture, metal work, textiles, ceramics, paintings and prints have been chosen with meticulous regard for quality and fitness of location. And every known material used in American houses is shown in Winterthur as it was originally used.

There is signed furniture by famous cabinetmakers of Salem, Boston, Newport, New York and Philadelphia. There are textiles of the colonial era. Blue and white checked linen draperies from old Pennsylvania mills in one room contrast with an adjacent room's pastel satins designed by Phillippe de Lassalle, the textile genius employed by Louis XVI. Walls of some rooms are covered with rare flock paper and decorated canvas. Neighboring rooms contain hand-painted Chinese papers and block-printed French scenic papers.

Paul Revere made some of the silver tankards and pitchers on display at Winterthur. Paintings include several by John Singleton Copley, Benjamin West, Gilbert Stuart and Charles Wilson Peale. On the floors are carpets from Persia and Asia Minor, famous weaves of Isfahan, Ushak and the Caucasus. They were the so-called "Turkey carpets" imported before the Revolutionary War. Of later date are the tapestry-weave Aubusson carpets, imported in the early nineteenth century, and colorful American weave woven strip carpets.

Typical room installations in the mansion include such items as the Port Royal Entrance Hall and Parlor from a house built in 1762 in Frankford, a town north of Philadelphia, by Edward Stiles, a wealthy planter and merchant from Bermuda. In this hallway the Doric entablature follows the severe pattern of classical architecture. Arched fanlights crowning the doors suggest the pierced shells seen in Chippendale ornamentation. A paneled dado skirts the lower walls; above it is eighteenth-century Chinese wallpaper painted with tree peonies, bamboo, birds and butterflies in muted colors.

The Readbourne Stair Hall was taken from a house built in 1733 near Centreville, Maryland for Colonel James Hollyday. The Latimeria Room was originally part of a

The Chinese Parlor at Winterthur has wallpaper painted in 1770 and Oriental art treasures that first reached Europe in Marco Polo's time.

house built in 1815 by William Warner in Wilmington from plans drawn by his friend, Eleuthere Irénée du Pont. The Blackwell Parlor and vestibule were formerly located in a Philadelphia house built in 1764 for John Stamper, a prosperous English-born merchant and mayor of that city. It later was the home of the Reverend Dr. Robert Blackwell, a leading clergyman.

The du Pont Dining Room has paneling from the Readbourne House near Centreville. The mantelpiece and overmantel are from Willow Brook, built in 1800 near Kernstown, Virginia. Over the mantel is a Stuart painting of George Washington. The Candlestick Room has cupboards and shelves from a 1800 store in Chelsea, Pennsylvania, which have been adapted to display the wide variety of candlesticks used in American homes from 1750 to 1850.

The Baltimore Rooms from eighteenth-century houses have decorations reminiscent of the Roman Republic. Inspired by the art objects found in excavations at Pompeii and Herculaneum, the classical ornamentation found here was extremely popular during this country's Federal period.

A graceful spiral staircase dominates the broad Montmorenci Stair Hall, formerly the outstanding feature of a mansion near Warrenton, North Carolina. Built in 1822 by General William Williams, who was known to all as "Pretty Billy" Williams, the mansion was a gift to his third wife. Many festive parties were held there. One of the guests at the Williams mansion was Lafayette.

The Marlboro Room was taken from a plantation house known as Patuxent Manor, built in 1744 for Charles Grahame in Calvert County, Maryland. A superb collection of furniture by the New York cabinetmaker Duncan Phyfe graces the Phyfe Room, illustrating the elegant simplicity of the Federal period and the American adaptations of the styles of Thomas Sheraton, French Directoire and English Regency.

Other rooms portray the Queen Anne, Chippendale, Classical, Empire and other periods. Among the ones open to the public are the Hart Room (Massacusetts, 1640), the Oyster Bay Room (Long Island, 1667), the Wentworth Room (New Hampshire, 1673), the Vauxhall Room (New Jersey, 1725), the Queen Anne Dining room (New Hampshire, 1760), the Flock Room (Virginia, 1714), the Chestertown Room (Maryland, 1762), the Chinese Parlor (China, 1770), and the Empire Parlor (Albany, 1830).

Noted for their colorful azaleas, dogwoods, broad lawns and winding paths, the gardens of Winterthur remain to this day a central feature of the museum. The magnificent spectacle of design and vegetation is a result of Henry du Pont's lifelong interest in horticulture and his careful supervision of the gardens throughout his life. The March Bank, which Henry began in 1909, features thousands of early blooming bulbs of lavender, yellow and white. The Pinetum features over fifty species and varieties of conifers, including the rare Dawn Redwood. The Azalea Woods features eight acres of red, pink, and white azaleas, originally hybridized in Japan. Gardens on the property also include a Reflecting Pool, a circular Sundial Garden of lilacs and honeysuckle, and the Quarry Garden, a naturalistic area of rock and bog plants that Henry du Pont designed himself.

Winterthur is not the only attraction associated with the du Pont family in this area. Longwood Gardens at nearby Kennett Square are among the most spectacular displays in the country. This site features formal flower gardens, an ensemble of fountains with colored lights playing on geysers of water, and a glass-colored arboretum covering the equivalent of three city blocks. Longwood was the estate of Pierre Samuel du Pont, who died in 1954. After opening the gardens to the public in 1921, he endowed a foundation in 1931 to operate them in perpetuity. They are open to the public from 9:00 a.m. to 6:00 p.m. daily, and occasionally throughout the evenings from May to October. The residence is not open to the public.

• • • • •

Winterthur is located in the Brandywine Valley, six miles northwest of Wilmington, Delaware, on Route 52, less than an hour's drive south of Philadelphia and halfway between New York City and Washington, D.C. It is just minutes from I-95 via exit 7 (Delaware Avenue, Rte. 52 North). The museum is open Monday through Saturday from 9:00 a.m. to 5:00 p.m., and Sundays from noon to 5:00 p.m.(Last tickets each day are sold at 3:45 p.m.). General Admission is $8.00 for adults, $6.00 for senior citizens, and $4.00 for children, ages 5-11. For an additional fee of $5.00, visitors can take a guided tour of a selection of period rooms; reservations recommended. Closed New Year's Day, Thanksgiving and Christmas. For further information call: (302)888-4600, or visit the museum website at http://www.winterthur.org

Photos courtesy of Winterthur Museum.

The Most Beautiful House in America

Carter's Grove Plantation

WILLIAMSBURG • VIRGINIA

UNITED STATES history might have been somewhat different if two rich and attractive young women of Carter's Grove Plantation had not been so finicky in choosing husbands. In this mansion, it is rumored that George Washington proposed marriage to Mary Cary and she rejected him. Here too, Thomas Jefferson is supposed to have proposed marriage to Rebecca Burwell, who also declined his offer. Consequently, the young swains did not join the sedate landed gentry of the plantation country along the James River; instead, they turned to more adventurous pursuits that led them into the forefront of the American Revolution. The two young men lost not only two beautiful belles of the Williamsburg social whirl but also a plantation/mansion that has since become widely acclaimed as "the most beautiful house in America." The accolade has been attached to so many houses across the country that it has become an overused statement at best, but to many persons it seems especially appropriate at Carter's Grove. Whether or not it is justified depends on individual preferences, but from an architectural standpoint the mansion is doubtless one of the very finest examples of red-brick Colonial elegance.

Carter Burwell, a member of Virginia's House of Burgessess under British rule, established himself at Carter's Grove in 1738 and soon began construction of the mansion complex, which would take fifteen years to complete. He was just thirty-four and he wanted a splendid home for his young family. The tract of land has a broad scenic frontage on the James River, six miles from downtown Williamsburg. The land had been inherited from Burwell's mother, Elizabeth, who had received it as a wedding gift from her father, Robert Carter, generally known as King Carter because of his vast wealth and power in the colonies.

King Carter owned 300,000 acres of prime Virginia land and over 1,000 slaves. In his will, he directed that the tract he had given to his daughter was "in all times to come be called and to go by the name of Carter's Grove." The name was used until the property passed out of Burwell family ownership, and so it is used today.

Burwell's enjoyment of the new household was short-lived. In the spring of 1756 he died unexpectedly. Burwell's widow and nine children moved away from Carter's Grove. His son Nathaniel returned to the estate in 1771, when he was twenty-one. He would reside in the house with his family for the next twenty years.

Carter Burwell hired skilled tradesmen to build the house. The contractor who supervised the job was David Minetree of Williamsburg. John Wheatley, also of Williamsburg, managed the carpentry work. The extraordinary pine paneling and decorative woodwork of the interior was the achievement of a skilled English woodworker, Richard Baylis. Burwell paid for the passage of Baylis and his family from London just to make certain that Carter's Grove would have some of the most talked-about rooms in Virginia. Burwell had the main house constructed as one unit, with separate dependencies flanking it and greens in between. A dependency on one side was an office. The one on the other side had quarters for servants and the plantation kitchen; food was carried across a green from the kitchen to the mansion. The structures remained unconnected until the present century, when brick linkages provided extra rooms and gave the mansion an uninterrupted stretch of 210 feet.

No original drawings or plans of the mansion have been found, but historians surmise that Burwell would have used popular architecture books of the era, such as *Palladio Londinensis*, as sources for the decorations.

Burwell's account books show that he was so pleased with the early construction that he paid the contractor an agreed price of 115 pounds for his services plus an extra twenty-five pounds "for work well done." They also show that leaders of the colony flocked to Carter's Grove to see the interior woodwork by the great craftsman from London. Architectural historians have since spoken of this woodwork almost reverently.

*The great hall, Carter's Grove. The magnificent finishes of the stairway are
a fine example of 18th century craftsmanship.*

There are records showing that Burwell advertised in the *Virginia Gazette* of Williamsburg for oyster shells. He offered three shillings a hogshead for all that would be delivered to his wharf on the James River. These shells were burned into lime for use in the colonial mortar of the mansion. The bricks were made at Carter's Grove by slaves. The walls of the buildings are three and four feet thick, with bricks of Flemish bond above ground and English bond below. The dependencies have patterned glazed-brick headers characteristic of some of the fancier buildings of early Virginia.

Cedars, poplars and locusts have grown to large size around the mansion, adding to its colonial charm. From the steeply pitched gray-slate roof of the three-story, thirty-one room mansion rise six massive chimneys and a series of dormers. Pilasters and pediments are of brick instead of the usual wood or stone. White trim and gray shutters provide color contrasts. A cornice has decorative modillions and dentils that still are widely copied in new houses of colonial design across the nation.

Inside, the pine paneling and the craftsmanship in the woodwork grip the attention of most visitors. The entrance hall has a beauty of proportions that has marked it among architects as "a masterpiece of early Georgian brought to its finest maturity." Stairs ascend on a west wall, then turn into two short flights before reaching the second floor. Even the dowels of walnut nosings of the stairs are lavishly carved with fleur-de-lis.

A suite of paneled rooms on the riverfront have doorways that provide a sweeping view of virtually the entire 210-foot stretch of rooms. They represent Carter's Grove in its greatest glory.

Among the many rooms of the house is the Refusal Room, named after the alleged rejection of two famous suitors, George Washington and Thomas Jefferson. The room is a southwest parlor, which has a mantel of white Sienna marble and a carved frieze from London, similar to those installed at Tryon Palace in New Bern, North Carolina. The story goes that Washington had come to Carter's Grove on a long visit and had fallen in love with Mary Cary, the daughter of a prominent tidewater citizen and the sister of Cary Fairfax (whose name has also been linked romantically with Washington's). When Jefferson allegedly made his proposal, he was a student at the nearby College of William and Mary, and a frequent visitor to the home. The last inhabitants of Carter's Grove also insisted that the room was haunted by the ghost of colonial society woman Evelyn Byrd, whose legendary love affair with the Earl of Peterborough was thwarted by her father.

From its earliest years the mansion was a meeting place of influential Virginians. The diary of John Blair tells of gay social events at Carter's Grove, with dances intermixed with cloakroom conferences of members of the House of Burgesses. Patrick Henry, James Mason, and James Madison were also visitors.

The mansion was still young when the Revolutionary War began. In the campaign of 1781, Colonel Banastre Tarleton commanded a force of British cavalrymen in the area. Legend tells of Tarleton riding up the stairs on a horse while he hacked on the staircase with a saber, in a fury because he could not get his men to report for duty. This is a legend that is discounted by historians, though the staircase does bear slashmarks. In the 1970s, however, archaeologists at Carter's Grove discovered a brass ornament embellished with Tarleton's family crest, suggesting that the Colonel's presence was known at Carter's Grove.

Lying at the foot of terraces laboriously cut out in the 1740s, the 18th century garden replicates an arrangement dating from the time of Nathaniel Burwell.

A dining room at Carter's Grove.

The last of the five generations of Burwell's to own Carter's Grove was Philip Carter Lewis Burwell. After the death of his wife and son, he sold the estate in 1838. A number of other persons, including Dr. Edwin Booth and Percival Bisland, later owned the property and occasionally renovated the buildings, but then the mansion became neglected and fell into disrepair.

In 1927 the property came to the attention of Archibald M. McCrea, a wealthy Pittsburgh industrialist, and his wife Mollie. Entranced by its architecture, its panoramic views and its history, they bought it, restored the buildings and connected the mansion with dependencies to make one large structure. They stripped paint from the woodwork and refinished the rooms until they were as fine as the Burwells had ever had them. The mansion became so interesting to so many people that even Hollywood took notice of it. In 1940, the movie *Howards of Virginia* was made at Carter's Grove.

The architect for the restoration by the McCreas was W. Duncan Lee of Richmond, Virginia, a contributor to the expansion of the Governor's mansion in Richmond. Under his guidance, the couple greatly enhanced the house through the addition of a steeply sloping roof to the main house, three additional bedrooms, two baths, and a large sitting room; all set off by new dormer windows.

In their determination to preserve the details of the house, the McCreas made certain that no paneling was removed, no walls were altered and no doorways were changed. To install modern electrical heating and plumbing systems, only floor boards were taken up; they could be replaced correctly without great difficulty.

The development of a national highway system in the 1920s and '30s made it easier for guests to visit Carter's Grove. Frequent visitors to the estate included such luminaries as Secretary Harold Ickes, Nelson Rockefeller, Gertrude Stein, and Walt Disney. Mrs. McCrea often entertained at Carter's Grove until her death in 1960.

In her will, Mrs. McCrea, who died after her husband, directed that Carter's Grove and its furnishings be sold to somebody who would appreciate and perpetuate the historic treasure. This, coupled with the fame of the Plantation, brought Carter's Grove to the attention of the Sealantic Fund, a philanthropic organization founded by the late John D. Rockefeller, Jr. In 1963 Sealantic Charitable Trust bought the property for the Colonial Williamsburg Foundation.

Archeological research begun in the 1970s has provided an additional focus to the public. Remains found there, particularly pottery, suggest that Europeans occupied the property in the early seventeenth century. Since the archeological work was completed in 1982, continued research has resulted in the recent opening of the Winthrop Rockefeller Archeology Museum. Located southeast of the mansion, the artifacts represented here offer another unique aspect of American history to the curious onlooker.

• • • • •

Carter's Grove Plantation is located six miles east of Williamsburg, just off U.S. Route 60 East. A country road (one way) runs between the Reception Center and the Historic Area. Pre-school children are admitted for free. Admission for adults is currently $17.00 and $10.00 for children ages 6-10. Hours of exhibition are 9:00 a.m.-4:00 p.m. Tuesday through Sunday and 9:00 a.m.-5:00 p.m. daily from June 13th-August 31st. Ticket prices and hours of operation vary seasonally. Tickets may be obtained by calling: 1 (800)HIS-TORY (447-8679). Further information on Carter's Grove may be obtained through the Colonial Williamsburg website at http://www.colonialwilliamsburg.org.

Photos courtesy of the Colonial Williamsburg Foundation.

A Family Legacy

Franklin D. Roosevelt's Springwood Estate

HYDE PARK • NEW YORK

AT THE EDGE of a high escarpment beside the Hudson River, eighty miles north of New York City, lays a plateau of gently rolling fields and wooded hills. A gray stucco mansion on the rim of the plateau dominates the countryside and has a panoramic view far across the river and into the mountains to the west. This residence, known as Springwood, was the lifetime home of the late President Franklin Roosevelt.

Born in the mansion in 1882, Mr. Roosevelt would return to his ancestral surroundings some 200 times for relaxation from the turmoil of public life and to ponder domestic and international problems. By 1944, ill and weary from the intensity of his last years in the White House, there was a note of finality when Franklin stated: "All

The living room of Hyde Park. Above the mantel is a portrait of Isaac Roosevelt, FDR's great-great grandfather, by artist Gilbert Stuart.

that is within me cries out to go back to my home on the Hudson River." Upon his death in 1945, Mr. Roosevelt was buried in the family rose garden beside the mansion, and his wife Eleanor was buried beside him in 1962.

Built as an ordinary small clapboard farmhouse around 1800, the dwelling was officially purchased in 1867 by Mr. Roosevelt's father, James Roosevelt, shortly after his first home was destroyed by fire. A dignified-looking man with a high-brow, deep-set eyes, and mutton-chops, James Roosevelt had been a successful investor and businessman. His maneuvers always made money, but never placed him on a par with the robber barons. Known in the Hudson Valley as "Squire James," FDR's father was acknowledged as a leader in the civic affairs of Hyde Park. When he traveled to Manhattan, it was to socialize with wealthy friends such as the Astors.

James and his first wife, Rebecca Howland, lived together at Springwood until her untimely death in 1876. In 1880, the fifty-two-year-old widower married the young and prominent Sara Delano, also of the Hudson Valley. James and Sara repeatedly enlarged and redeveloped Springwood until it approached the mansion it is today. Their only child, Franklin, played in the fields and gardens, built tree houses and river rafts, learned the lore of the woods, the joy of freedom and the effects of collectivism. Then, at fourteen, he was sent away to school. When he married his cousin and childhood playmate, Eleanor Roosevelt, the mansion became their property and the place their five children were reared.

From Springwood Mr. Roosevelt embarked on his political career. Some biographers contend that the New Deal was born there, and with it Mr. Roosevelt's concepts of social responsibility. As early as 1917, he and his wife had a heated discussion about the home with his mother, who had been widowed in 1900. Sara asked Franklin and Eleanor to promise that the Hyde Park estate remain in the family after she died. She wished for it to be the private home of the Roosevelts for many more generations. Her son and daughter-in-law objected, Franklin entering into a vigorous exposition of his social and political philosophies, and the rights of the poor to enjoy some of the properties and opportunities of the rich. Sara Roosevelt was shocked, and later correspondence between mother and son showed that Franklin was already moving rapidly towards ideas that became the foundation of the New Deal.

It was from the Hyde Park mansion that Mr. Roosevelt first successfully ran for public office; from 1911 to 1913 he represented his neighbors as their New York State Senator. He was Assistant Secretary of the navy from 1913 to 1920, and then he set forth from Hyde Park to campaign successfully for Vice President.

Stricken with poliomyelitis in 1921 while at his summer home in Campobello, New Brunswick, Franklin waged his long fight against the ailment at his home in Hyde Park. Here he greeted his friends in 1928 and in 1930, when elected and reelected governor of New York. During his three successive terms as the thirty-second President of the United States and for part of the fourth term, when death intervened, the Hyde Park mansion remained his favorite home. In compliance with his wishes, Franklin's body was returned here after his sudden death in 1945 at Cold Springs, Georgia.

Now the public may visit his work rooms, trophy collections, personal bedrooms, recreation facilities and gardens to view in depth the intimate surroundings of the late President and the many social changes he helped initiate. Visitors sometimes wonder if the furniture and art treasures from many nations inspired the late President's famous comment: "Remember, please, that you and I are descended from immigrants and revolutionists."

Countless transformations in the mansion's design and contour since James Roosevelt bought it include the addition of two rooms, enlarged servants quarters, and the erection of a large carriage house for James' prized horses and carriages. He also added a porch with a sweeping balustrade and a white colonnaded portico on the front. In 1915, under the guidance of Franklin Roosevelt, the final major changes were made. These included the addition of an elevator and replacement of all the clapboards from the original farmhouse - now the central part of the dwelling - with gray stucco. Two-story wings of fieldstone on each end now give the whole structure an H shape. Franklin also planted over 500,000 trees on the property, enlarging the estate to 1,600 acres and eventually turning large sections of the property into an experimental forestry station. No further revisions were made or are likely to be made. The mansion now stands three stories high and has thirty-five rooms and nine baths.

A place where such notables as Prime Minister Winston Churchill and British royalty were entertained, visitors to the home are struck by the comfortable setting of the Hyde Park mansion, with all the treasures and knick-knacks dear to the hearts of millions of families. The interests and customs of the Roosevelt family are evident to visitors when they first step into the large front hall. The room is dominated by family antiques and pictures, chiefly naval prints. To the left of the front door are a massive oak wardrobe and eighteenth-century grandfather clock. Both were purchased in the

Netherlands by FDR's parents on their wedding trip in 1880. Against one wall is a sideboard bought by James Roosevelt in Italy in 1869. In a corner is a life-size bronze statue of the President at the age of twenty-nine, executed by Russian sculptor Prince Paul Troubetzkoy (1866-1938) in 1911. Behind the statue is a wall-case of stuffed birds that Franklin collected as a boy.

The south hallway leads to the Roosevelt "snuggery" - a small, cozy sitting room - and on to the living room, which occupies the entire lower floor of the south wing. It is a cheerful and spacious room in which the family met, played, read and entertained. Two portraits over the fireplace are of Roosevelt ancestors. One is a Gilbert Stuart painting of Isaac Roosevelt - the late President's great-great grandfather, a Revolutionary War leader and a state senator. The other is a portrait of FDR's great-grandfather - James Roosevelt, a New York City merchant, state assemblyman and the first Roosevelt to come to the Hyde Park area in 1819. A large portrait of Franklin Roosevelt in this room was painted at the mansion in 1932 by the eminent American portrait painter Ellen Emmet Rand (1875-1941). Two high leather chairs were Mr. Roosevelt's in Albany, when he served as Governor of New York in the late 1920s.

In this living room Mr. Roosevelt carried on the family tradition of trimming Christmas trees with real candles. It was here that he read Dickens' Christmas story of Old Scrooge and Tiny Tim, sitting at the fireside and making an evening event of the eloquent presentation. Here too, Roosevelt could pursue his favorite hobbies, which included stamp collection and building ship models. Roosevelt had a lifelong interest in ships and the sea, particularly in U.S. Naval history.

The Dresden Room near the living room is a light and elaborately formal parlor, taking its name from a delicately wrought Dresden chandelier and mantel that James Roosevelt bought in Germany in 1866. The rug is an Aubusson and the floral drapes and upholstery were installed especially for visits of English royalty in 1939.

The dining room is dominated by heavy, dark furniture. The oak dining table is now permanently set for two persons but can be extended to seat twenty. Antique sideboards were acquired by James Roosevelt in Italy and the Netherlands about 1800. In this room and the Dresden Room, formal entertaining took place.

On the second floor is further evidence of Franklin's formidable presence. On display are the Birth Room, including the bed in which he was born, his Boyhood Bedroom, which was later used by each of his sons, and a large bedroom at the end of the hall that the former president used in his later years. After his poliomyelitis attack the large bedroom became a great favorite of Roosevelt's, since its windows provide a panoramic view of the Hudson and the mountains beyond. Here he surrounded himself with his favorite oil paintings, naval prints and family photographs. Scattered about the room are books and magazines that were at Hyde Park just before Roosevelt's death, as well as the leash and blanket of his pet Scottie, Fala.

Congress designated the mansion as a national historic site in 1939 when Mr. Roosevelt gave it to the nation, along with some thirty-three acres and subsidiary buildings. Members of the Roosevelt family continued to retain life interests in the property. In 1945, the Secretary of the Interior received full title to Springwood when FDR's widow and children relinquished all claims to the estate after his death. In 1952, a sixty-acre tract between the house and the river was given to the government by the Franklin D. Roosevelt Foundation. The site now contains ninety-three acres.

The rose garden near the northeast corner of the mansion, almost surrounded by a century-old hemlock hedge, was chosen by Mr. Roosevelt as his burial place. This was a symbolic choice because the surname Roosevelt was derived from the Dutch "fields of roses" in the family's ancestral land. The rose symbol is perpetuated in the family coat of arms, which has three roses on a shield, surmounted by a casque and three feathers.

A white marble gravestone, with a slight trace of color highlighting its natural beauty, has been placed at the late President's grave. Known as Imperial Danby, the stone is from a Vermont quarry that produced the marble for the Thomas Jefferson Memorial in Washington. Plans for the stone were drawn by Mr. Roosevelt in a memorandum written the day after Christmas in 1937. In it he stated:

"It is my hope that my dear wife will on her death be buried there also, and that the monument contain no device or inscription except the following on the south side:

"Franklin Delano Roosevelt

"1882. 19-

"Anna Eleanor Roosevelt

"1884. 19-"

The Dresden Room is named for the chandelier and mantelpiece bought by the President's father on a visit to Germany in 1866.

The grave of FDR and Eleanor is located in the rose garden.

His instructions were followed precisely.

Adjacent to the mansion is the Franklin D. Roosevelt Library, administered by the National Archives. Built by Mr. Roosevelt six years before his death, it contains his papers, books, letters and other historical materials. It was from an office in this building that the former President delivered many of his radio addresses to the nation.

The library contains more than 44,000 volumes of reference works and 15,000 volumes of books from the President's personal collection. From boyhood, Mr. Roosevelt collected books on history, economics, government, public affairs, travel and other subjects. After he became President he received books as gifts from authors, publishers and friends. In addition, the library contains a complete accumulation of Mr. Roosevelt's Presidential and political papers, naval manuscripts, 109,000 still pictures, 4,000 sound recordings, 700 reels of motion pictures and 24,000 artifacts, including a wide variety of art objects.

From the time of George Washington, the papers that accumulated in the White House during the tenure of a President have been his property when he left. Such papers have met varying fates. Some have been destroyed, many have been acquired by private buyers and others have been deposited in the Library of Congress. The establishment of the Roosevelt Library as a repository of presidential papers set a new precedent.

The Roosevelt Library collections include gifts received by Mr. Roosevelt from heads of state and other notables throughout the world. There is a gold inkwell from King George VI of England, Chinese and Korean relics, a silver urn from Denmark, a gold-and-porcelain tea set from Norway, a gold filigree tiara and bracelets presented to Mrs. Roosevelt by the Sultan of Morocco, a large aquamarine given to Mrs. Roosevelt by the President of Brazil, a gold globe of the world from Emperor Haile Selassie of Ethiopia, and a 200-year-old Torah manuscript rescued from a burning synagogue in Czechoslovakia.

The well-worn desk and chair used in the White House by Mr. Roosevelt and some of the curios that he liked to keep on his desk are now in the library. A cabinet contains china used in the White House as well as two Arabian swords with sheaths of gold and diamonds given to Mr. Roosevelt by King Ibn Saud of Saudi Arabia. Four brocade wall hangings were sent by the Dalai Lama of Tibet.

There are cabinets filled with Mr. Roosevelt's rings, watches, cigarette cases, membership cards, medals, baptismal and marriage certificates, and school essays. In some rooms are the ship models Mr. Roosevelt collected, ranging from Chinese junks to modern battleships. His favorite was a model of the U.S.S. Constitution, which was 100 years old when he bought it. He personally rerigged the model.

A large Persian rug in the library was given to Mr. Roosevelt by the Shah of Iran at the Teheran Conference in 1943. Some rooms are filled with clocks, urns and paintings from world notables. In the basement is a ceiling-high statue of Mr. Roosevelt as the Sphinx, inspired by his refusal in 1939 to admit whether he would run for President again in 1940.

Other objects include carriages, iceboats, cars and sleighs that the late President used. This includes the manually operated 1936 blue Ford convertible that Roosevelt often drove on inspection trips around the Hyde Park estate and which he was often shown in photographs.

· · · · ·

The Roosevelt shrine is located on the Albany Post Road (U.S. Route 9) at Hyde Park and is accessible from the New York State Thruway and the Taconic State Parkway. Ticket prices are $10.00 for adults (FDR Home & Library/Museum). Children under seventeen are admitted free of charge. The mansion is open daily throughout the year and is closed Thanksgiving Day, Christmas, and New Year's Day. Hours of operation are 9:00 a.m. to 6:00 p.m. For further information call: (914) 229-7770 or visit the National Park Service website at http://www.nps.gov/hofr.

Photos courtesy of The National Park Service, Roosevelt-Vanderbilt National Historic Sites, Hyde Park, New York.

An American Monaco

Photo by John Hill.

John D. Rockefellers' Kykuit

POCANTICO HILLS • NEW YORK

SITUATED HIGH on a hilltop in Sleepy Hollow, Kykuit (pronounced Kye-cut), commands stunning views of the Hudson River and the Palisades. The 4,180-acre estate was the principal home of the family and descendants of John D. Rockefeller - founder of Standard Oil Company - a man history often judges as the "representative American of the Gilded Age." Ten times larger than Monaco and five times the size of Central Park, the mansion in its heyday was the playground and palace of four generations of American royalty, as well as countless leaders from around the world. As one Broadway wit of later years wisecracked, the Pocantico estate was an example of "what God could have done if He'd only had the money."

The dining room, Kykuit. Photo by Ron Blunt.

Born on a farm in upstate New York and raised in Cleveland, John D. Rockefeller entered the oil refinery business in 1863. Seven years later, he and his partners incorporated the Standard Oil Company, which despite a nationwide depression, quickly grew to become a monopoly among its competitors. By the latter half of the nineteenth century, Rockefeller assumed control of ninety-five percent of all the oil refinery business in the nation-a prize he shared with his hand-chosen partners Samuel Andrews and Henry M. Flagler. Alternately admired and scorned, JDR was soon to become one of the wealthiest men in the world, as well as the nation's greatest philanthropist. While still living in Cleveland, he had purchased Forest Hill, a nearby rural retreat, which he used as a summer home. But soon after he moved to New York City in 1884, Mr. Rockefeller began to seek a place outside of the city where he and his family could spend the spring and fall. At fifty-four years old, he wanted to mold a small community to his own fancies while keeping an eye on business.

John D. Rockefeller's initial purchase included seventeen tracts of farmland on Kykuit Hill, an exposed hilltop site situated five-hundred feet above sea level. The property is located on a high ridge between the Hudson and Saw Mill River valleys, with panoramic views of thirty miles. Known as Signal Hill, the ridge had been used by Indians to send up smoke signals. Dutch settlers had called the hill Kykuit, meaning Lookout Hill in English.

With a pick and shovel, Mr. Rockefeller joined with workmen in planting trees and shrubs, moving stone walls and laying flagstones just as he wanted them. John D. Rockefeller, Jr., a recent graduate of Brown University and now a worker in his father's corporation, took the same personal interest in Kykuit as his father.

On the hilltop was an old mansion with broad verandahs. It was the first Kykuit. When the family moved into it, Mr. Rockefeller wrote to friends that "the fine views invite the soul" and that he and his wife, Laura Spellman, could "live simply and quietly here."

The old frame house burned in 1902 and the family moved to a smaller dwelling on the property for five years while a fifty-room stone house - the present Kykuit - was constructed. The elder Rockefeller displayed little initiative in construction of the final mansion. The real inspiration and planning for it was initiated by John D., Jr. In 1902, without his father's knowledge, Junior called upon the architect Chester Homes Aldrich (1871-1940), a friend and distant cousin of his wife Abby, to draw up plans. Aldrich and his partner, William Adams Delano (1874-1960) had once been employees of Carrère and Hastings, the architectural firm responsible for construction of Flagler's Marble Casa, New York City's Public Library, and the Metropolitan Opera. Later, John Jr. hired prominent decorator Ogden Codman, Jr. (1862-1951)- a foremost leader of classical revival in America-to design the elegant interior of the new family mansion, as well as landscape architect William Welles Bosworth (1869-1966), who would establish his reputation through the Rockefeller name.

Portrait of John D. Rockefeller, Sr. by John Singer Sargent. Photo by Ron Blunt.

By 1906, Rockefeller's son John was given full command of Kykuit's construction. It was his duty to maintain contact with architects, contractors, and supply companies, while overseeing every detail, large and small, of construction. Kykuit was one of the first major undertakings Junior would perform for his father, and its outcome would play a major role in how he earned his father's trust. The outcome of this test was positive, for soon after Kykuit's completion, John Jr. began to assume a greater share of the family business and philanthropic concerns.

Classical Revival emulated the design principles of ancient Greece and Rome, as well as Renaissance Italy, generally viewed as the greatest intellectual and cultural traditions of the western world. John D., Jr. felt that by designing Kykuit in this style, he could associate the family name with these ideas. Both Codman and Bosworth were accorded heavy responsibilities as designers. While making decisions about furniture, curtains, carpets and decorative work in the house, Codman personally selected many of the furnishings which arrived from London, Paris, Boston and New York. Bosworth's gardens at Kykuit, which survive virtually unchanged, are considered the best work he ever performed in the United States, where he worked until 1919. They include a series of hilltop terraces, from which are visible the magnificent cliffs and undeveloped hills of the Palisades Interstate Park. The terraces, gardens, and stone walls are planted with roses, ivy, climbing hydrangea, perennials, an extensive collection of rhododendrons and magnolias, and splendid trees and shrubs. There are also grottoes, garden pavilions, large wrought iron gates, and glorious fountains.

John D. Rockefeller, Jr., whose new duties also included philanthropic concerns, used his expertise in this area to enlarge the Pocantico Hills holdings. The New York Central Railroad was given close to one million dollars to close the Pocantico Hills station, move the tracks a mile to the east, and raise an unsightly trestle and other structures that marred the appearance of the Rockefeller properties. Hotels, candy stores and shops were bought, closed and razed by the Rockefellers. Roads that bisected the estate were rebuilt at the Rockefeller's expense, bridges were built over, and tunnels dug under roads to link the various parts of the estate. The post office, gasoline stations and even public telephones were removed from the face of Pocantico Hills.

As they became the owners of ninety-eight percent of the property in Pocantico Hills, the Rockefellers increased their benefactions. They contributed playgrounds, a school, a firehouse, and even churches. To the nearby Union Church, which the Rockefellers sometimes attended, nine stained-glass windows by Marc Chagall were donated in the 1960s, as well as a stained-glass window by Henri Matisse in 1954 - the last art object the French master ever produced.

Events both gay and tragic have taken place at the estate. The Cinderella story of Anne Marie Rasmussen began there in the fifties; she was a Norwegian maid for the Nelson Rockefellers and married their son Steven. Michael, one of Steven's brothers, lived at Kykuit until he went on an exploration in the South Pacific and was lost at sea. Winthrop, one of Nelson's brothers, lived there during his romance with Bobo Sears, a Lithuanian model, whom he married and later gave $5,500,000 to in a divorce settlement. The Nelson Rockefellers lived there from 1963 until his death in 1979.

Kykuit underwent two renovations, the first of which ended in 1908 and the second in 1913. The second renovation involved the addition of two-and-a-half floors to the house as well the complete redesign of the façade. Inside their walled estate the Rockefellers built a private golf course and a million dollar recreation center with bowling alleys, tennis courts, and indoor and outdoor swimming pools. A generator in the Coach Barn brought electricity to the house, which was also equipped with central heating, a central vacuum system, and an Otis elevator. John D. Rockefeller, Sr. would move back into the main house with his wife in 1913. Although his wife died two years later, the elder Rockefeller would enjoy the house immensely until his death in 1937.

Like many mansions of the time, Kykuit bears the distinct hallmark of those who inhabited it. However, distinctions changed as new generations of Rockefellers claimed principal ownership. The noticeable lack of a ballroom reflects the personality of the elder Rockefellers. Strict Baptists who allowed no dancing or drinking in the house, John D. and Laura Rockefeller, Sr., entertained only on a modest scale. A hidden staircase discouraged anyone, including guests, from a vain display of fashionable clothes. A central feature of many fine houses, grand staircases which opened onto huge halls were built with the purpose of display in mind. Similarly, there is little decorative gilding at Kykuit. Most of the walls are white.

The influence of several generations of Rockefellers may be seen in the music room. Codman's most ambitious design at Kykuit, it was modeled in the English style of Christopher Wren (1632-1723). The oval opening, or oculus, in the ceiling, reveals the second floor gallery leading to the bedrooms. Originally surrounded by eight sets of glass double doors, the room also included a pipe organ with three keyboards. Frequent family get-togethers often ended in the music room, and sometimes organists such as H.R. Shelley, of New York's Fifth Avenue Baptist Church, provided entertainment. Nelson Rockefeller later replaced the organ with a replica of the large oil painting, *Hirondelle Amour*, by the great Spanish Surrealist painter Joan Miró (1893-1983), the original of

Frequent family get-togethers often ended in the music room at Kykuit, which once featured a large organ. Photo by Ping Amranand.

which he gave to the Museum of Modern Art in 1976. John D. Rockefeller, Jr.'s Chinese ceramic collection has also been on display in this room since the 1930s.

The collection of art became a principal hobby of many members of the Rockefeller family in later years. Associations at Kykuit to the world of art began with Abby Aldrich Rockefeller (1874-1948), wife of John D. Rockefeller, Jr. A preeminant collector of American folk art in this century, her collection is now part of Colonial Williamsburg. She was also one of three female collectors who founded the Museum of Modern Art (MoMA) in New York City. In her memory, Nelson created a special place of honor at Kykuit, the Alcove Room, where a seventh-century statue of Bodhisattva, one of Buddha's divine attendants, now stands.

By the time he came to live at Kykuit Nelson Rockefeller was actively engaged as a major player in the nation's art world. He had already employed his position as governor of New York State to create the New York State Council on the Arts, the first governmental program on the arts in the country. Nelson proceeded to convert much of the mansion's ground-floor spaces into four separate galleries. On display here are more than 100 works, mostly from American artists of the twentieth century, including Max Ernst, Andy Warhol, George Segal, and Alexander Calder. Governor Rockefeller also added over seventy pieces of twentieth-century sculpture to the gardens. Included here are works by Pablo Picasso, Alberto Giacometti, Constantin Brancusi, Isamu Noguchi, Louise Nevelson and David Smith. Most of the works are abstract, avant garde, and modern - a remarkable departure from the classical legacy of the gardens.

A handsome Coach Barn, located just below the summit of the hilltop, houses carriages and coaches, several of which belonged to John D. Rockefeller, Sr. and his son. The collection of automobiles housed there today includes an electric car, a 1918 Crane Simplex, a 1939 Cadillac, a 1959 Chrysler limousine that Nelson Rockefeller used while governor, as well as a group of children's pony carts and wicker carriages. A state-of-the-art conference center, operated by the Rockefeller Brothers Fund, is now located on the first floor of the building, which is closed to the public.

John D. Rockefeller, Jr. died in 1960. Over the course of his life it is estimated that he donated over $400,000,000 to philanthropies, including building projects and historic preservation. He provided funds for the restoration of Rheims Cathedral and the Versailles Palace, located outside of Paris, after they were damaged during World War I. He also financed the development and construction of Colonial Williamsburg in the 1920s, bought property for and financed construction of The Cloisters Museum in New York in 1935, financed development of Sleepy Hollow Restorations, and used his influence to preserve many national parks across the United States.

In 1976, the house and gardens at Pocantico Hills were dedicated as a National Historic Landmark, with an address from Gerald R. Ford, under whom Nelson Rockefeller had served as Vice President. Following the death of Nelson Rockefeller in 1979, Kykuit was left to the National Trust for Historic Preservation. The house and garden were opened to the public in 1994. Today, Historic Hudson Valley, a restoration organization founded by John D. Rockefeller, Jr., operates the museum program.

● ● ● ● ●

Kykuit is located in the hamlet of Pocantico Hills, which is part of the village of Sleepy Hollow. It is open daily from May-October except on Tuesdays. Tours are offered to the public from 10:00 a.m. to 5:00 p.m. All tours to Kykuit begin at historic Philipsburg Manor in Sleepy Hollow. Tickets must be purchased in advance. Admission fees are $20.00 for adults, $19.00 for senior citizens, $17.00 for people 18 and under. For further information please call: (914)631-9491, or visit the Kykuit website at http://www.hudsonvalley.org. Tickets purchased on-line are discounted.

Photos courtesy of Historic Hudson Valley

The Largest House in Vermont   *Photo by Joseph Mehling.*

Shelburne Farms

LOCATED ALONG Lake Champlain in northern Vermont, the spectacular vistas of the Adirondack Mountains stand opposite the magnificently restored Queen Anne Revival style Shelburne House, now known as the Inn at Shelburne Farms. The setting is sublime - the views are among the most beautiful in the world. But Shelburne Farms, established in 1886 by Dr. William Seward Webb and Lila Vanderbilt Webb, has always been more than a grand house.

William Seward Webb was the grandson of General Samuel B. Webb who, after serving in the Revolutionary War, became aide-de-camp to General Washington and held the Bible on which the first President took his oath of office. As a reward for his

The Marble Dining Room at the Inn at Shelburne Farms. A portrait of Lila Vanderbilt by Jules LeFebvre (1836-1912) hangs to the left of the fireplace. Photo by Gary Hall.

loyal service, General Webb was deeded property, fortuitously, in Vermont. William's father, James Watson Webb, was a fiery independent man who ran away from home at the age of seventeen to join the military and later became the owner and editor of the *New York Courier* and *Enquirer*. William Seward Webb was graduated from Columbia University's College of Physicians and Surgeons in 1875. He then pursued his medical studies for two years in Vienna before returning to New York. Soon after, he became captivated by the young Eliza (Lila) Osgood Vanderbilt, daughter of William Henry Vanderbilt, at the time the richest man in the world. When the couple first met, Mr. Webb had recently abandoned his medical training and to impress Lila's father, had chosen a less risky career on Wall St. He would later go on to work as a businessman for her father's railroad company, proving his business acumen by rescuing a floundering Wagner Palace Car Company from the economic doldrums.

Lila was the youngest of William Henry Vanderbilt's daughters. Born in 1860, and a graduate of Miss Porter's School in Connecticut, she had spent most of her life secluded in her father's brownstone mansion at 459 Fifth Avenue. Much to her father's dismay, the nineteen-year-old Lila fell very much in love with the worldly Seward Webb, who was ten years her senior. Had it not been for the efforts of Lila's sister Emily Sloane, who acted as secret postmistress between the lovers, the relationship would have surely foundered. After a lengthy courtship, protracted by her father's opposition to the union, the couple married in 1881.

One might wonder how this young couple, securely ensconced in the social milieu of Victorian New York City, came to establish their home in the remoteness of northern Vermont. Lila had spent the early impressionable years of her childhood on a farm in rural Staten Island, New York. There she may have grown fond of flowers, carrying this influence with her to the Shelburne Farms house and gardens decades ahead. Dr. Webb was immediately entranced by the extraordinary beauty of Vermont's landscape after first visiting the state on a hunting trip; he would later firm up plans to live there while on business in VT for the New York Central Railroad.

Soon after their marriage, the young couple moved to Burlington, Vermont, a little city on the shore of Lake Champlain, and proceeded to build a modest home - Oakledge - in 1883. In 1885, William Henry Vanderbilt died, and it was Lila's ten million dollar inheritance that allowed her and Dr. Webb to realize their dream of establishing a model agricultural estate. The matter took careful planning, for as evidence of his continued distrust for Dr. Webb, William Henry had placed Lila's money in a trust that was not to be available until she turned thirty.

Assembled from the purchase of thirty-two small farms, Shelburne Farms originally encompassed approximately 4,000 acres and was planned to utilize the most innovative agricultural and land use techniques. Dr. Webb engaged one of the era's most talented architects, a New Yorker named Robert Henderson Robertson (1849-1919), to perform the architectural design. His magnificent buildings were sited in a pastoral landscape that was shaped with the assistance of Frederick Law Olmsted (1822-1903), considered the father of American landscape architecture. Winding roads were laid out so that as one drove through the property, curiosity and anticipation would be raised as each vista, more beautiful than the last, was revealed around the curves.

The establishment of Shelburne Farms bore the imprint of Seward Webb's mania for scientific modernism and passion for horseflesh. A superb equestrian with a lifelong interest in horses, Webb concentrated the agricultural emphasis of his new estate on perfecting the breeding of the American horse. The Farm Barn was the center of agricultural operations and the Breeding Barn stabled imported English Hackney horses. Dr. Webb intended to use these buildings to breed a superior variety. The Breeding Barn and Farm Barn were so technologically advanced in their operations and output that Webb, who hoped to set an example across the state, soon earned the scorn and resentment of his less well-to-do farming neighbors.

When the shingle-style house was first constructed in 1887, it was meant to be a temporary residence until a more lavish house could be built on Lone Tree Hill, the highest site on the property. Dr. Webb and Lila occupied the cottage with their

The library at the Inn at Shelburne Farms contains over 6,000 volumes. Photo by Gary Hall.

younger children: Frederica, James Watson, and W. Seward,Jr.- a fourth son, Vanderbilt, was born in 1891. The couple grew increasingly enamored of the site with its gorgeous lake and pastoral views; so instead of building on Lone Tree Hill, they decided to expand the existing house. The addition, completed in 1900, comprised 110 rooms, including the servant's wing. In keeping with the Queen Anne style after which it was designed, the façade of the house was eclectic. Architectural details included windows of many shapes and sizes, dormers, clustered chimneys and lovely conical roof porches. The house, like the agricultural operations, was modern and up-to-date. Unlike many of their wealthy contemporaries, the Webb family did not collect rare and expensive art. Hand-crafted objects were valued and savored in an otherwise fast-paced age of mechanization, and the artwork in the house celebrated rural lifestyles and values. Most food products, including vegetables, dairy products, lamb, beef and poultry were grown on the farms.

Differences in farming techniques were not the only way in which Webb and his family were distinguished from their rural neighbors. The family also possessed a private railroad car, a mark of exceptionally high status for that era. Complete with a dining car, a wine cellar, servants, and a library, it allowed the family to travel virtually at will-even to such destinations as New York's Grand Central Station. Frequent hosts, the Webbs lavish style of entertaining soon established a name for Shelburne Farms among the nation's social elite. In the winter, guests could go sleighing, iceboating, skating or tobogganing on a private run. A fall visit might include a shoot in

The East Room once belonged to Seward Webb. Photo by Gary Hall.

Dr. Webb's private pheasantry, while in the summer they could golf on the Webb's private golf course or pass away leisure time sailing on the Webbs 117-foot steam yacht, the *Elfrida*.

Lila's love was the garden which evolved from the geometric French formal parterre style to incorporate a mixture of styles. She was influenced by European gardens on trips abroad and introduced into her garden many architectural elements, including statues, a stone balustrade, and a water garden derived from classical villas. Lila also amassed an impressive collection of garden books which would often serve as a source of inspiration. Most influential among the writings were those of Gertrude Jekyll, an English artist and gardener responsible for the exuberant English cottage style of flower border. The grand allée in the formal gardens at Shelburne Farms was planted in this style and included a lavish collection of hollyhocks, poppies, delphinium, lilies, irises, and many other perennials. There was also a peony border and a rose garden.

At the height of its splendor, Shelburne Farms was a sparkling jewel. The model farm supplied all the butter used on New York Central's dining cars, plus a large portion of the railroad's milk and cream supply. A large portion of apples, oats, wheat and rye was also exported, which a large staff of over 300 employees helped to tend. Changing economic times, however, soon brought trouble to the Webb's rural utopia. Mr. Webb's own railroad firm, The Wagner Company, was taken over by the larger Pullman Company at the end of the 1890s, forcing his resignation. The rise of the internal-combustion engine also destroyed Mr. Webb's dream of enlarging his horse breeding business. Seward Webb soon began suffering excruciating migraine headaches, which he turned to morphine to relieve. Unable to break the habit, he increasingly withdrew from his family and public life until his death in 1926.

The Farm Barn, center of agricultural operations at Shelburne Farms. Photo by Marshall Webb.

Throughout this time, Lila did her best to manage the estate, despite the fact that she was faced by mounting debt. While she did her best, farm management was not her forte. Mounting deficits were paid out of her own capital, while no alternatives were presented and no solutions considered. She was also faced with the onset of deafness. With the cash portion of her inheritance gone and Seward Webb's career in ruins, Lila was forced to turn to her relatives for assistance. This she received from her brother Fred, whose inheritance she had once helped to secure. His contributions, coupled with Lila's shrewd frugality, maintained the property in her name despite increasing misfortune.

Following Lila's death in 1936, the property was divided among the Webb's four children, most of whom were already living on the vast estate at least part-time. Vanderbilt Webb inherited the house and the northern section of the property. Derick Webb, Vanderbilt's son, managed the Farm and dedicated himself to rebuilding the agricultural operations. The Big House was used only during the summers. Although the agricultural operations were self-supporting, by the 1960s, with mounting expenses and taxes, Derick found it impossible to envision the Farm's survival. He gathered his children, and from a deep commitment to saving the property, vowed to find a way to conserve Shelburne Farms. Their resolve resulted, in 1972, with the formation of the nonprofit Shelburne Farms Resources, endowed with the mission of utilizing a place of astonishing beauty to teach and demonstrate the stewardship of natural and agricultural resources.

Chief responsibility for the restoration project was given to Burlington architect Martin Tierney in the early 1980s, an expert on old houses. Local businesses and members of the community contributed cash and donated building resources to enable the restoration, which amounted to $1.4 million. Although latent, the state's acceptance of the Webbs had finally arrived.

From a modest start as a site for concerts by the Vermont Mozart Festival and limited special events, the Big House began its new life as an Inn. Completely renovated in 1987, it was the recipient of a Presidential Award for Historic Preservation the following year. The Inn at Shelburne Farms now welcomes guests from mid-May through Mid-October, continuing the tradition of gracious hospitality established by its founding family. The drive from the main gate to the Inn has been maintained as a pastoral working landscape, still nourishing Olmsted's original vision. Upon arrival, visitors enter the Main Hall which is separated into a reception area and a comfortable living area. Today guests may be seen using first-floor rooms much as they would have been used by the Webbs in the late 1800s — reading, relaxing, enjoying the views or the coziness of a fire, chatting together or finding a nook for quiet contemplation.

The library contains over 6,000 volumes reflecting the wide-ranging interests of the Webbs in the areas of literature, politics, art, travel, history, and religion. Lila's gardening books are also on display, many containing notes in the margins made as she planned the gardens at Shelburne Farms. There is a lush, low green velvet couch, circa 1890s, made for the house by a local furniture maker.

In the elegant tearoom — originally the kitchen and pantry area prior to the 1900 addition— guests are now served afternoon tea. The room contains a carved Colonial Revival woodwork ceiling. Family portraits hang on all of the walls, including an etching of Cornelius Vanderbilt, as well as portraits and photographs of the Webb family and four Webb children. The sideboard and serving table are from General Samuel B. Webb's house in Wethersfield, Connecticut.

The Marble Dining Room is now used for the service of breakfast, dinner, and Sunday brunch for the Inn's guests and visitors. The room contains a striking portrait of Lila during her courtship to Seward Webb by Jules LaFebvre. The black and white all-marble floor of this room was purchased from VT Marble Co. in 1899. Silk damask wall coverings that are original to the room adorn the walls, and the views of the gardens, lakes and mountains through the glass French doors are unsurpassable.

Upstairs each guest room is unique. Throughout, tiles surrounding the fireplaces often inspired the colors in the fabrics, upholstery, and wallpapers. During the restoration, many of the wallpapers were reproduced based on surviving swatches of the original papers. From a simple, bright family member's bedroom like the East Room, which was once belonged to W. Seward Webb, Jr., to the more elaborately decorated Louis XVI Room, guests can delight in imagining life as it once was. The style of the Louis XVI Room celebrated the French ruler and contains pastel wallpaper and pastel bedspreads. This room was often used by visiting family members, including Lila's mother, Maria Vanderbilt, who enjoyed the formal decor.

Lila's room, Overlook, is so named because of its views of her beloved gardens. The bedroom furniture in Dr. Webb's adjoining room belonged to William Henry

Vanderbilt and was shipped from New York to Shelburne following Vanderbilt's death. The wallpaper in this room is a dark and elegant William Morris pattern. The Brown Room, once Vanderbilt Webb's bedroom, contains a collection of marquetry pieces with holly and sycamore inlaid in mahogany. The Dutch Room, constructed in 1899 as an addition to the house, was originally a guest room. The mantle of this room has delft tiles, no two alike.

The Inn, lovingly restored and alive with guests, supports programs of a larger venture. Shelburne Farms is now a 1,400-acre working farm, historic site and non-profit environmental education organization whose mission is to cultivate a conservation ethic in students, teachers and the general public by teaching and demonstrating the stewardship of natural and agricultural resources. Shelburne Farms welcomes more than 120,000 visitors annually. Guests are free to participate in school field trips and educator workshops, stroll miles of walking trails, visit the Children's Farmyard and its cheesemaking facility, attend concerts and special events, or tour the historic buildings and landscape. The landscape and buildings of Shelburne Farms are now on the National Register of Historic Places.

• • • • •

Shelburne Farms is located at the junction of Harbor and Bay Roads in Shelburne. The Inn is open from mid-May through mid-October for overnight accommodations, breakfast, dinner, and Sunday brunch. For reservations at the Inn, call: (802) 985-8498. There are five regular property tours daily, walking trails are open year round - weather permitting - and more extensive "tea tours" of the house are offered three times weekly from June -September. The Children's Farmyard is also open from Mid-May through Mid-October. For information about programs, walking trails, property tours and special events, call: (802) 985-8686 or visit the Shelburne Farms website at http://www.shelburnefarms.org. Admission is charged, advance reservations suggested.

Photos courtesy of Shelburne Farms, Shelburne, VT.

A Palace in the Wilderness

The Hampton Mansion of the Ridgelys

TOWSON • MARYLAND

IN MARYLAND'S PICTURESQUE old horse country, a few miles north of Baltimore, stands one of the great post-Revolutionary era mansions, a National Park Service acquisition. Built on a high plateau commanding a ten-mile panoramic view of Baltimore County, Hampton Hall, with its late Georgian architecture, formal gardens and original furnishings, is a unique tribute to one family who lived on the property for eight generations.

Financial contributors to the salvaging and restoration of the estate have included notables such as Mrs. Alisa Mellon Bruce, heiress to much of the fortune of her father, Andrew W. Mellon. In recognition of the faded glory of the thirty-three room house, Mrs. Bruce and others donated the property to the nation, using Hampton as a prece-

The great hall of Hampton. The large portrait, "Lady with a Harp," by Thomas Sully (c. 1818), is of Eliza Ridgely, third mistress of Hampton.

dent to the establishment of the National Trust for Historic Preservation.

The Hampton estate was home to five Charles and five John Ridgelys. The first Charles, known as the Colonel, purchased the property in 1745. Colonel Charles Ridgely established the Northampton Iron Works, a thriving business during the colonial period. His son, Captain Charles Ridgely, made a fortune from the iron works during the revolutionary period, producing cannons and other armaments. He also speculated in confiscated British lands and operated mills, quarries, plantations, and a mercantile business. Immediately after the Revolutionary War, Captain Ridgely began constructing his "Palace in the Wilderness." Hampton Hall, as it was known by the Ridgely family, was built between 1783 and 1790, and was destined to become a future model of self-sufficiency. Before the Civil War, it was the centerpiece of a 24,000-acre agricultural, industrial, and commercial conglomerate. Jehu Howell, a master carpenter, supervised the construction for Charles Ridgely, and was according to newspaper accounts, an "ingenious architect."

Ridgely knew what he wanted - a house to impress and intimidate his contemporaries. Hampton Hall would resemble an English manor, and would include a preeminent dome atop the urn-decorated roofline. Ridgely spent considerable time in England prior to the war, and was familiar with the fashionable Baroque and Palladian-style designs.

When completed, Hampton was one of the largest and most elaborate houses in eighteenth-century America. One hundred and seventy-five feet wide, it is fifty-five feet deep. The center section has three stories, plus a cellar and attic, ornate dormers, and an octagonal cupola that is five stories above ground. Two-story wings extend from each side of the center section. The five-part house is built of stone, with a stuccoed exterior which is naturally pale peach in color.

Some architects are critical of the exterior design, contending that the pillared portico and massive pediment are too large, the pillars spaced too far apart, and the discrepancy in size between the center structure and wings disproportionate. Other architects acknowledge the house as distinctive, a symbol of the evolution from early Georgian design to newer forms. Most agree on the magnificence of the mansion's size and spread, the elegance of the cupola and decorated dormers, and the arresting animation of the finials located above the pediment and corners of the roof.

The great hall of the mansion is fifty-three feet long and twenty-two feet wide. On display here are eighteenth-century English cut-glass chandeliers, Baltimore painted furniture, family portraits, and the Ridgely family crest, displayed in stained glass mounted in fanlights over doors,

The dining room at Hampton.

gilded curtain cornices and curtain pins. A portrait of Eliza Ridgely by Thomas Sully, entitled *Lady With A Harp*, dominates the room. Considered one of the artist's best, it attracted the interest of the Mellon family and the National Gallery of Art in 1944. When representatives visited Hampton to purchase the painting, they were so impressed with what they saw that efforts were made to restore and donate the house to the National Park Service.

Whether the Ridgeleys entertained fifty or more for dinner, or 1,500 persons for an afternoon reception, tables were set up in the great hall. Entertainment often spilled out into the gardens, which were used by family members as an extension of the house. The great hall was also used as a reception room, ballroom, and scene for occasional snowfights among the Ridgely children. It spanned the length of the house, opening to the carriage drive on the north and the formal terraced gardens to the south. A walled family cemetery, with an elaborate classical-style vault remains part of the historic site.

Formal garden at Hampton, south of the mansion. Two greenhouses survive from the 19th century.

The first Ridgely to be buried at Hampton was its builder. A portrait of Captain Charles Ridgely by John Hesselius shows him as a heavy-set man, with a low forehead and the disposition of a successful business mogul accustomed to luxurious living. He served in the Maryland Legislature before and after the war and as a drafter of the State's constitution. Despite his fortune, Ridgely perceived himself to be a man of the people, and was considered a bit of a rabble-rouser.

Ridgely's wife was the former Rebecca Dorsey, a devout Methodist who spent many hours worrying about her husband's apparent lack of religious faith. Family tradition relates that while Captain Ridgely celebrated the completion of his house with a convivial card party and drinking, Rebecca held a prayer meeting to both bless the house and pray for the men's souls.

Ridgely farmed some of his land and kept over 100 slaves for hard labor. The Hampton Estate, which in the early years was composed of 1,500 acres, was kept largely productive in this manner for over three generations, with the upkeep of the family's agricultural, industrial, and mercantile aspects of the estate largely in the family's hands. Three slave quarters survive for architectural study.

Captain Ridgely died of unknown causes, childless, six months after Hampton was completed. The mansion and most of his wealth, including 12,000 acres of property, went to his sister's son, Charles Carnan. To comply with the provisions of the will, the nephew changed his name to Charles Carnan Ridgely. Charles Carnan Ridgely made Hampton a showplace, and used it as a setting for lavish and frequent entertaining.

The combined effect of the formal terraced gardens, English-style landscaped park, commercial orchards, and ponds and streams, created an idyllic setting for one of the country's largest houses. He also bred race horses, entered state politics, and built Hampton up into a self-sufficient economic unit composed of 25,000 acres of land. Charles married Rebecca Dorsey's younger sister, Priscilla, who bore fourteen children between 1783 and 1803, including three sons to carry forward the Ridgely name. Priscilla was responsible for a large and ever-growing household, which included the welfare of indentured servants, over 300 African-American slaves, craftsmen, laborers, and professional staff, including a high-priced gardener and foreign chef.

Rebecca Dorsey Ridgely (1739-1812), wife of Captain Charles Ridgely and first mistress of Hampton Hall. Portrait by John Hesselius, c. 1770.

Charles Ridgely and his wife loved to entertain and found plenty of room for celebration within their household. The house contains four parlors, two on either side of the great hall. Located to the right side of the great hall is the drawing room. Gilded cornices, large looking glasses, marble-topped consoles, and black and gilt painted furniture, all emphasize the formal use of this room. John Finlay of Baltimore, known as the best painted furniture maker in early America, made this suite in 1832. At Christmas time the drawing room was the scene of merriment for slave children. Eliza Ridgely (b. 1828), a later owner's daughter, would decorate the room with greenery and bring in the slave children to say prayers, sing hymns, and receive gifts. An itemized list of these gifts, preserved in the Hampton archives, is used to contrast lives of slave children with those of the Ridgely sons and daughters.

The dining room, located in the southeast corner, was refurbished in "the newest taste" by Charles Carnan Ridgely between 1810 and 1815. Elaborate wallpaper and a Brussels carpet, silk window treatments, copious silver, and French porcelain all bear witness to this owner's grand lifestyle. Grocery bills of this time period do not record the sale of flour, meat, fish, or local pro-

Captain Charles Ridgely (1733-90), first owner and builder of Hampton Hall. Portrait by John Hesselius, c. 1770.

duce; all of these were provided from the farms at Hampton. Exotic food, however, was purchased in abundance; from fine Madeira wine, champagne and other wines, to spices, English cheese and mustard, pineapples, tea and chocolate. Ridgely was said to "keep the best table in America" during his tenure at Hampton.

The house has sixteen bedchambers, six large rooms on the second story, and ten chambers on the third. The southwest bedchamber on the second story, or master bedchamber, is furnished in the style of the late eighteenth century. The room contains numerous examples of Priscilla's domestic accomplishments and Charles Ridgely's scientific interests, and was elaborate enough for Priscilla to entertain friends stylishly when confined throughout her numerous pregnancies. Several generations of Ridgely brides and grooms have etched their names in one of the windowpanes, a feature that lends the room significant added charm.

Priscilla Ridgely died in 1814, leaving eleven surviving children. Soon after her death, Charles Carnan would ascend to the position of state governor, where he would remain for three terms until 1818. He lived as a widower until his death in 1829. Ownership of the estate was then passed on to his second son, John Ridgely, a worldly man in his thirties who did not expect to inherit the estate. John's wife Eliza (b. 1803) was an heiress in her own right and was well-known as the former darling of the Marquis de Lafayette. An accomplished linguist and musician, she traveled widely, frequently acquiring exotic new furnishings for the mansion. Known to be more retiring than his wife, John would frequently escort her and the children to Europe or an American "spa," and then retreat to Hampton to await his family's return.

John and Eliza had five children, two of which survived into adulthood. Their surviving son, the fourth Charles Ridgely, would marry his first cousin, Margaretta Sophia Howard, a granddaughter of Charles and Priscilla Ridgely. Margeretta and Charles were witnesses to the changes wrought at Hampton by the Civil War. The estate was reduced to about 4,000 acres, and the industrial and mercantile interests were gone. Charles died in Rome in 1872, but Margaretta continued to control the estate until her death in 1904. Hampton remained an elegant seat of hospitality during this period, but fell into a decline in the twentieth century.

Helen West Stewart Ridgely, Margaretta's successor, was an author and artist. She greeted life as a challenge, producing two books and over one hundred watercolors, which currently remain in the Hampton collection. Her husband, John Ridgely, son of Margaretta and Charles, disliked automobiles, and prided himself on walking into town for the newspaper and the latest gossip. Similarly, Helen thought electricity was a fad. Despite the fact that Hampton had been lit by gaslight for over fifty years, she refused to allow electric circuitry at Hampton on the grounds that it was dangerous and unsafe. Upon Helen's death in 1929, John Ridgely immediately installed it throughout the mansion.

The twentieth century brought other changes to Hampton. By 1900, the estate had declined to less than 1,000 acres, and there was inadequate income to keep it thriving.

Family members were moving away to resettle, both within and outside of Baltimore. Land was divided to provide homes for John's younger brothers. Labor became expensive and more difficult to obtain. Many family treasures were sold to pay the bills. The garden staff was reduced, and some of the formal gardens levelled to grass.

John Ridgely died in 1938, and was succeeded by his son, John Jr., who soon came to recognize the futility of any further efforts to maintain the estate. In a last ditch effort to save the estate, John Jr. sent his eldest son to Newport, hoping he would marry an heiress. John III, however, fell in love with a registered nurse from New York, and lived happily ever after in modest style. John III and his wife served in the Army during World War II and by the time their service ended, negotiations were already underway to transfer Hampton to the American people as a national park.

Today, a friends' group, Historic Hampton, Inc., assists the National Park Service in preserving and interpreting the remnants of the Hampton estate, including the mansion, privies, ice house, Orangery and garden structures, as well as the home farm. The c. 1720 farmhouse, three slave quarters, barns and a dairy contrast the former lives of slaves and hired help with that of the big house. A large collection of original furnishings and artwork, formal gardens, and extensive archives provide a detailed, accurate glimpse of three centuries on an American estate in the English country house tradition.

• • • • •

Hampton National Historic Site is located at 535 Hampton Lane, off Dulaney Valley Road (State Road 146), at Towson, MD. Hampton may be reached from Baltimore via exit 27B of Interstate 695. The mansion is open daily from 9:00 a.m. until 5:00 p.m., excluding Thanksgiving, Christmas, and New Year's Day. Tours of the mansion are conducted on the hour until 4:00 p.m. Admission is charged. For further information call:(410)823-1309, or visit the Hampton website at http://www.nps.gov/hamp.

Photos courtesy of Hampton National Historic Site

A Prelude to the Gilded Age

The Lockwood-Mathews Mansion

NORWALK • CONNECTICUT

BY 1863, the American Civil War was in its second year. President Lincoln had freed the slaves with his Emancipation Proclamation and delivered his Gettysburg Address at a battleground cemetery in November. It was also the year that LeGrand Lockwood, a New York investment banker, returned to his boyhood home of Norwalk to purchase land on which to build his summer "cottage." The *New York Sun*, upon completion of Lockwood's vacation home, would designate it "the most magnificent country seat in America."

LeGrand Lockwood and his wife, Ann Louisa, were American trendsetters of their day. Lockwood was recognized as a business leader in New York society, renowned for his integrity and philanthropy. His successful promotion of the sale of U.S. war bonds abroad, as well as his involvement in the railroad and steamship business, made him one of the country's first millionaires.

Lockwood married nineteen-year-old Ann Louisa Benedict in 1842. She too was born in Norwalk where her father, Seth Williston Benedict, had published a local paper, the *Gazette*. At the time of the couple's wedding at the Presbyterian Church on Allen St., Mr. Benedict was publisher of another paper, the *New York Evangelist*. The couple produced eight children, six of whom lived to adulthood. Lockwood's three eldest sons, LeGrand Jr., Williston and Henry Benedict, went on to join their father in the brokerage and banking business.

To fulfill his architectural fantasy, Lockwood engaged the services of one of the foremost architects of the time, Detlef Lienau (1818-1887), who had trained in Munich and Paris before moving to the United States in 1848. More than three decades before the famous

The entrance hall features four pillars and four pilasters of Florentine marble on poryphyry bases. The custom-made mantel of English and American walnut reaches almost to the ceiling.

mansions of Newport and Long Island's "Gold Coast," Lienau introduced the style of building that would typify the American Gilded Age. Commissioned to design a summer house unequaled in America, Lienau chose the latest and most fashionable style, that of the French Renaissance Revival. He combined a classic plan with contemporary European and American features, and satisfied the Victorian demand for the picturesque by including two turrets and a large verandah.

The mansion Lienau constructed included the finest Italian marbles, exotic ebony and rosewood, and specially designed Aubusson carpets. Completed in 1868, the entire project cost Lockwood nearly two million dollars. A staff of gardeners were utilized to landscape the grounds which contained greenhouses, an arboretum, grape arbors, a large orchard, a small lake, and a carriage house large enough to contain seventeen carriages.

A number of European artists and artisans were selected from Europe to work on the Lockwood's new home. Stonemasons and woodworkers from Italy arrived aboard the same ships that transported rare varieties of wood and marble in the holds. During construction, these craftsmen lived in outbuildings located on the property. Stonecutters earned $1.00 a day, woodworkers 50 cents a day, in an era when a trained artisan, like a blacksmith, might make $14.00 a week.

One worker's fate was unusually tragic. A story in the *New York Sun* on October 2, 1869 tells of "A terrible accident resulting in the death of Mr. Samuel Stevens on the premises of LeGrand Lockwood . . . A large bed of mortar had been mixed, which had become frozen and hard on the surface . . . on Friday morning, Mr. Stevens went for the mortar as usual, when the bed caved in and buried him up. He was soon dug out but life was extinct . . ."

Constructed of granite from nearby Branford, CT, the mansion was designed in the shape of a Greek cross; four arms of equal length, with the arms filled in. In the center of the house a great octagonal rotunda rises forty-two feet to a skylight and acts as a light well, bringing natural light into the center of the building. LeGrand Lockwood made sure the house was also equipped with the latest technology of the day, including a central air heating system, gaslights, plumbing, and up-to-date burglary devices. All of these systems are still intact and evident.

The Lockwoods and Lienau also worked closely with the cabinetmakers who designed the interiors of the house. A pair of wooden doors opens into a vestibule painted in dun, with accents of coral and blue, and a groined ceiling of pale blue. A second pair of doors with etched glass panels leads to the entrance hall, with its four great columns and four pilasters of Florentine marble on porphyry bases. A great carved mantelpiece of English and American walnut with finely carved caryatids dominates one side of the room which originally held two sculptures by Joseph Mozier: *Pocahontas* and *The Wept of Wish-Ton-Wish*, part of Mr. Lockwood's art collection. To the right another great pair of doors leads to the library designed in the Renaissance Revival style by Leon Marcotte, a former business associate of Detlef Lienau. At that time, the room featured a Turkish divan on one wall, four great bookcases of English and American walnut, and another magnificent fireplace, which are still part of the decoration. On the west side of the library, Lienau added a semicircular conservatory, with glass panels painted in a pattern of deep blue fleur-de-lis, which can be closed off with a pair of great pocket doors, also incorporating etched glass panels.

An ingenious pair of pocket doors leads to the music room, designed in the neo-Grec style by Christian A. Herter (1839-1883) and Gustave Herter (1830-1892), famed designers to notables Mark Hopkins, J.P. Morgan and William Henry Vanderbilt. The music room walls are painted a pale lavender and bordered with a classical pattern of laurel leaves. The ceiling incorporates musical motifs which are echoed by the marquetry of the doors. Above the Italian marble mantelpiece, a panel of etched glass depicting the Roman goddess Pomona allows light to stream in from the great rotunda. The original carpet of this room was woven in France, as were all the carpets on the first floor.

A central feature of the mansion is located in the drawing room, also designed by Herter Brothers. This room contains a magnificent ceiling painting, *Venus at Play with her Cupids* by the French artist Pierre-Victor Galland, who also created the etched-glass *Pomona* panel in the music room, two painted panels in the library, and the wall paintings in the small octagonal card room which opens off of the drawing room.

The dining room was designed by New York cabinetmaker George Platt, and features a carved wooden mantelpiece and an eight-foot mirror, designed to reflect a pair of gas chandeliers which once illuminated the room. Many of the dining room motifs, both carved and painted, represent the harvest, the vintage or the hunt. The room originally held two circular tables, one of which could be extended to seat twenty-four. The second smaller table was probably used by the family and is now located near a bay window in the room. It currently displays part of the museum's decorative arts collection of china, glass and silverware, as well as other period artifacts, including candle-shades, linens and serving pieces.

The great central rotunda, with its magnificent parquet floor of five different woods, was designed to house Mr. Lockwood's private collection of paintings and sculptures, which included works by some of the finest artists of the Dusseldorf and Hudson River Schools. Mr. Lockwood was considered a major patron of the arts. He frequently sponsored the travel activities of artists and commissioned such works as Albert Bierstadt's *The Domes of the Yosemite*. In addition, Lockwood owned works by the contemporary Arctic painter William Bradford, the nineteenth-century American landscape painter Jaspar Cropsey, and William Sidney Mount, one of the first and best American genre painters.

A grand staircase with 250 carved and inlaid balusters rises on the north side of the rotunda to a landing. It then divides to reach the second floor, where bedroom suites, each decorated in a specific style and color scheme by Herter Brothers, and a family sitting room are located. The grand staircase presents a sweep that architectural experts have termed "unparalleled in American domestic architecture." The former children's rooms, nursery and a children's theater once occupied the third floor, which is no longer open to the public.

Unfortunately, the Lockwoods were not able to enjoy their country seat for very long. Before the house was fully furnished, Mr. Lockwood suffered the loss of his extensive fortune in the gold crash of September 24, 1869, known as Black Friday. To reestablish his business and help pay off business debts, Lockwood mortgaged the great house in Norwalk. Sadly, he died of pneumonia less than three years later, leaving as survivors his wife, four young children and two grown sons.

Mr. Lockwood's mortgage had already passed on to the Lake Shore and Michigan Railroad, then controlled by Commodore Vanderbilt. Mrs. Lockwood sold her hus-

The library at Lockwood-Mathews mansion was designed in the Renaissance Revival style by Leon Marcotte. The parquet floor is made of eight different woods.

band's art collection in the spring, and the furnishings at auction the following October. The following year, the house and property were advertised for sale. Several New York papers speculated on possible new owners, including Cardinal McCloskey, the Catholic Archbishop of New York. However, there was no sale, and Mrs. Lockwood was unable to make a final payment of $80,000. The Railroad foreclosed and Mrs. Lockwood returned to live in Manhattan with her son LeGrand, Jr., and his wife. In 1876, the property was purchased by Charles Drelincourt Mathews, a provision merchant from Staten Island, who moved into the house with his wife Rebecca and their four children. Mr. Mathews, like Mr. Lockwood, was a man of great integrity and business acumen, as well as taste and culture. He greatly prized his new possession, and made very few changes to the house. He did, however, paint the great rotunda a deep Pompeiian red, and added a classical Greek key border to the walls.

Mr. Mathews made a concerted effort to acquire furniture and other items on a par with the former owners. He obtained matching French wallpaper to cover bare spots on the library walls revealed by the removal of furniture. He was also able to reacquire the original bookcases. He ordered a library table from Leon Marcotte to match the carvings, metal bosses and strapwork ornamentation of the library mantelpiece. Mathews contacted Mrs. Lockwood to purchase the original Aubusson carpets for the drawing room, the dining room, the music room and the second floor Moorish sitting room. He even consulted noted landscape designer Frederic Law Olmsted (1822-1903) for ideas on completing the grounds.

Like Mr. Lockwood, Mr. Mathews did not enjoy his prize for long. In 1879, while his family was traveling in Europe, he died in Norwalk, probably of a stroke. His funeral was held in the mansion upon the family's return two weeks later. The family continued to use the house in all but the coldest months, while maintaining residences in Manhattan. Florence Mathews, the last member of Charles D. Mathews' family to inhabit the house, died in 1938.

The City of Norwalk purchased the property from Miss Mathews' estate in 1941 for use as a public park. Following a final auction of the contents, the mansion and the outbuildings were later used for offices and

The conservatory, destroyed by a falling tree, has been completely restored.

storage during World War II. Community meetings were also held in the mansion until 1950, when the house was declared a fire hazard and closed to the public. In 1955, the Connecticut Turnpike acquired the southern end of the property, and a police station was built on the east side of the park. When threatened with demolition, the mansion made headlines in the early 1960s, as a number of concerned local preservationists, known as the Common Interest Group, succeeded in saving the building. In 1965, the Junior League of Stamford-Norwalk was granted a lease on the building for the purpose of restoration, and in June 1967, the building was opened as a museum. The mansion was designated a National Historic Landmark in 1971, cited as "the most sumptuous private home built in America up to that time. . . a prelude to the opulence of the Gilded Age."

In the years since the establishment of the museum, significant restoration and conservation work has been accomplished. Curators at the mansion have actively and successfully sought return of objects and furnishings sold at both the Lockwood and Mathews auctions, and descendants of both families have generously donated a number of heirlooms. Of central importance to the mansion is the preservation of the original decoration and interior design of the 1860s. Visitors to the mansion will also be intrigued by a remarkable collection of nineteenth and early twentieth-century musical boxes, currently on loan from the Musical Box Society International. The mission of the Lockwood-Mathews Mansion Museum is to preserve the building while creating educational programs on the material, artistic, and social culture of the Victorian era. Annual summer exhibits on these issues have explored such themes as the position of Northern women in the Civil War, daily life in a Victorian mansion, and children's role in Victorian Society. The building may also be familiar to many people as the setting for two films of the 1970s: *The House of Dark Shadows* and *The Stepford Wives*.

• • • • •

The Lockwood-Mathews Mansion Museum is located at 295 West Avenue, Norwalk CT., just off I-95 (exit 14 northbound, exit 15 southbound). The mansion is open for guided tours of the first two floors from mid-March through December; Wednesday through Sunday from 12:00 to 5:00 p.m. From January to mid-March, the museum is open during the week by appointment only. The museum is closed on Mondays, Tuesdays, President's Day, Thanksgiving, and Christmas. There is an admission fee of $8.00 for adults, and $5.00 for seniors and students. Members and children under twelve are admitted free of charge. For further information call: 203-838-9799 or visit the mansion website at http://www.norwalk.com/mansion.

Photos courtesy of The Lockwood-Mathews Mansion Museum of Norwalk, Inc.

Romanov Treasures and Capitol Splendor

Marjorie Post's Hillwood

WASHINGTON • D.C.

NESTLED IN AN EXQUISITE twenty-five acre site in the northwest quadrant of Washington, D.C., is the palatial residence of Marjorie Merriweather Post, former businesswoman, socialite, philanthropist and art collector. Named Hillwood after her former Long Island home, the mansion reflects a gracious way of life long associated with successful Americans earlier in this century. Yet Hillwood is also a museum, the original accomplishment of a passionate art collector whose famed pursuit of some of Russia's greatest masterpieces would make her a legend in the art world. It now houses the largest collection of imperial art objects outside of that country.

The only child of C.W. Post, inventor of the coffee substitute Postum and Grape-

Hillwood 237

The foyer of Hillwood features portraits of Russian tsars and tsarinas. To the center is a portrait of Catherine the Great by Dimitrii Levitskii (1735-1822).

Nuts cereal, Marjorie would be known throughout most of the twentieth-century as the world's wealthiest woman. She was born in Springfield, Illinois, on March 15, 1887, the daughter of Charles W. Post (known as C.W.) and Ella Merriweather Post. Her father, who became gravely ill when she was three years old, responded so well to the vegetarian diet prescribed by his Christian Science caretakers that he immersed himself in finding ways to help others. After purchasing an inn outside Battle Creek, Michigan, C.W. began experimentation with grains, bran and molasses, and in 1895 perfected a coffee substitute he dubbed Postum. Soon after, C.W. also developed a new high-fiber breakfast food he named Grape Nuts. From Grape Nuts and Instant Postum he made a fortune that Marjorie later parlayed into the General Foods Corporation with its Jell-O, Swan's Down Cake Flour, Minute Tapioca, Baker's Chocolate, Log Cabin Syrup, Maxwell House Coffee, Birdseye Frozen Foods and other items.

In 1905, the beautiful and sought-after Marjorie married Edward B. Close, who went to work for her father's company. They had two daughters, Adelaide, born in 1908, and Eleanor, born eighteen months later. To pass time, Marjorie studied art and architecture courses at a nearby private school. Marjorie's attempt at domestic bliss was soon overturned, however. In 1912 her mother died in her sleep; two years later, the severely depressed C.W. committed suicide, leaving the twenty-seven-year-old

The Louis XVI drawing room contains original 18th century French furniture. Beauvais tapestry on right.

Marjorie a multi-millionaire and sole heir to the Postum Cereal Company. The distraught Marjorie soon became consumed in a whirlwind of business-related activities and a move to one of the finest mansions on New York's prestigious Fifth Avenue, then known as Millionaire's Row.

In 1919 Marjorie's marriage to Close came to an end. This was followed by marriage to Wall Street financier Edward F. Hutton in 1920. They had one daughter, Dina, known in later years as Dina Merrill, the actress. The Hutton marriage made Mrs. Post an aunt of Barbara Hutton, the Woolworth five-and-dime heiress. Mr. Hutton became board chairman of General Foods in a marriage that would be celebrated in the nation's highest social circles. It was at this stage in her life that Marjorie began acquiring art objects, including French furniture from such leading New York dealers as Duveen and paintings from Wildenstein and Company. Under the recommendation of Duveen, Marjorie documented her new treasures, illustrating her growing seriousness as a collector.

At a time when Mr. Hutton was criticizing President Franklin D. Roosevelt and Mrs. Post was praising him, the marriage broke up, ending Mr. Hutton's connection with General Foods. In 1935 Mrs. Post married Joseph E. Davies, who was to become U.S. Ambassador to the Soviet Union and other nations. Roosevelt's decision to send Davies to the Soviet Union was a calculation that involved the pairing of an American with cunning negotiation skills accompanied by a wife who symbolized the essence of capitalism.

Disappointed at first in her husband's new position, Mrs. Post soon adjusted to her new lifestyle abroad, becoming the chatelaine of the U.S. embassy in Moscow from 1936 to 1938. Enthralled with Russia's exotic culture, it was then that she began collecting great Russian artifacts, icons, jewels, and other treasures. She found many of the items under dust in warehouses, where they had lain since their expropriation from Russian Imperial families. Available to Mrs. Post and her husband were such exotic pieces as silver niello boxes, enameled kovshi from Moscow, and pieces of imperial porcelain. Mrs. Post was greatly excited by her new hobby, which would soon grow into her lifelong passion.

Following a divorce from Davies in 1955, Mrs. Post purchased Abremont in Washington, D.C. - originally built in 1922 for Mrs. Parsons Erwin - enlarging it and transforming it into a thirty-six room mansion. Mrs. Post would rename the three-story Georgian structure Hillwood, after a former estate she once owned in Roslyn, Long Island. She moved there in 1957, just before her marriage to Mr. May, her fourth husband.

Hillwood, Mrs. Post's final home, was designed by New York architect Alexander McIlvaine. New York decorators McMillen, Inc., were chosen as the principal interior decorators. Former clients of Eleanor McMillen Brown, the last of the old guard decorators, included such notables as Henry Ford, Doris Duke, and Jacqueline Kennedy Onassis. As early as 1952, Mrs. Post had decided that her growing collection of fine and decorative art should be preserved for future generations; therefore she had the mansion reconfigured to function not only as a home for grand entertaining but also as a future museum.

The mansion's rooms are logically articulated to provide excellent circulation for entertaining. Guests enter the home facing an opulent two-storied foyer with a sweeping staircase. Displayed on the walls are portraits of tsars and tsarinas. Transversing the foyer is a regal hall decorated with French eighteenth-century paintings, furniture and imperial Russian objects. The hall leads to Hillwood's formal display and entertaining rooms. A porcelain display next to the French dining room features eighteenth-century French Sèvres soft-paste porcelains; and at the opposite end of the hall, next to the small Russian Icon display Room, is a hexagonal space with displays of imperial Russian porcelains.

Included also on the first floor are four large spaces for entertaining. These include a dining room, paneled with

The Icon Room at Hillwood Museum features rare Russian icons and liturgical items and over ninety decorative objects by Karl Fabergé (1846-1920).

original eighteenth-century French boiseries, an English Georgian-style pine-paneled library, a French salon or drawing room displaying three eighteenth-century Beauvais tapestries designed by François Boucher, and a pavillion designed in an early nineteenth-century classical style that was used by Mrs. Post for dancing or showing movies. Smaller rooms on the first floor include a treasury or "cabinet of curiosities" for the display of Russian icons, liturgical objects and Fabergé bibelots, as well as a beautifully scaled breakfast room that was based on a similar room from her New York apartment.

The second floor of the mansion contains Mrs. Post's regal Louis XVI style bedroom suite, two guest bedrooms-one decorated in English eighteenth-century Adams style

Marjorie Merriweather Post (unfinished portrait by Douglas Chandor).

and the other in English-Georgian, a small pine-paneled library, and various spaces for supporting Mrs. Post's lifestyle. The third floor originally contained living quarters for her female staff of servants, but now houses climate controlled art storage, conservation laboratories, a photography laboratory and various office spaces to maintain current museum function.

Conscious that eighteenth-century Russians usually decorated their palaces with a mix of European and native pieces, Mrs. Post intentionally combined French and other European furnishings with her Russian ones to create an appropriate balance. Her home reflects the profusion of a serious collector. Displayed throughout the mansion is her extensive collection of over 16,000 art objects. Extremely particular about what she chose, Mrs. Post's criteria was to purchase objects of exceptional beauty, superb craftsmanship and important historical associations. Among her numerous treasures are over ninety objects by Karl Fabergé including two imperial Easter eggs, one of the largest collection of French Sèvres porcelain in America, Russian Orthodox liturgical objects including an extensive icon collection, and the largest holding of Russian eighteenth- and nineteenth-century porcelains outside of Russia. One of her final acquisitions was a gold chalice commissioned by Catherine the Great in 1791 for a monastery in St. Petersburg. Studded with thousands of diamonds and eight cameos, it stands out as one of the finest Russian Orthodox chalices ever created.

Parallel to the elegance of her mansion, Mrs. Post also insisted that the grounds of her estate be elegantly landscaped. She hired the fashionable landscape architectural firm of Innocenti and Webel to design a series of pleasure gardens, or outdoor rooms, which on warm days she used to extend her entertaining spaces. Among the specialized gardens, there is a formal French-style parterre adjoining her interior French drawing room, a lunar-shaped garden overlooking a spectacular view of the Washington Monument, and a sunken Japanese-style garden designed by the noted landscape architect, Shogo J. Myaida. Possessing a great love of flowers, Mrs. Post also created a large cutting garden with an adjoining greenhouse for growing orchids and tropical plants. To complement this setting, Mrs. Post also added various auxiliary buildings, most notably a one-room adaptation of a Russian country house, or dacha. It is now filled with rare Russian decorative objects acquired by her good friend Madame Augusto Rosso.

In her final years, Mrs. Post generously prepared the way to donate Hillwood mansion to the public as well as her remaining properties, Mar-A-Lago and Camp Topridge in New York State's Adirondack Park region. In 1969, Hillwood was accepted by the Smithsonian Institution with the understanding that she would have life tenancy. However, three years following her death in 1973, the Smithsonian returned Hillwood to the foundation she established due to operational complexities. In 1977, Hillwood was opened to the public by the Marjorie Merriweather Post Foundation, under the leadership of her daughter, Adelaide Riggs. It now remains the sole monument to Mrs. Post.

Mrs. Post's single desire in life was always to be surrounded by sheer, resounding beauty - a feat she managed to accomplish in every one of her properties. However, at Hillwood she created her last and great masterpiece. Today it is open as a museum. There are currently a total of thirteen structures on the grounds including a café, gift shop, library and additional exhibits. Hillwood Museum and Gardens is accredited by the American Association of Museums.

• • • • •

Hillwood is located at 4155 Linnean Avenue, near Connecticut Avenue, in Washington, D.C. The museum and gardens are undergoing restoration and are temporarily closed to the public until the fall of 2000. During the period that the museum is closed, Hillwood's educational and travel programs, library, and on-line museum shop will continue to operate. Further information may be obtained by calling Hillwood at:(202)686-8500, or visiting the museum website at http://www.hillwood-museum.org.

Photos courtesy of Hillwood Museum, Washington, D.C.

The Orange Grove Haven of the "Blue Boy"

Henry E. Huntington's Treasure-Trove

SAN MARINO • CALIFORNIA

FEW MANSIONS IN THE ENTIRE WORLD offer the impressive array of treasures the Huntington does. The home of former transportation magnate Henry E. Huntington, the site features one of the most important private art collections in the world, a library which spans ten centuries of British and American history and literature, and a 130-acre botanical garden. Located eleven miles from Los Angeles in the foothills of California's Sierra Madres, this Georgian-style palace is considered to be the owner's biggest stride toward immortality.

Henry Edwards Huntington was born on February 27, 1850, in the small town of Oneonta in the Susquehanna Valley of Central New York State. A direct descendant of religious philosopher Jonathan Edwards, Henry was also directly related to members of the Continental Congress, generals in the American Revolution, and a signer of the Declaration of Independence. Yet despite Henry's impressive pedigree, his family was of modest financial circumstances. Solon, Henry's father, supplied the needs of the farming community with his general store, while his mother Harriet devoted her energies to the upbringing of seven children - three of whom would die before Henry was ten. A cheerful boy, Henry is known to have had his first experience as an entrepreneur at age eight or nine when he built a covered booth to sell lemonade and peanuts.

The emergence of Mr. Huntington as a shrine builder had a dynamic background. In 1870 when Henry was twenty years old, he took a job as a porter in a New York City hardware store rather than go to college. Big fortunes were being made in business after the Civil War and he wanted to get started in one of his own while he was still young. Tireless and meticulous, he soon was promoted to a clerkship, and in time moved on to the ownership of a sawmill. After these jobs he went to work for his uncle, Collis P. Huntington, in the development of the Chesapeake, Ohio & South Western Railroad, the Kentucky Central Railroad and other lines. When he was forty-one years old, Henry joined Collis in San Francisco to manage the Southern Pacific Railroad and to develop street transportation systems in San Francisco and Los Angeles.

As though he had undertaken to prove the wisdom of Horace Greeley's well-known advice to young men, Huntington went on to become a director of sixty corporations on the West Coast and a dominant power in politics. Although kind and gentle with his friends, he was known to be shrewd and ruthless in business. Revered in California, Henry was given much of the credit for its economic boom between 1900-1910. The street railways were known as "Mr. Huntington's lines" and all extensions and improvements were attributed to "Mr. Huntington."

Mr. Huntington gained his first fortune by earning it. He gained another by inheritance from his uncle Collis in 1900, who left one-third of his $50 million dollar estate to his nephew. He gained a third by marrying his uncle's widow, Arabella Duval Huntington, in 1913, six years after divorcing his first wife Mary, who was the mother of his four children. Marriage to Arabella meant a merger of the fortunes Henry had variously earned, inherited and married. Although the union created some family tensions and sensational headlines: "Bride is an Aunt of Husband"- the new couple were extremely compatible, particularly in their passion for the art world, where Arabella was already known as one of the most important collectors of her generation.

While traveling through the Los Angeles area in 1892, Mr. Huntington had visited The San Marino Ranch, owned by J. de Barth Shorb. The view of the sunset from the south verandah, overlooking the San Gabriel Valley, made a lasting impression upon him. To the north of the ranch could be seen the majestic Sierra Madre range of mountains, with Mount Wilson, Mount Lowe and Old Baldy. To the south was the rolling countryside of citrus trees and fields of hay and grain; to the southeast, a panoramic view of the Whittier hills.

*The main hall of the Art Gallery, with the bronze statue Diana Huntress, c. 1782,
by Jean-Antoine Houdon (1741-1828).*

The name "San Marino" was first used on the West Coast by Mr. Shorb, who called his estate The San Marino Ranch because his grandfather had owned a plantation of that name in Frederick County, Maryland. Shorb's grandfather had used the name because he was fond of the tiny independent San Marino nation in the mountains of Italy.

As the years passed, Mr. Huntington became convinced that someday Southern California would be a cultural center of the world. Certain that it was his favorite place to live, he bought vast properties there. In 1902 he purchased 550 acres of The San Marino Ranch, part of which was in Pasadena. While he still spent considerable time in the East on business, Henry's affections for his adopted state grew.

Rough sketches for the San Marino

The moon bridge in the Japanese garden.

The mausoleum of Henry and Arabella Huntington by John Russell Pope (1874-1937), one of America's most distinguished architects.

The Huntington Library, exterior view.

mansion Huntington hoped to build were made in 1905 by E.S. Code, a railroad engineer. In 1906 Mr. Huntington hired Myron Hunt and Elmer Grey of Los Angeles as architects for the mansion. The Shorb house, a Victorian structure built in 1878, was razed and its lumber used for six houses of workmen. The Huntington mansion began to rise on the site of the old residence. It was completed in 1910 but Mr. Huntington did not continuously occupy it until 1914, after marriage to Arabella and his first trip to Europe. By that time he had decided to strengthen and remodel the second floor for some of the heavy works of art he was collecting.

The design of the building, called "modified Georgian" by the planners, is similar to that used for small palaces in England and France in the eighteenth century. The house has three floors and the exterior is of white cement, with black iron railings, Georgian pillars, red-tile roofs and terrace floors, marble steps, and three-foot cement urns containing evergreens. The width of the house, with its covered portico, is 344 feet.

On entering the great hallway, visitors see a broad double stairway of marble, which swoops upward in two directions. There is also an elevator. The overall structure of the building has changed little over the years, yet former living quarters on the first and second floors have all been converted into galleries. The first floor originally contained a drawing room, library, terrace, dining room, kitchens and service rooms. The focus of this floor is now the main gallery, which showcases a group of twenty full-length portraits created between 1770 and 1780 by Sir Joshua Reynolds, Thomas Gainsborough, George Romney, Thomas Lawrence, John Constable, William Hogarth, Sir Henry Raeburn, Gilbert Stuart, Benjamin West and J. M.W. Turner. Many leading painters of the French "ancien régime" are now represented on the second floor, which once contained seven bedrooms with marble fireplaces, six master baths, sitting rooms and dressing rooms, as well as seven servants' rooms and baths. Galleries on this floor now contain works by Boucher, Fragonard, Drouais, Greuze and Prudhon. The third floor contains ten rooms, which are now closed off to the public and used as an art reference library.

The northeast section of the huge basement once contained a large wine cellar. Mr.

Huntington owned the San Gabriel Winery, which he obtained in a land deal, and he kept large supplies of its product in hogsheads, as well as rare vintage wines from France. He drank little of the wine himself but served it liberally to guests.

Mr. Huntington was a naturally frugal man but he permitted no scrimping in the construction of the mansion. All interior woodwork received six to ten coats of paint, each rubbed smooth before the next one was applied and the final coat of enamel rubbed with pumice and rottenstone to produce a satin finish.

One of the extravagances at San Marino was a railroad spur to the door of the mansion that enabled Mr. Huntington to ride from his home to Grand Central Terminal in New York without leaving a private car. He had three private cars at the estate and a big concrete garage to keep them in. The cars were called the "Alabama", "San Marino No. 1", and "San Marino No. 2." Often Mr. Huntington would ride in one of them and have another one attached to the same train for servants, baggage and some of the statues and paintings that he was transporting across the country.

Mrs. Huntington, who liked birds, had an aviary at the mansion with twenty-six varieties of parrots and sixty-five other species of birds, including blue-crowned Victorian pigeons, pheasants and talking mynahs. One of her favorite mynahs made trips to New York with her and Mr. Huntington, talking all the way and apparently enjoying the travel. The couple also built a lily pond for waterfowl, houses for a thousand chickens, as well as garages and stables.

Early in the development of his estate, Mr. Huntington began building an arboretum, cactus garden and vast flower beds with plantings from all the hemispheres in the world. As a director of this work he hired William Hertrich, a young horticulturist from Germany, who laid out the gardens, pagodas, ponds and groves of citrus and redwood trees. Visitors to the museum today can explore over fifteen different gardens containing about 14,000 different kinds of plants as well as distinctive garden sculpture; much dating from the late seventeenth and early eighteenth centuries.

In his search for unusual foliage, Mr. Huntington obtained palms from all parts of the Los Angeles area, as well as from San Diego, Ventura, Santa Barbara, England, Belgium, Germany and Japan. There were ferns from New Zealand, Australia, Mexico, Central America; and cyclamens, primulas, azaleas and rhododendrons from many nations. When Mr. Huntington wanted a Japanese garden, Mr. Hertrich found one in Pasadena whose owner agreed to sell the entire property intact including buildings and bridges. It was bought and in 1911, construction was begun to build terraces, ponds, and paths. The purchase included an authentic five-room Japanese house, a temple bell and moon bridge. In 1968 the garden was expanded with the addition of a Zen garden reached by a zigzag bridge.

Mr. Huntington, wanting a mature forest at once, had fifty-foot trees weighing twenty tons each transplanted, as an ordinary home-builder would put shrubs around a foundation. No heavy tractors or power-shovels were available at that time, so all digging and boxing of the trees had to be done by hand. When one of the trees fell from a truck and interrupted highway traffic for days, Mr. Huntington made a

*Gainsborough's Blue Boy was acquired
by Huntington in 1921.*

decision to build the railroad spur to his home to facilitate further transplants.

Inside the mansion there were many conferences to plan new acquisitions of art objects and books. Participants often included Sir Joseph Duveen, later Lord Duveen of Milbank, who advised Mr. Huntington on art, and Dr. A.S.W. Rosenbach, the bibliophile, who considered Mr. Huntington the biggest private collector of books the world has ever known. House guests also included John D. Rockefeller, Jr. and his family, Prince Paul Troubetskoy, who modeled a bust of Mr. Huntington, shipbuilder Homer Ferguson, New York financier Mortimer Schiff, and Crown Prince Adolf and Prince Louise of Sweden. The Huntington collections began with a focus on eighteenth-century British and French art, and today also feature American art ranging from the early eighteenth century to the early twentieth. The Virginia Steele Scott Gallery, a large skylight gallery opened in 1984, showcases American art painted between the 1740s and 1930s, including works by John Smibert, John Singleton Copley, Walter Kuhn and Edward Hopper.

One of the most important art treasures that Mr. Huntington acquired for the mansion is Thomas Gainsborough's famous painting, the *Blue Boy*, which now hangs in the main portrait gallery of the first floor. Whether the *Blue Boy* rates among the finest paintings in the world is a moot question; certainly it is one of the most popular, being the magnet that attracts the most attention from the 500,000 persons who visit the Huntington mansion every year. It is now flanked by paintings such as Sir Thomas Lawrence's *Pinkie* - a portrait of Sarah Moulton-Barrett - who would have been Elizabeth Barrett Browning's aunt if she had lived to adulthood; and Sir Joshua Reynold's Sarah Siddons as the *Tragic Muse*, generally regarded as one of the artist's greatest works.

French porcelains, European furniture, Renaissance bronzes, statues and primitives are among Mr. Huntington's collection of decorative arts. His first art acquisitions, ten Boucher wall tapestries woven in the royal factory as Beauvais in the reign of Louis XV, are generally considered the most distinguished items now on display. The success of the eighteenth-century French factory was due partly to its wealthy, luxury-loving patrons, but mainly to the superb designs of François Boucher - and Mr. Huntington bought some of the best. The Sèvres porcelains of the Marquise de Pompadour in the collection have blues and greens that stir the enthusiasm of the experts. To protect these and other delicate items from earthquakes, Mr. Huntington had them fastened down securely. The home of his uncle, Collis, had been wrecked in the San Francisco earthquake, with a loss of more than $1,000,000 worth of Rembrandts, Van Dycks, and other art objects.

As a collector, Mr. Huntington distinguished himself at San Marino by acquiring incunabula - venerable volumes printed before 1500. The greatest of these is the Gutenberg Bible, generally considered to be the first important book ever printed with movable metal type. The two volumes of this work are printed on vellum, probably sheepskin, and are bound between heavy wooden boards. Over the boards is stretched the original fifteenth-century stamped leather, held fast by metal bosses. Four hundred bidders sought this work when it was auctioned in New York City in 1911. The bidding started at $10,000 and

Pinki (Sarah Moulton-Barrett) by Sir Thomas Lawrence (1769-1830).

when Mr. Huntington purchased it for $50,000 everybody stood up and cheered.

One of Mr. Huntington's first big book purchases was that of the Henry W. Poor library in 1909, which included 1,600 lots of beautifully printed and bound volumes, illuminated manuscripts and incunabula. Subsequently, he bought more entire libraries, competing with the biggest dealers in the world. His collection also includes an illuminated manuscript of Chaucer's *The Canterbury Tales*, an unsurpassed collection of Shakespeare's early editions, manuscripts of Washington, Jefferson, Lincoln, Walt Whitman, Emily Dickenson, and Charlotte Brontë, and the neatly penned autobiography of Benjamin Franklin, written in his own hand. The library, which includes a wing Mr. Huntington built as a memorial to his wife, is 200 feet east of the old residence.

A perpetual deed of trust for the maintenance of the estate, now reduced to 207 acres, was signed by Mr. Huntington in 1919. The instrument centers the responsibilities within a small board of directors, the first five members of which were Howard E. Huntington, Henry's son by his first marriage; Archer M. Huntington, Arabella's son by her first marriage; Dr. George E. Hale, then the director of the Mount Wilson Observatory; and George S. Patton and William E. Dunn, friends and business associates of Mr. Huntington.

After completing his home, Mr. Huntington joined with friends and neighbors in founding the city of San Marino. He donated much of the property for it, built broad highways and planted its trees and flowers. He also contributed a site for the city hall when incorporation papers were drawn. Under his planning the city became a community of fine homes, ornamental highways and little commerce. In 1926 Mr. Huntington commissioned John Russell Pope (1874-1937), the distinguished New York City architect, to plan a mausoleum for a high knoll of his estate at San Marino. Constructed in the form of a Greek temple, Pope later employed the same design in the construction of the Jefferson Memorial in Washington, D.C. It was under construction when Mr. Huntington died, and he and his wife are now buried there. Except at the estate, Mr. Huntington had tried to avoid the limelight and when asked to write an autobiography he had declared: "No never. This home and library will tell the story. They represent the reward of all the work I have ever done. The ownership of a fine home, a fine collection and a fine library is the swiftest and surest way to immortality."

• • • • •

The Huntington Library, Art Collections, and Botanical Gardens is located twelve miles from Los Angeles, just south of Pasadena. The museum and grounds are open to the public Tuesday through Sunday. It is closed Mondays and most holidays. Hours are 12:00-4:30 p.m. Tuesday-Friday; 10:30-4:30 p.m. Saturday and Sunday. Summer hours (June through August) are 10:30-4:30 p.m. daily, excluding Mondays. Admission is $8.50 for adults, $8 for seniors, and $6 for students. Children under 12 are admitted for free. For further information, contact general information at (626) 405-2141, or visit the Huntington website at: http://www.huntington.org.

Photos courtesy of The Huntington Library.

The Collection of A Lifetime

The Baum-Longworth-Taft House

CINCINNATI • OHIO

KNOWN AS THE first great mansion of the Middle-West, the Baum-Taft house is also one of the oldest surviving wooden structures in Cincinnati. Known today as the Taft Museum, the building was originally erected circa 1820 for the Cincinnati merchant Martin Baum. Significant today for its outstanding collection of paintings, porcelains and decorative arts, the museum's reputation rivals collections established by a select group of millionaires with a similar flair for the ornate, including Isabella Stewart Gardner, Henry Clay Frick, and Henry E. Huntington.

The twenty-room mansion has been owned by several Cincinnati millionaires, including Nicholas Longworth, David Sinton, and Mr. and Mrs. Charles Phelps Taft, whose

The music room, Taft Museum. Charles and Anna Taft were married in this room in 1873. Their portraits now hang above the fireplace.

The dining room, Taft Museum.

strong commitment to both philanthropy and culture transformed the home into the museum showcase it is today. All spoke with pride of the stately Federalist portico with its Tuscan columns and dentilated cornices, and its spacious rooms for entertaining.

Cincinnati was a village of cotton brokers, cattle dealers, Ohio River roustabouts and waterfront brothels when Martin Baum, a native of Maryland, established residence in the city in the early 1790s. A man of significant business acumen, Baum added a sugar refinery, an iron foundry and a steam mill to the small village of ninety-four cabins and ten frame houses. With his economic status seemingly assured, Baum focused on philanthropic pursuits, including the addition of a local college, literary society, and museum to the city.

By 1820, Mr. Baum began to build on Pike Street - not far from the Ohio River - the mansion that the Tafts later acquired. Baum's original design includes many of the same features as Thomas Jefferson's Monticello, a popular style in that era, including a large center hallway, a Federal exterior, and a building site with gentle slopes. The front of the Taft house is one story high, with broad steps rimmed by winding iron railings leading up to a pillared portico with a stately pediment and interesting fanlight that lifts the house out of the ordinary.

In the rear, the house is two stories high, with a porch that could once be reached through exceptionally large triple-sash sliding windows. The design of the house, which features a high center core and low side wings, permits the reception rooms to have very high ceilings and the bedrooms in the wings to have lower ceilings. On the ground floor were the kitchens and housekeeping quarters.

Mystery has surrounded the identity of the mansion's architect. For many years speculation shifted back and forth between Benjamin Henry Latrobe and James Hoban, both highly prominent architects of the nation's capitol. These attributions were later proved un-

The entrance hall of the Taft Museum features murals by Robert S. Duncanson (1821-72).

founded, and it is now believed that the house was the work of local carpenters and masons who worked from architectural handbooks such as those published by Asher Benjamin and Owen Biddle, two well-known builders from Philadelphia.

Mr. Baum's reputation as a mogul of Cincinnati came to an abrupt end in 1825 when a financial debacle forced him to deed the home to the Bank of the United States along with a four-and-one-half-acre tract of land. The bank held the property for a short period of time, during which it served a new purpose as the Belmont Boarding School for Young Ladies. In 1829, another newly-made millionaire came along to buy the residence for reconversion into his private home. His name was Nicholas Longworth, great-grandfather of a future U.S. representative by the same name who would later marry President Theodore Roosevelt's daughter.

For the family he was then rearing, Mr. Longworth bought the mansion Mr. Baum had begun. He also purchased the vineyards that Mr. Baum had laid out on nearby property and made a second fortune in Catawba and Isabella wines.

Records of the period indicate that Longworth "finished" the house, a logical argument considering the distressed financial condition of the original owner. Mr. Longworth enjoyed the arts and so was a patron for Hiram Powers (1805-73), the sculptor, and Robert S. Duncanson (1821-72), an African-American painter. Improvements included the addition of two side wings in the 1830s, an enhanced entranceway, and new

The former parlor of the Tafts' home, the Gray Room, features artwork by the English masters Sir Joshua Reynolds and Thomas Gainsborough.

fireplaces. Duncanson's murals, a series of eight romantic landscapes, launched the young artist's career. Painted in the 1850s, they are among the few mural projects created prior to the Civil War still remaining in their original location. Duncanson's work may be seen today in the entrance hall.

Longworth loved to entertain and his improvements were noted by many, including a variety of presidents, governors and senators who came to the fashionable parties the Longworths threw at their mansion. Nicholas Longworth died in 1863, and by the early 1870s, the house was transferred to David Sinton, a Cincinnati industrialist. Sinton's philanthropic efforts, particularly as a founder of the Cincinnati Art Museum in 1881, established a legacy in the art world that his heirs would perpetuate.

The last private owner, Charles Taft, was the proprietor and publisher of the *Cincinnati Times-Star*. A lawyer and a philanthropist, Charles was also the elder half-brother of William Howard Taft. As such, he provided the guidance and financial backing that historians have said lifted the younger Taft from political obscurity onto the path that led to the White House. On the front steps of Charles Taft's mansion, William Howard Taft accepted the Presidential nomination in July, 1908, followed by some of his most effective political campaigning. Charles Taft became the co-owner of the residence upon his marriage to Sinton's nineteen-year-old daughter, Anna. After their well-publicized marriage, Charles and Anna Taft took up residence with her father in the house on Pike Street, beginning a relationship that would have a strong impact on Cincinnati's future.

The illness and death of David Sinton in 1900 brought great wealth to the Tafts. Sinton, perhaps the richest man in Cincinnati, left an estate valued between seven to

$8,000,000, which fell mostly into the hands of Anna. Besides the majority of the estate, Anna and her husband also inherited the house on Pike Street, which they would remain in and improve over the duration of their lives.

The couple began their mutual career as art collectors on a visit to Europe soon after the death of Mr. Sinton. His death had taken a considerable toll on Anna Taft and neither she nor her husband had "anticipated the extent of her reaction." After her recovery, the couple took a trip to Europe where they acquired "ceramics, rock-crystals, and other objets d'art" before expanding their collection to include paintings. Early in 1903, with the first year of serious acquisition completed, Charles wrote, "Annie and I have about made up our minds that it would be just as well to invest money in pictures as to pile it up in bonds and real estate. At all events, we get a good deal of pleasure out of pictures."

The Taft collection of paintings grew rapidly between the years 1902 and 1927, the year in which the Tafts pledged their museum to the public with a matching gift of $2,500,000 from the citizens of Cincinnati. In all, the Tafts collected over 690 pieces of art, and as the years passed, their reputation as connoisseurs grew. In 1909, the couple placed some of their paintings in exhibits around Manhattan; and in 1919, the King and Queen of Belgium visited the Tafts' home for the purpose of viewing the famous collection. Works the couple collected over the years include important pieces by John Singer Sargent, Jean-Baptiste-Camille Corot, Thomas Gainsborough, James Abbot McNeill Whistler, Anton Mauve, Jan Steen, a collection of watercolors by Joseph Mallord William Turner, and even an authentic Rembrandt. One of the museum's most popular paintings today is *The Song of Talking Wire* by Cincinnatian Henry Farny. The painting features a native American in a winter landscape who has put his ear to that ominous portent, a telegraph pole. It is widely featured in art books and history books across the country.

The Tafts also delighted in collecting European decorative arts. From the Paris art dealer Jacques Seligmann, they acquired a collection of forty-nine seventeenth and eighteenth-century watches. These had formerly been in the possession of a Spanish count, making "quite an addition" to their collection. One of the couple's finest objects from this category of art was one of the last to be bought: a Gothic ivory Virgin and Child (ca. 1260-80) from the Abbey Church of Saint-Denis. A piece that measures just under fourteen inches, it is believed there are only two similar works remaining in the world today. It is the only such piece in the museum's decorative arts collection and is currently on display in the Violet and Gray Room.

The Taft collection also includes 224 pieces of precious Chinese ceramics, including a Chinese ewer in the form of a phoenix mounted in porcelain with silver-gilt mounts from the Ming Dynasty (ca. 1570-80), an intriguing pair of Buddhistic Lions from the Qing Dynasty (ca. 1700-30) and a rare set of Baluster vases, also from that time period. The most extensive collection in the house today, various pieces from this exhibit may be seen throughout the house.

Today, the couple's beloved collection is showcased throughout their former home in a highly accessible manner. The collection of seventeenth and eighteenth-century pocket watches is mounted in a vertical wall case rather than a traditional display table so that details can be seen clearly. Some of the rarest porcelains have been taken out of their traditional cases and displayed without glass, so that no reflections interfere. The rooms have been completely restored and are painted in Federal shades of gray, terra cotta, yellow and green; the colors determined by analyzing paint and wallpaper. Featured throughout the house is Federal furniture from the New England workshops of Duncan Phyfe and his contemporaries, which came from the sale of the Louis Guerineau Myers collection.

The Tafts' role as collectors was only equaled by their role as philanthropists. In a time of increased citywide industrialization, their active involvement in Cincinnati's urban renewal and culture came at a time when many of their wealthy local counterparts were fleeing to the suburbs. Not wanting to move from their home of thirty years, the Tafts instead invested their money in improving the city's environment. Their efforts resulted in the creation of a citywide Park Commission in 1906, a spacious home for local working women in 1909, and the creation of the Cincinnati Institute of Fine Arts (CIFA), which was incorporated as a non-profit organization in 1927. Within the same year, the couple made the decision to bequeath their home and art collection to the board, granting ownership to it upon the couple's deaths.

Charles P. Taft died at his home in late 1929, one year after he completed arrangements with the Cincinnati Institute of Fine Arts to transfer ownership of the Taft house to the public as a museum. Thirteen months later in 1931, Anna Taft, who had remained active after her husband's death, passed away unexpectedly. "The two were inseparable in business, social and philanthropic ventures" noted the *Cincinnati Enquirer*. With Anna's death, the Taft house was officially turned over to the CIFA and opened to the public as a museum in 1932. The house is now a National Historic Landmark and is today considered one of the finest small art museums in America.

• • • • •

The Taft Museum is located at Fourth and Pike Streets, five blocks from the center of Cincinnati. It is open Monday through Saturday from 10:00 a.m. to 5:00 p.m. and from 1:00 p.m. to 5:00 p.m. on Sundays. It is closed Thanksgiving, Christmas and New Year's Day. A nominal admission fee is charged. Further information may be obtained by calling the Taft Museum at: (513)241-0343. Interested parties may also visit the Taft Museum website at http://www.taftmuseum.org.

All photos by Tony Walsh, courtesy of The Taft Museum.

Statesmen, Massacres, Bourbon and Thanksgiving

Berkeley Hundred Plantation

CHARLES CITY • VIRGINIA

BERKELEY HUNDRED PLANTATION sprawls across 1,000 scenic acres along the north shore of the James River. The stream broadens there into a two-mile-wide estuary to become a safe and inviting harbor for small ocean-going ships. The fields beside the river are fertile and attracted the earliest British settlers. Situated in the heart of the South's most concentrated historic area, midway between Williamsburg and Richmond, the plantation has more claims to fame than any such property.

This was the ancestral home of four Benjamin Harrisons who were members of Virginia's ruling House of Burgesses. Also born in the mansion was a fifth Benjamin Harrison, who signed the Declaration of Independence. The mansion later became the birthplace of William Henry (Tippecanoe) Harrison, the ninth President of the United States, whose grandson, another Benjamin Harrison, became the nation's twenty-third President.

Berkeley Plantation can boast to being the site of many important events. Generals of the Revolutionary and Civil Wars made the plantation their headquarters. Once with 140,000 soldiers encamped on the grounds, Berkeley served as headquarters for the Army of the Potomac. The beautiful manor house was later used as a hospital and as a prison for Confederate prisoners of war.

Although some encyclopedias overlook it, Berkeley was the setting for the first official Thanksgiving in America. On December 4, 1619, a weary band of thirty-eight settlers arrived at Berkeley on the ship *Margaret*. After stepping ashore they opened sealed orders carried aboard ship from England. The orders, from the British Crown, instructed the settlers that "the day the ship arrived at the place assigned for the plantation in the land of Virginia shall be yearly and perpetually kept holy as a day of Thanksgiving to Almighty God." Accordingly, the colonists, led by Captain John Woodlief, knelt in prayer and proclaimed a day of Thanksgiving. The word "hundred" was attached to the plantation's name because it symbolized the number of men and women the property could accommodate. The first band of settlers was assigned 8,000 acres.

Former President William Harrison's chambers at Berkeley.
The Harrison family maintained control over the estate from 1691-1846.

Mayflower descendants are known to be shocked by such sacrilegious thinking. When the *Saturday Evening Post* related the Berkeley story, they wrote scathing rebuttals, but Berkeley has a monument to memorialize its Thanksgiving claim and the new York Public Library has documents to substantiate it. One year a Presidential proclamation gave all the credit for Thanksgiving to Plymouth. In November of 1962, the attention of Arthur Schlesinger, Jr., then a White House aide, was called to this controversial debate by irate Virginians. After an investigation he responded that the omission of Berkeley in the proclamation was an unfortunate error. "You are quite right," Mr. Schlesinger wrote in his apology, "I can only plead an unconquerable New England bias on the part of the White House staff. We are grateful to you for reminding us of the Berkeley Hundred Thanksgiving and I can assure you that the error will not be repeated in the future."

Berkeley is also famous for the potent liquor brewed there in the early seventeenth century from cornmash. Later called bourbon, it was first made at the plantation by George Thorpe, an English clergyman. Thorpe wrote back to England that "the concoction is better than British ale, and it does not sicken the mind or body."

In 1691 the Harrison family bought Berkeley; four years later they began construction. They named the waterfront Harrison's Landing and proceeded to build tobacco warehouses, wharves, dry-docks and a thriving shipbuilding business. They also carded wool, tanned hides, made wrought-iron objects and planted fields. Ultimately they controlled 50,000 acres and held 200 slaves.

The present house was completed in 1726 under the supervision of Benjamin Harrison IV, who had the manor house built for his bride, Anne Carter. Anne was the daughter of Robert "King" Carter, of neighboring Carter's Grove Plantation, which is now a property of the Colonial Williamsburg Foundation. Shipwrights supervised Berkeley's construction for the bride and groom, and the rugged construction with hand-hewn timbers and three-foot-thick brick walls would endure for many centuries. The original datestone, which is still visible today, bears the initials of Anne and Benjamin Harrison and the date the house was completed. Tragedy would beset the couple soon after; in 1744, Benjamin and two of his ten children were killed in a thunderstorm. They had gone upstairs to close a front bedroom window to keep out rain. A bolt of lightening struck and killed them all.

The Harrisons were something less than favorites of the British during the American Revolutionary War. When Benedict Arnold, the American traitor, camped near the mansion with British troops; he had all of the Harrison portraits and furniture piled on the front lawn and burned. The Harrisons later restored the house and hosted visits by many famous people, including Presidents George Washington and Abraham Lincoln.

During the American Civil War the plantation was occupied by Union forces led by General George M. McClellan. In 1862, the general displeased the President by not marching on Richmond after several bloody struggles that had discouraged him. Instead, McClellan had settled down with his troops at Berkeley. Slaves had been left there with orders to burn the buildings if Yankees arrived, but they failed to do it.

Gardens at Berkeley. The James River is in the distance.

Confederate cavalrymen and gunboats in the river fired on the mansion, immediately causing damage.

It was during this time that Daniel Butterfield, a general at Berkeley, composed the tune called "Taps." He had long been dissatisfied with the bugle calls the Army had been using. He summoned his staff bugler, a soldier by the name of O.W. Norton. Butterfield whistled a tune that he had improvised. The two men experimented for a few minutes until the haunting melody of "Taps" was produced. General Butterfield ordered it used to signal "lights out" at night. Other commanders heard and adopted it, and later it came into use for military burials.

Balloons were first used in warfare at Berkeley during the Civil War by Professor Lowe, a Scotsman, who rented them to the Army of the Potomac. They were used in July and August of 1862 for observational purposes.

The sixteen-room main house of Berkeley is built in the Georgian style of architecture. It is flanked on either side by two similar buildings. One of the small, well-proportioned brick buildings on the property was the guesthouse formerly used for male visitors, the other housed the kitchen and servants' quarters. The residence stands in a grove of magnolias on a hill overlooking the James River and a bridge named in honor of Benjamin Harrison.

The mansion has the first decorative cornices to appear in Virginia. The red bricks used for construction of the building were made on the property and much of the timber cut there also. Doors and windows are occasionally off center, indicating that the structure was built by eye rather than from detailed drawings. A broad center hall connects all of the downstairs rooms.

The Harrison family ultimately lost control of Berkeley in 1846 as they were unable to pay taxes on the plantation. After the Civil War Berkeley became dilapidated as tenant farmers kept cattle and sheep in the formerly elegant mansion. Fences tumbled and unfertilized fields turned brown. Unwanted, the plantation fell into the hands of receivers until 1907 when the property was purchased by a new owner, John Jamieson.

John Jamieson, a native of Scotland, was an engineer with the New York Port Authority who had worked on the development of the Statue of Liberty in New York Harbor. At the age of ten he had been a drummer boy in General McClellan's Army at Berkeley and had developed a fondness for the plantation. As an adult, he had developed a fondness for its timber, too, and he bought the entire property, reduced to 1,400 acres.

In 1927, John's nineteen-year-old son Malcolm inherited Berkeley. He immediately began work on the restoration of the estate. "The mansion was in terrible shape when I took over," he recalls. "Somebody had even put red paint on the red bricks and it took me weeks to scrub it off." Malcolm Jamieson spent nearly seventy years making the plantation the showplace it is today. He was often called the "Father of the Virginia Plantation County." In 1997 he was honored by the Congress of the United States for "His tireless efforts in the historic preservation of Berkeley Hundred Plantation." John died in November of that year. He is survived by his wife, Grace, who, following their marriage in the 1930s, took over the interior decoration of the plantation.

Berkeley Plantation is now owned by Malcolm's son, Malcolm E."Jamie" Jamieson. Jamie plans to continue the work begun by his father.

• • • • •

Berkeley Plantation is located on State Route 5 near Charles City. It is open to visitors from 9:00 a.m. to 5:00 p.m. daily except Christmas. Admission is $8.50 for adults, $6.50 for students ages 13-16, $4.00 for children ages 6-12. Children under the age of six are admitted free. Discounts are provided to senior citizens, members of the military, and AAA members. Further information can be obtained by calling: (804)829-6018 or by visiting the Berkeley Plantation website at http://www.berkeleyplantation.com.

Photos courtesy of Berkeley Plantation.

Tarheel Elegance

Tryon Palace

NEW BERN • NORTH CAROLINA

BEFORE SAILING for the colony of North Carolina in 1764 with his wife, Margaret Wake Tryon, and his three-year-old daughter, Margaret, newly appointed Lieutenant Governor William Tryon must have planned to build a grand government building. Why else would a temporary replacement for Royal Governor Arthur Dobbs (who wished to make a trip to England) bring along English architect John Hawks?

Whatever Tryon's plans, they were disrupted when he found that Dobbs did not intend to turn the colony over to him for some months. Tryon grumbled in a letter to a friend: "this I own was a Thunderbolt to me." A resourceful man, Tryon spent his time waiting for Dobbs to leave by traveling around the colony, acquainting himself with the people, the land, and the waterways.

Dobbs never made his trip to England. He died in March of 1765 and Tryon succeeded him as governor. By 1766 Tryon had designated New Bern, an eastern North Carolina port town at the confluence of the Neuse and Trent Rivers, as the new capital city.

Before Tryon's time, there was no fixed seat of government in all of North Carolina. The Colonial Assembly met to conduct the business of the government in whatever town was convenient, and state documents frequently had to travel the uncertain roads and rivers between towns. Tryon put an end to this situation. He arranged for his architect, John Hawks, to build the largest and the most elaborate building in the colony. This Government House would serve many functions; the Council (the upper house of the colonial legislature) would meet there, the governor would receive and entertain official visitors there, and the governor's family would live there.

Governor Tryon obtained from the Colonial Assembly of North Carolina a grant of 15,000 pounds, or about $75,000, to begin building the palace in 1767. Finished within three years, the new Government House or palace was constructed of local brick, with pine and cypress timbers felled in nearby forests. Skilled craftsmen were brought to the site from as faraway as Philadelphia and London, as were certain building materials - such as lead, glass, and ironwork - that were not available locally. John Hawks, who trained under the English master-builder Stiff Leadbetter, was the first professionally trained builder and architect to practice in the colony of North Carolina, and one of the few then working in any of the colonies. As his elegant plans illustrate, Hawks brought a knowledge of up-to-date English architecture to North Carolina. With its two flanking dependencies or "offices," the new palace showed a formal Palladian composition, very much in imitation of the finest Georgian country houses then being built in England. The arrangement of the wings, connected to the main building by curved colonnades, created a forecourt where visitors could approach and enter the edifice.

Elegance came at a cost however. The poll and liquor taxes levied to pay for construction of the palace inflamed the sentiments of many North Carolinians, particularly those in the west who were already unhappy with high taxes and corruption in their local governments. Loosely organized under the name "Regulators," these dissatisfied colonists attempted to reform government, but their increasing violence caused Tryon to lead the North Carolina militia against them, defeating them at the 1771 Battle of Alamance.

The Tryons moved into the palace in 1770, and in December of that year hosted "a very grand and noble Entertainment and Ball" to celebrate its completion. Their enjoyment of the home would be short-lived however, for in the following year Governor Tryon was transferred to New York. Josiah Martin, the new royal governor, immediately moved into Tryon Palace and also retained Mr. Hawks to add rooms and auxiliary buildings to it. At the onset of the American Revolution in May of 1775, Martin fled the capital, having already sent his wife and children to New York for safety.

During the Revolution, there was some discussion between the continental army

The Council Chambers at Tryon Palace, from which North Carolina was governed in pre-Revolutionary times.

and the provisional governor about plundering the palace's roof for much needed lead. Although the roof was initially spared, by war's end some "nonessential" lead had been removed. Because the lead may not have been as "nonessential" as the revolutionaries thought, and because of general neglect, the palace slipped into genteel decay. When President George Washington visited New Bern in 1791, he was entertained there but was housed at another residence. He wrote, "Dined with the Citizens at a public dinner given by them; & went to a dancing assembly in the evening; both of which was at what they call the Pallace, formerly the Government House and a good brick building but now hastening to ruin." After 1794, the palace's rooms were used variously for classrooms, meetings, dancing lessons, and storage.

On the night of February 27, 1798, fire swept through the palace. Accounts from the time say the fire began in hay stored in the cellar. The central building was destroyed but townspeople prevented the fire from spreading to the dependencies by pulling down the connecting colonnades. Although the Kitchen Office (east wing) was demolished in the nineteenth century, the Stable Office (west wing) remained standing, and was eventually converted to a residence that remained in use well into the twentieth century.

After the fire, it appeared that the palace was lost to North Carolina forever. In 1800, New Bernian Frederick Beasley wrote to his childhood friend William Gaston, "Shall I begin with talking of the palace? ….I am afraid she will never revive like the regenerated phoenix from the fury of the flame." What was once palace land was divided into lots and a house-lined street soon passed right over the palace's foundations. Soon the building existed only as a memory to North Carolinians.

A movement arose in the 1920s and 30s to reconstruct the palace on its original foundations. With donations and two trust funds totaling well over $1,100,000 from Mrs. Maude Moore Latham, the wife of a prosperous businessman in Greensboro, the plan to rebuild began in earnest after World War II. Mr. and Mrs. John A. Kellenberger, Mrs. Latham's daughter and son-in-law, continued to support the restoration after Mrs. Latham's death in 1951. To bring the palace back to life, the state of North Carolina purchased and removed over fifty buildings from the original property, rerouted Highway 70, and moved the Trent River Bridge.

The walls of the wing that survived the 1798 fire were found to be ninety percent intact, with bricks from the eighteenth century; but the roofs had to be renovated to comply with the original design while all remaining rooms had to be rearranged. Gradually the palace was reconstructed, with walls three feet thick, mahogany doors and shutters and other details modeled on surviving Georgian country houses. Typically British cornices were installed and Italian marble mantels were used where the old plans called for them.

Fragments of the ten original red sandstone steps located at the entrance to the palace were found when the new foundation was built. Stones to match were obtained from an unknown quarry in England. Surviving pieces of the old plaster were also retrieved, which provided the architect with more clues to the appearance of the original interior. Wrought-iron gates imported from an eighteenth-century English home were donated to the reconstructed palace by the Garden Club of North Carolina.

Mrs. Latham's daughter, Mrs. Kellenberger, and the acquisitions committee they

This formal, colonial revival garden honors Maude Moore Latham, the major benefactor of the Palace reconstruction.

The kitchen office wash house recreates the lost world of the servants who worked to maintain the home.

worked with, saw to it that no expense was spared when the palace was furnished two centuries later, and many of the furnishings in the house date back to 1770 or earlier. These include English cut-glass chandeliers, a walnut spinet from London made in 1725 by Thomas I. Hitchcock, antique highchairs, a desk which may have stood in the original palace and a tall clock made in 1736 by Charles Clay. In the first-floor parlor sits a mahogany card table of pierced flower design attributed to William Vile of London. Vile, a contemporary of Thomas Chippendale, was a premier cabinet maker who secured many royal commissions from George II and III and other members of the royal family. The clock, located in the Council Chamber, has chimes and bells that play operatic tunes; it also records the day, the month and the position of the moon. Unlikely to have existed in the colonies at the time the Tryons occupied the palace, the curious timepiece fascinates today's visitors.

No known record exists of the palace's original furnishings; however, when the Tryon's New York home burned in 1773, the family made a complete list of the furnishings that were lost in hopes of being reimbursed. Since the discovery of that list in the 1940s, much effort by curators has been spent recovering items at least similar to those lost in the fire. Tryon listed over 400 books - by short titles only, often with no author's name - and about eighty-five percent of these titles have been acquired in their original, eighteenth-century condition. Besides the expected books on law, history, geography, mathematics, and the classics, Tryon's library included a wide range of timely literature, including Milton's *Paradise Lost* and works by Alexander Pope, Jonathan Swift, John Locke, and Miguel de Cervantes. After the New York fire, Tryon is recorded to have said to his friend William Smith, "I am not much used to reading, but I have made Notes which helped me to References I shall miss."

Landscape architect Morley Jeffers Williams could find no documentation of the garden's original appearance when he created the majestic gardens that surround the palace. It was not until 1991 that a garden plan was discovered in Caracas, Venezuela. John Hawks, who remained in North Carolina after the American Revolution, gave the garden plan drawn by C.J. Sauthier to a South American visitor, Francisco de Miranda, in 1783. Visitors currently enjoy gardens in the Colonial Revival style installed by Morley Jeffers Williams and, as research continues on the gardens of Governor Tryon, they will eventually see gardens that resemble those of the eighteenth century.

One of the most unique features of recent preservation efforts at Tryon Palace is the kitchen office, which recreates the lost world of the servants who worked to maintain the home. The rooms duplicate Hawks' 1767 plans, which show a secretary's office, a kitchen, a scullery, and a wash house on the first floor. Governor Tryon identified the second floor room in a letter as "intended for Servants Chambers, and a Laundry." Today, costumed interpreters cook "the Governor's" meals at the open hearth of the massive kitchen fireplace, using reproduced utensils. The beehive oven, specified by Hawks in his plan, bakes a variety of savory eighteenth-century items.

Since it has reopened in 1959, the reconstructed palace has evolved into Tryon Palace Historic Sites & Gardens, an agency of the North Carolina Department of Cultural Resources charged with presenting the history of New Bern from its first settlement in 1710 through the Reconstruction era. Visitors now tour the John Wright Stanly House (1779), the Dixon-Stevenson House (1830), the Robert Hay House and the New Bern Academy (c. 1806-1810) as well as the palace.

• • • • •

Tryon Palace Historic Sites & Gardens is located on U.S. Routes 17 and 70 and State Route 55 in downtown New Bern. It is open from 9:00 a.m. to 5:00 p.m. Monday through Saturday and from 1:00 p.m. to 5:00 p.m. on Sunday. During the summer months, the hours of operation are extended. The palace is closed on New Year's Day, Thanksgiving Day, and December 24th - 26th. An admission fee is charged. For more information, call: 800-767-1560 or 252-514-4900. Interested individuals may also visit the Tryon Palace website at http://www.tryonpalace.org.

Photos courtesy of Tryon Palace Historic Sites and Gardens.

Christopher Gore's Country Home

WALTHAM • MASSACHUSETTS

JUST NORTH of the Charles River in the suburban Boston community of Waltham, Massachusetts, lies a 45-acre estate of fields, orchards, and gardens, that frames one of the most magnificent Federal mansions in the United States. Built by Christopher Gore and his wife Rebecca in 1806, Gore Place reflects the lifestyle of a wealthy gentleman-politician of New England in the early 1800s. The red-brick mansion is a striking example of neoclassical architecture conceived on a grand scale. The five-part plan is perfectly symmetrical, extending about 200 feet from end to end. The exterior follows very simple lines, while the interior reveals large formal rooms for entertaining and luxurious furnishings. Together, the house and grounds stand out as one of the great estates of the Federal era.

The grand staircase in the formal entrance hall spirals upwards without any visible means of support. Portraits of Gore family members hang on the wall to the right. Photo by David Bohl.

Christopher Gore was born in Boston in 1758, the tenth of thirteen children of Frances and John Gore. John Gore, a successful merchant and artisan, was able to send Christopher to Harvard College, enrolling his son at the age of thirteen (class of 1776). The Gore family exemplifies the political divisions that occurred during the American Revolution. John Gore, a Tory, fled the country after Massachusetts patriots confiscated his property and banished him. An older son, Samuel, joined the Sons of Liberty and participated in the Boston Tea Party. Following his graduation from Harvard, Christopher served in the Continental Army as a clerk with the artillery regiment of his brother-in-law Thomas Craft.

After the war, Christopher Gore chose the law as his profession and apprenticed himself to John Lowell. He was admitted as an attorney to the Bar of Suffolk County and opened his office on State Street in Boston. Gore was unquestionably bright and ambitious, and his practice flourished with the increased demand for legal services brought about by the Revolutionary War. Gore also invested in revolutionary scrip and the many new mills and toll roads that sprang up on rural land west of Boston, greatly increased his wealth.

Marriage in 1785 to the socially prominent Rebecca Armory Payne, the daughter of a wealthy merchant and maritime insurer, cemented Christopher

The parlor features a reproduction of the original "Birds of Paradise" French wallpaper and a portrait of Rebecca Gore by John Trumball (1756-1843). Photo by David Bohl.

Gore's place in Boston society. Rebecca's dowry helped the couple make their first purchase of land in Waltham. They gradually enlarged their holdings to 400 acres and dreamed of establishing a country estate and summer home. It would be an easy horseback ride from Mr. Gore's law office. In 1793 they built a wooden mansion to replace an earlier farmhouse on the property. The new owners named the estate Gore Place.

Planning for the new estate was interrupted by Mr. Gore's rapid ascension in the world of government and politics. In 1788, Gore was elected to represent Boston at the Philadelphia convention to ratify the new United States Constitution. A year later, George Washington appointed Gore the first United States Attorney for Massachusetts. In 1796, Washington reappointed Gore to a diplomatic position - settling mercantile disputes based on the treaty John Jay had negotiated with Britain in 1794.

Still abroad in 1799, the Gores received news that their house in Waltham had burned, leading them to plan a new mansion for the site. Rebecca Gore was particularly interested in architecture, and her husband gave her free reign in the new design. The Gores had visited many homes in England and traveled throughout France, Belgium and Holland. Not surprisingly, many of the ideas garnered for the Gores's new home came from the buildings they most admired. A major influence on the Gores was Jacques-Guillaume Legrand, an architect they met in Paris. The new design featured an interplay of geometrical shapes, including carefully laid out oval parlors, and restrained neoclassical ornamentation adapted from the buildings of ancient Greece and Rome.

Another influence was Humphrey Repton, the English landscape architect who was at the height of his popularity. He advocated broad lawns, open fields, ponds, clumps of trees and inconspicuous gardens, while eschewing formal gardens and abundant shrubbery. The location of the new mansion on a hilltop overlooking the Charles River permitted full application of the Repton philosophy and eventually included broad lawns, tree-lined walkways, a kitchen and flower garden, and plantings that isolated the stables and farm buildings from the mansion. A variety of fruits, vegetables and grain was also cultivated on the estate, including expansive fields of wheat, rye and corn.

The Gores finally returned to Massachusetts in 1804 and work on the new brick mansion commenced in 1805. The cost of construction totaled just under $24,000, a very large sum of money for its day. Mr. Gore's records detail expenses for everything from Pennsylvania marble floor tiles to imported English hardware, even though Mr. Gore said he had "no desire to vie with his neighbors" in the elegance of his house.

The house consists of a large central block with two symmetrical wings, over thirty rooms on three levels, plus attics and a basement. The ceilings of the largest rooms soar to over fifteen feet, while lesser spaces are built to accommodate mezzanine rooms. The center section of the south-front is bow-shaped; this permits an oval drawing room with an oval family parlor above it. The great hall on the north side was used for multiple functions, including a reception hall, dining room and ballroom. The Gores decorated these rooms with elaborate French wallpapers, fragments of which still survive. The west wing was devoted to servants' quarters, servants' hall and kitchen. The east wing includes a large library as well as Mr. Gore's billiard room, which contains an impressive Boston-made billiard table. Daniel Webster, a protégé of Mr. Gore, the Marquis de Lafayette and James Monroe were guests who visited.

The upper floors include a series of comfortable bedchambers and connecting dressing rooms, designed for comfort and convenience. The oval family sitting room contains three windows that offer excellent views of the grounds and capture summer breezes. A cupola with an open shaft above the center hall was built to provide additional light and ventilation.

Soon after completion of their new summer home, Christopher Gore returned to the Massachusetts legislature and a leadership role among Massachusetts Federalists.

He ran for Governor of the Commonwealth in 1807 and 1808 before winning a one-year term in 1809. In the spring of 1813, Gore was appointed to the U.S. Senate, and he and Rebecca spent three years in Washington. Retiring to Waltham in 1816, the Gores made some changes to transform their mansion into a year-round residence. They installed "double windows" in four rooms, added coal-burning grates, and installed woolen carpets in several spaces. The most dramatic change was the addition of a grand, curving staircase in the formal entrance hall that spirals upward without any visible means of support.

The Gores remained in Waltham until 1822 when Mr. Gore's declining health forced them back to Boston for the winter season. For the last two years of his life, Christopher Gore employed an experienced African-American butler, Robert Roberts, who would later become active in Boston's abolitionist movement. Roberts also wrote *The House Servant's Dictionary*, a popular manual for household servants and their employers that ran through numerous editions.

Following her husband's death in 1827, Rebecca continued to use Gore Place for the remaining seven years of her life. Following her death, the house and all its contents were sold at auction, in accordance with the terms of Mr. Gore's will. Several families lived at Gore Place for the next ninety years and continued the growing of crops, breeding of cattle, and cultivation of gardens that the Gores had started. In the 1920s, the mansion became the clubhouse of the Waltham Country Club. When that venture failed in 1935, the bank was about to tear down the buildings and sell off the land for housing, when Mrs. Helen Patterson, a Boston preservationist, gathered her friends and the financial resources necessary to save it. The Gore Place Society was founded the same year. For more than sixty years, Gore Place has been lovingly restored and open to the public.

• • • • •

Gore Place is located between the centers of Waltham and Watertown on Route 20, Main Street. The house is open for tours from April 15th through November 15th. Hours of operation are 11:00 a.m. to 5:00 p.m., Tuesday through Saturday; 1:00 to 5:00 p.m. Sundays, and by appointment. Admission is charged. Further information may be obtained by calling: (781)894-2798, or visit the Gore Place website at http://www.goreplace.org.

Photos courtesy of Gore Place, Waltham, MA

Cà d'Zan, bayside view from the north lawn.

A Three-Ring Venetian Palazzo

John Ringling's Cà d'Zan

SARASOTA • FLORIDA

JOHN RINGLING, the lusty, free-spending king of the American circus, adored the West Coast of Florida. At Sarasota he built a Venetian palazzo that speeded the transformation of the cow-town of saloons and barnyards into a winter wonderland for tourists, much as Henry Flagler's casa had done at Palm Beach on the East Coast. Mr.

Cà d'Zan 275

The inner court, or great hall, of Cà d'Zan was the main living room. The floor has black marble from Belgium and white marble from Alabama. The chandelier once hung in New York's old Waldorf-Astoria Hotel.

Ringling called his home Cà d'Zan-Venetian patois for "House of John." At his death he left a legacy to Florida that is now a star attraction of the state park system.

John Ringling was born in McGregor, Iowa, in 1866. His father, from Hanover, Germany, was a harness maker. The original family name, Rungeling, remained so in this country until a newspaper misspelled it "Ringling." When John and some of his brothers went into the circus business at Barnaboo, Wisconsin, where the family finally settled, they adopted the newspaper's version of the name.

John's five older brothers: Albert, August, Otto, Alfred and Charles; his younger brother and sister, Henry and Ida, all appreciated Baraboo. John's siblings enjoyed the quiet lifestyle of the Midwest and were happy with the middle-class lifestyle that came with their early collective involvement in the Circus world as traveling musicians. John, however, wanted broader horizons. Leaving the Midwest, he roamed the world collecting acts for the circus, and soon became the family celebrity.

Traveling to Europe as a young man in the 1890s, Ringling became interested in paintings. He began an intensive self-education in art - visiting galleries, studying techniques and reading constantly. The knowledge he acquired still amazes art connoisseurs. His first acquisition is supposed to have been an unknown nude of little value; but over the years his skills improved and John soon became one of the shrewdest buyers in the auction rooms of Europe. He assembled one of the largest and finest collections of paintings by Peter Paul Rubens (1557-1640), foremost painter of the Flemish school. He also bought works by Tintoretto, Rembrandt, Veronese, Reynolds, Gainsborough, Hals, El Greco, Velázquez and other masters. Overall, it is estimated that Mr. Ringling collected over 600 paintings in his lifetime. An admirer of Michelangelo's statue of David, Ringling had a copy almost twice as large made for himself. All of these art objects are now part of the Ringling shrine.

As he acquired culture, Mr. Ringling also gained polish. He shaved off his bushy mustachios, switched from store-bought clothes to the latest fashions from Saville Row, filled his garages with Rolls-Royces and Pierce-Arrows and stocked his cellar with vintage wines and old Curio Scotch. Mr. Ringling also began investing in oil wells and railroads, sometimes conducting deals while at the bar of the old Waldorf-Astoria Hotel in New York. At the height of his fortunes, Mr. Ringling's estimated worth was $200,000,000.

In 1903, at the age of thirty-seven, Mr. Ringling married Mable Burton. Born Armilda Burton in Moons, Ohio, little is known about Mable's background; however it is possible she may originally have been a circus performer in one of Mr. Ringling's acts. Eleven years his junior, she possessed a dark complexion, large laughing eyes and a piquant little face. John and Mable Ringling were constant and devoted admirers of each other throughout their marriage. When Mr. Ringling began purchasing property in Sarasota in 1912, he started to think about building a palace for Mable and his art objects.

John Ringling and his brother Charles first spotted Sarasota in 1909 while looking for winter quarters for their animals. The area was largely a wilderness of tangled semitropical vegetation and great stretches of white-sand beaches. John bought thirty-seven acres of land for a home beside Sarasota Bay, with Longboat Key in the distance and the open gulf beyond. Mr. Ringling also purchased additional property on the coastal barrier islands of Bird, St. Armand, Coon, Otter Keys and several miles of Longboat, building a million-dollar causeway to link them.

Several of the Ringling brothers ultimately moved to Sarasota, and intense rivalry developed between John and Charles. When John founded the Bank of Sarasota, Charles founded the Ringling Trust and Savings Bank. After John bought the big yacht *Zalophus*, Charles purchased a bigger one, the *Symphonia*. While John was planning Ca'd'Zan, Charles built a nearby mansion of his own in a more classical beaux-arts design, which has since been converted into a college. But when John finally completed his home in 1926, it was, and remains, the most grandiose showplace of the area.

A massive wrought-iron fence around Cà d'Zan contains a picturesque gateway of pink stucco and terra cotta, embellished with glazed tile and the name of the estate. Near the mansion is a Florentine museum that houses the bulk of Ringling's art works, a museum of circus relics, and the Asolo Theatre, which was built on a hill near Venice circa 1883. It was brought to Florida in pieces beginning in 1949, and reconstructed by the state on its present site in 1957.

Mable Ringling's vision guided the design of Cà' d'Zan. Initially, she hired local Sarasota architect Thomas R. Martin to design her Venetian palazzo, with Martin's son Frank responsible for the preliminary design drawings. According to some, John Ringling found the Martin's cost estimate too high and hired prominent New York architect Dwight James Baum to refine and reestimate the design. The reserved Baum and the bombastic Circus king soon clashed. Most of the on-site supervision of the project then fell to Baum's young associate, Ralph Twitchell, who later fostered the regional variation of high modern architecture known as "The Sarasota School." Twitchell and Mable Ringling made the day-to-day design decisions that made Cà' d'Zan a unique and personal expression of a Mediterranean fantasy come to life.

A variety of influences were incorporated into the final design of the mansion. Viewed from the bayside, the patterned marble terrace, checkerboard masonry walls

Mable Ringling's bedroom has Louis XV furniture of inlaid sandalwood. The pillow covers were made by Mrs. Ringling from Venetian, Belgian and Irish laces that she collected.

John Ringling admired Michelangelo's statue of David so much that he purchased a copy cast from the original for the garden of the museum he built beside his home.

and traceried west façade of Cà' d'Zan immediately recall Venetian landmarks, most notably the Doges' Palace in Venice. From her travels, Mable Ringling would have been familiar with other well-known buildings facing the Venetian lagoon, and may have even stayed at the luxurious Hotel Danieli, a converted fourteenth-century palazzo in the heart of Venice. The hallmark, spiral-staired tower at the center of the property may derive from the Stanford White-designed old Madison Square Garden Building, where the Ringling Brothers Circus performed in New York. Inspiration for its design may have also come from the tower of William Randolph Hearst's Casa Grande at San Simeon. A profusion of strange and fanciful emblems, many recognized as Masonic in origin, suggests that John Ringling (a high-level Mason) may have had Baum and Twitchell incorporate a secret symbolic program into the design of Cà d' Zan.

While the house was under construction, the Ringlings hired theatrical designer, children's book illustrator and muralist Willy Pogany to execute a series of octagonal panels of "Dances of the World" for their music room ceiling. Pogany also executed a whimsical and somewhat bizarre ceiling painting for the L-shaped third floor game rooms. Ladies in Venetian carnival attire flirt and frolic with fairy-tale creatures, some

John Ringling was aghast when he discovered that the architects had portrayed him and his wife as Adam and Eve on the front of the mansion.

rumored to be caricatures of Ringling's business associates. In the center of the room, Pogany placed a life-sized portrait of John and Mable Ringling in carnival costume. The artist's own portrait, with brush and paintpot in hand, appears near the door, laughing at the scene he has just created.

Baum faced a special problem in finding materials suitable in color and texture for the ornate Venetian-inspired structure, that could also withstand the intense heat, pervasive damp and punishing tropical storms of the Gulf Coast climate. For stability, a state-of-the-art steel frame was used and then encased in interlocking hollow terra-cotta blocks, known as "t-bricks." The use of cast terra cotta for the Gothic traceries and blue, green and rose relief panels of flowers, fruit, animals and zodiac signs enabled Baum to produce an elaborately ornamented building without the restrictions of time, cost or structural weight of hand-carved stone.

Subtly shaded marble and ashlar masonry of many tints were also used on the exterior of the building, its steps and terraces. The Venetian terrace on the waterfront, where Mrs. Ringling kept an authentic gondola until a hurricane wrecked it, is 200-feet long and paved with imported and domestic marbles of many colors, set in a spectacular chevron pattern. From Barcelona, Mr. Ringling brought thousands of old red barrel tiles for the roof of Cà' d'Zan and related buildings. Ships were chartered to transport the tiles to Florida's ports of Tampa and Miami. Terra-cotta balustrades, columns veneered with Mexican onyx from Southern California and rounded arches add to the majestic appearance of the exterior.

Many windows in the mansion have panes of hand-blown European "lac" (lake in French, in reference to the watery ripples in the material) glass, delicately tinted in watercolor hues of rose, gray, straw and blue. The prismatic dappled effects of colored light in Cà d'Zan are most immediately apparent in the Court, the two-story central living space. The Court, remarkable for its coffered ceiling of Florida pecky cypress in late Medieval style, serves as the focal space of Cà d'Zan, with all the other formal living areas and bedrooms radiating from it. In addition to twenty-one "formal" rooms in the main block of the house, a wing to the south contains fifteen additional rooms for service areas, including nine servants' bedrooms.

A gallery encircling the Court once contained many of the Ringlings' collection of seventeenth and eighteenth-century Flemish and French tapestries. Renaissance and

Baroque-era altercloths and church vestments of silk and velvet, embroidered in gold and silver floss as well as multicolored silks, are displayed along the gallery railing. The centerpiece of the Court is the Aeolian Duo Art organ, custom-designed for the house so that its 2,100 pipes could be arranged throughout the building for maximal acoustical impact.

Many of Cà' d'Zan's furnishings reflect a lingering Victorian sensibility in the taste of the Circus tycoon and his wife. As a farmboy in Iowa, John Ringling surely was aware of the legendary fortunes of families such as the Astors and the Vanderbilts. As fate would have it, these particular Victorian-era Fifth Avenue mansions were being deserted at precisely the time Cà d'Zan was being built. As a result, Ringling was able to acquire furnishings and even entire rooms of paneling for incorporation into his own house and museum. These included such treasures as Mrs. Astor's Louis XIV revival-style gilded parlor furniture and selected items from Alva Belmont's collection of Medieval and Renaissance decorative arts, long housed in the gothic room at Marble House on exclusive Bellevue Avenue in Newport.

In contrast to the strong Medieval and Renaissance character of the first floor rooms, the bedrooms tend to have a lighter, Rococo-inspired flavor. Mr. Ringling's bedroom on the second floor is decorated in French Empire style, with gilded framework on doors and windows, a floor of black marble, and a mythological eighteenth-century ceiling painting which originally adorned the townhouse of a wealthy merchant in Amsterdam. Off the bedroom is an ornate bath, with walls and a tub of yellow Sienna marble and fixtures of gold. A modern barber's chair, where Mr. Ringling was shaved every morning by his valet, stand - an anachronism - near the tub.

Near Mr. Ringling's bedroom are the bedrooms of his first and second wives. Mable Ringling's bedroom adjoins her husband's and features inlaid sandalwood furnishings embellished with gilt-bronze figures, in the style of Louis XV. The ceiling of her room is notable for its whimsical design - a series of heraldic shields animated by commas, exclamation points and other punctuation marks. In tribute to Mable, John Ringling maintained this room in its original fashion after her death.

It is estimated that Cà'd'Zan cost Ringling almost $2,000,000 to build, and he spent about the same amount for the adjacent art museum. Art dealers estimate that Ringling spent around $3,000,000 for paintings and other art objects that are today worth well over $20,000,000.

Entertaining at Cà'd'Zan was on a grand scale. Visitors included Florenz Ziegfeld and his wife Billie Burke, James J. Walker, Alfred E. Smith, Will Rogers, Irvin S. Cobb and other prominent persons of politics and the entertainment world who could match Mr. Ringling's quick wit and storytelling skill. Adjacent to the dining room is a barroom complete with bar, cabinets, windows and brass rail, that Mr. Ringling brought intact from Old Cicardi's Winter Garden Restaurant in St. Louis.

The end of a Florida land boom in the late 1920s ushered in a dark period in John Ringling's life. Mable died in 1929, only three years after Cà d'Zan was completed. Her unexpected passage left a huge gap in Mr. Ringling's life, for he had never contemplated life without her. Later that year. however, Mr. Ringling married Mrs. Emily Haag Buck, a divorcée and former New York socialite. Just before the ceremony, Mr. Ringling had Emily sign a waiver of rights to his estate, since he was determined to donate Cà' d' Zan and the adjacent museum to the public as a memorial to Mable and himself. The ink of the marriage certificate was barely dry when Emily tore up the waiver. The two were soon in court, with sensational charges and counter-charges flying back and forth.

Another crushing blow for Ringling was his loss of the family's circus. Hard-pressed for cash after the stock-market crash of 1929, he refused to sell even one of the mansion's valuable paintings, believing that good times were just around the corner. His financial troubles led to the loss of a lease on the new Madison Square Garden in New York to a rival show, the American Circus Corporation. Mr. Ringling turned the tables by buying the American Circus Corporation, but in the process he saddled himself with a debt of $1,700,000 that he could later not repay.

In his comparative poverty, Mr. Ringling retired to Cà' d'Zan to live with a skeleton staff of servants. When he died in 1936 he had $311 in the bank, although his entire estate was later appraised at $23,500,000. Cà' d'Zan and related buildings were left to the state. Emily was left one dollar. Their divorce suit was near completion when he died. Long litigation over the estate ensued but Florida obtained full possession of Cà' d'Zan and its related buildings in 1946. Since that time, the museum's art collection has been increasing along the lines John Ringling laid down. Following an extensive $20,000,000 restoration project that began in 1982, the museum reopened to the public in January, 1991.

• • • •

The museum is now under renovation and will re-open in the Spring of 2001.

The entrance to the Ringling residence and other buildings is from U.S. Route 41 at 5401 Bay Shore Road in Sarasota. The buildings are open to the public from 10:00 a.m. to 5:30 p.m., Monday through Sunday, except on Christmas and Thanksgiving and New Years Day. Guided tours of the residence are conducted. An admission fee of $9.00 is charged for adults; children under twelve are admitted free. Further information can be obtained by calling: (941) 359-5700, or visit the Ringling Museum website at http://www.ringling.org.

Photos courtesy of The John and Mable Ringling Museum of Art, the State Art Museum of Florida.

A Southern Legacy

The White House of the Confederacy

RICHMOND • VIRGINIA

SITUATED ON A HILL overlooking Shockoe Valley in Richmond's historic Court End neighborhood, the White House of the Confederacy is one of the nation's finest historic, architectural and decorative treasures. The official residence of the first and only Confederate President - Jefferson Davis - the building has earned a unique stature in American history as the social, political and military center of the Old South.

Little is mentioned about this stately home in the voluminous literature of the Civil War. In its heyday as the South's Executive Mansion, it functioned much like its Northern counterpart, as a hub of social activity and strategic decision making. And like some of its more prestigious counterparts in the north and south, a battle was

The State Dining Room is the largest and most elegant room in the house.
The room features Rococo Revival furniture and symbols of Southern nationalism, including
a copy of Gilbert Stuart's portrait of George Washington.

waged to maintain its existence as a historic site long after its principal function was completed. Now a National Historic Landmark, this Southern treasure maintains the most comprehensive collection of Confederate art and artifacts anywhere in the nation.

Long before its official designation, the residence enjoyed an illustrious history as the home to a succession of wealthy Virginia families. Construction of the property was initiated by Dr. John Brockenbrough and his wife Gabriella Harvie Brockenbrough, whose fortunes had recently increased with the physician's new-found role as president of the Bank of Virginia in 1811. His predecessor in that role had died in the tragic Richmond Theater fire of the same year. As a result of their elevated social position, the Brockenbroughs felt compelled to move one block east, to the smarter area of Richmond on the southeast corner of 12th and Clay Streets.

The status-conscious Brockenbrough did not hesitate to spend whatever money was necessary to advance his new image. The ambitious new financier invested the substantial sum of $30,000 to buy property and construct his home - over five times the average amount being spent on a middle-class dwelling of that time period. The large residence would for decades be known as the Brockenbrough house.

The plan of the house was typical of Richmond's finer nineteenth-century dwellings. The brick exterior walls were stuccoed and painted to resemble masonry. The principal floor contained a parlor, drawing room, dining room and three bedrooms on the upper level. It also included an adjoining outbuilding for use as a kitchen and servants' quarters and a large garden, complete with terraces. Brockenbrough made additional improvements soon after, including altering the entrance hall's shape from a rectangle to its present oval. The formal rectangular staircase was replaced with a handsome circular one, and classical detail was added to the house's woodwork - particularly on the first floor.

There is no definite record indicating who the architect or builder of the Brockenbrough residence actually was. Possibilities indicate that the architect may have been Robert Mills (1781-1855), a prominent American neoclassical architect well-known in Richmond. Later appointed architect of public buildings in Washington, Mills also designed the Washington Monument, the Treasury Building, the Patent Office, and the old Post Office Building. The city's own building community probably supplied the talent for the construction of the new residence.

Additional improvements to the house were made over the years with the passage of each new owner. Soon after Brockenbrough sold the house to James M. Morson, in 1844, a carriage house and stable were added. Morson lived in the house for three years and then sold it to his sister-in-law, Sally Bruce. Bruce, a Richmond socialite, subsequently married James Seddon, a Virginia lawyer and statesman who would later serve as secretary of war under the Davis administration. Mr. Seddon, who would often return to the familiar rooms in later years, would enjoy occupancy in the house for a decade before selling it to Louis Crenshaw, a wealthy Richmond manufacturer.

Lewis Dabney Crenshaw, co-owner of the successful Haxal-Crenshaw flour mills and a pioneer of the profitable flour-for-coffee trade with South America, personified the economic success of Richmond in the 1850s. The father of eight children, he used his considerable wealth to make important contributions to the home. These included the construction of a third story as well as the addition of elaborate gas-burning chandeliers, called gasoliers. Crenshaw also added plaster ceiling ornamentation to complement the new fixtures, as well as a major refurbishing and redecorating of the house. The individual furnishings and overall interior decoration of Crenshaw's home reflect the popularity of the American Rococo Revival style, or "French taste," which was popular in the 1850s and was also featured in the Washington White House.

By 1859, Richmond was considered the most important industrial complex in the South. Virginia's capital since 1780, the city on the James River still reveled in its glamorous history as a major Revolutionary War outpost - the place where Patrick Henry had bravely challenged George III to "give me liberty or give me death." A city rich in culture, theaters played host to stars such as Jenny Lind and various members of the prestigious Booth family of actors, while local hostesses vied with each other in elaborate forms of entertaining.

Newly elected President Davis was not eager to carry out his duties in this illustrious city, where he felt dangerously exposed to enemy attack. Many natives of the area, still proud of what their grandfathers had accomplished, were also not eager to receive him when secessionist states began to burn Lincoln's image in effigy by late 1860. Southern leaders, anxious for the prestige of ties to this mother state, appeased state leaders by offering to make Richmond the capital of the Confederacy. Soon after, at Crenshaw's invitation, the City of Richmond purchased his house and its contents for use as the official Executive Mansion. In May, 1861, the Southern Congress moved to the colonnaded city from its provisional seat at Montgomery, Alabama. President Davis and his wife Varina followed separately shortly after.

Jefferson Davis was, by his wife's admission, "a nervous dyspeptic of supersensitive temperament." Born in Kentucky on June 3, 1808, he was raised by a family of yeoman farmers. His grandfather, Evan Davis, was a Welsh Quaker who was born in Philadelphia in 1702. Land-hungry and uneducated, Evan's eventual move Southward was typical of many Scotch-Irish immigrants of that time. Evan's stepson, Samuel, served in the Revolutionary Army and was given land in Augusta, Georgia for his services. Like his father, he possessed a frontiersman spirit. In 1792, Samuel and his growing family left Georgia for the Kentucky wilderness where a greater fortune was to be made raising horses and growing tobacco. His tenth and last child, Jefferson, who was named for the current President, was born shortly before the family's final move to Mississippi, where King Cotton was establishing a fixed rule.

Samuel Davis knew the value of education and was determined that his son receive only the finest training. Jefferson attended Kentucky's Transylvania University - the South's Harvard - and the U.S. Military Academy at West Point, where a fondness for drinking and socializing earned him only average grades. During time at a frontier military post in Wisconsin, Mr. Davis met his first great love, Sarah Knox Taylor, the daughter of his commander - future president Zachary Taylor. The couple were married in September, 1835, despite strong objections from Sarah's father who opposed his daughter's union to a penniless soldier. Sarah died of malaria three months after, leaving the grief-stricken Davis to retire to his Mississippi plantation, "Brierfield," for nine years.

Jefferson Davis met his second wife, Varina, a cultivated seventeen-year-old from Natchez, in 1843, on a visit to his brother's plantation, "Hurricane." Varina's father, William Burr Howell, was the son of Richard Howell, a Revolutionary war hero and later eight-term governor of New Jersey. The couple was married at the bride's home a year later, shortly before Mr. Davis was elected to the U.S House of Representatives from Mississippi. Their marriage, though sometimes stormy and often punctuated by long separations, would last forty-five years. The two enjoyed prominence in Washington social circles until Mississippi's secession from the Union in early 1861 forced the Senator's retirement. Soon after returning to his plantation, the future Confederate president was informed of his new role while clipping roses in his garden. Varina would report that he received the message "as if some calamity had fallen upon him." Davis accepted his new duty however, hurriedly packed, and left for Montgomery the next day.

Jefferson Davis arrived in Richmond with great fanfare on May 29, 1861, where he reportedly was greeted with the "honor due to a new Washington." His wife arrived three days later, with street crowds and flowers along the way. The new couple were given the finest accommodations in the nearby Spotswood Hotel while the Executive Mansion was redecorated and refurbished. Richmond citizens wished to give the couple the house as a gift, which Davis did not accept. Upon moving into her new residence, Varina Davis exclaimed: "One felt here the pleasant sense of being in the home of a cultivated, liberal, fine gentleman." Although Varina would have liked more and smaller rooms - some were forty-feet square - here at last, the family felt "somewhat at home."

The center parlor. Examples of "prisoner-of-war art" and reproductions of the first and second national flags of the Confederacy have been placed on the Carrara marble mantle below a portrait of Jefferson Davis by John Robertson.

The Civil War had been underway for four months when the Davis family settled into their new home in August, 1861. Richmond already faced the threat of invasion, forcing President Davis' entire attention to military matters. While Davis spent his days at his executive office in the Treasury Building (formerly the Federal Customs House on Main St.), his fabled devotion to work and frequent illnesses forced him to conduct much business at home where he often met with military advisers and cabinet members. He selected the rooms for his private office and bedchamber on the second floor of the mansion, which was also used as the family's living quarters. On April 4, 1865, shortly before the South surrendered, President Lincoln came to visit the former capital and the deserted Confederate White House. Escorted into Davis' office he sat at the empty desk and declared with a dreamy expression, "This must

Jefferson Davis, circa 1860.
Photo by Mathew Brady.

have been President Davis' chair." Today, the desk and swivel chair that Mr. Davis used are still on display, as well as an original 1853 roller map of North America, period prints, and Davis' 1829 commission to the United States Army.

Flanking the office space are the mansion's most private rooms, including the master bedchamber, Varina Davis's dressing room, and the children's nursery. The two bedrooms are furnished with a few pieces of bedroom furniture once used in the house and furnishings from other period houses. Much of the furniture in this room was used by the Davis family, including the mahogany bed, an Empire style wardrobe, a marble- top washstand and a marble-top dressing bureau which features a "secret" compartment below the lower front drawer. A cylindrical night stand, two marble-topped washstands, a dresser, and two gilt-framed mantel glasses are the only original pieces of furniture featured in the nursery. Toys, including a small working cannon that belonged to Jeff, Jr., as well as games and miniature furniture, suggest the presence of small children.

Despite the tragedy of war, the Davises maintained a warm and active family life. The pregnant Varina brought three young children with her to Richmond in 1861 and two more were born in the Confederate White House by June of 1864. Both first families would lose a son while in office at this time; tragically it was four-year-old Joseph, "Mr. Davis's hope and greatest joy in life," who died after a fall from the east portico of the Confederate White House on April 30, 1864. In the decades following the war, three more Davis children succumbed to disease; ultimately only one daughter, Margaret, survived her parents.

Mrs. Davis often threw parties in the evening between limited hours, which were attended by any member of Richmond's social hierarchy not in deep mourning. Guests to the White House entered from Clay Street into an elliptical entrance hall. Sparsely furnished, the area is dominated by two life-sized statues representing "Comedy" and "Tragedy" by English artist Humphrey Hopper, and were added to specially created niches in the entrance hall between 1825 and 1830. Facing this passage is a grand circular stairway, an 1895 cast-iron replica of the 1820s original. The marble figures of Athena and Hera standing in niches along the staircase wall are features original to the house as is a unique lighting fixture at the foot of the stairway.

The apartments used for entertaining are in the rear and *en suite*, with a parlor between the drawing room and the dining room. The center parlor and drawing room were the setting for many public occasions, including receptions and Christmas celebrations. The space features large, sliding pocket doors that allow the rooms to be closed off or used in combination, Carrara marble fireplaces, as well as furniture and artwork original to the mansion. Among the most important pieces of art are a portrait of Jefferson Davis by John Robertson and bust by Frederick Volck (1833-91), both of which Davis sat for, and which appeared in the Executive Mansion during the war. The drawing room also features a pair of landscapes by the Virginia born artist William D. Washington, also original to the mansion.

The Confederate White House also served as the part-time residence for many others besides the immediate Davis Family. These included extended family members - particularly Varina's sister Margaret Howell, Varina's mother Margaret Kempe Howell, and a large assortment of aides and military personnel. They would stay on the third floor, which served as a dormitory space for guests at this time. Varina's younger sister Margaret brought with her the whirlwind of Richmond's singles scene. "The fascinating Miss H- at the White House," as one young officer called her, was known to have many suitors and was notoriously outspoken.

When the fall of the Confederate capital was imminent on April 2, 1865, Davis fled Richmond. Fleeing southward by train, he was captured with his wife and children and members of his cabinet and staff by Union troops on May 10, 1865, near Irwinville, Georgia. Without benefit of a trial, Davis would remain in Federal custody for two years in Fort Monroe, Virginia, before finally resettling in Mississippi, where he wrote his memoirs. Davis, who would lose his U.S. citizenship after the war, never set foot again in the Confederate White House. He was later laid to rest in Richmond's distinguished Hollywood Cemetery, four years after his death in 1889. Varina, who enjoyed a brief writing career in New York following his death, was also buried there in 1906. The plot is also the resting place of all the Davis children.

Federal military occupation of the Confederate White House began immediately after Jefferson Davis' departure and continued for five years. Upon reclaiming its property in January 1870, the city of Richmond used the house as a school. Over 600 students attended every year until 1889, when city officials decided that the mansion was no longer fit for occupancy. A proposal was made to raze the building and replace it with a modern facility. The house seemed doomed to destruction.

In May, 1890, the Confederate Memorial Literary Society (CMLS) was born with Isobel Stewart Bryan serving as its first president. Following the example of societies which had rescued such important historic sites as Washington's Mount Vernon and the Hermitage (President Andrew Jackson's home in Tennessee), the group was composed entirely of women. The influential group was already known for its successful efforts in relocating Confederate soldiers from graveyards at Gettysburg and battle-

Most private of the first floor rooms is the library, which the Davises used as a study and intimate meeting place.

fields around Richmond.

To raise money to preserve the Confederate mansion, the CMLS held a memorial bazaar in the spring of 1893. Representatives from fourteen states sold native goods and commemorative objects. In three weeks the group raised $31,315.-well over what was needed to purchase the property from the city a year later. Immediately the building was completely fireproofed and prepared as a future repository for Confederate artifacts. On February, 22, 1896, exactly thirty-four years after Jefferson Davis's inauguration, The Confederate Museum was opened. It would prove to be an immediate success with the curious public.

The CMLS remained an entity and in 1975-76, the group initiated a three-phase plan to restore the Confederate White House to its wartime appearance. A large grant was obtained from the state of Virginia by 1978, followed by intensive historical research on the house that would continue into the next decade. Archeological investigation of the rooms took place and restoration architects were called in to determine details of the original building obliterated by post-war occupation. Furniture, sculpture and lighting fixtures were also restored to their wartime appearances. After being designated a National Historic Landmark in 1966, the newly restored Executive Mansion was officially reopened to the public in June 1988.

Today, the museum houses more than 15,000 artifacts, including hundreds of uniforms, flags and the personal effects of many Confederate generals, including Robert E. Lee's sword, the bible Thomas "Stonewall" Jackson carried and the personal effects of J.E.B. Stuart. The Eleanor S. Brockenbrough Library, housed within the museum, maintains over 20,000 books, photographs and currency pieces and 540 cubic feet of manuscripts. The White House period rooms display over 1,000 objects, including paintings, sculpture, furniture and decorative objects - the majority of which have a Davis family provenance. Exhibitions, lectures, special events and educational programs are also held on a scheduled basis throughout the year.

• • • • •

The Museum of the Confederacy is located on 1201 East Clay Street, in downtown Richmond two blocks from the State Capital. Tours are conducted daily. Hours of operation are Monday through Saturday, 10:00 a.m. to 5:00 p.m., and Sunday, 12:00 to 5:00 p.m. The museum is closed Thanksgiving Day, Christmas Day and New Years Day. A tour of both the museum and the White House is $9.00 for adults, $8.50 for seniors and $5.00 for students. Group rates are available, by pre-arrangement, for groups of ten or more. For further information call: (804) 649-1861 or visit the museum website at: http://www.moc.org.

Photos by Katherine Wetzel, courtesy of The Museum of the Confederacy and the National Archives.

The House with Nine Lives

Boscobel - the Manorial Mansion of States Morris Dyckman

GARRISON • NEW YORK

LOCATED IN THE HEART of the Hudson Highlands, Boscobel commands a panoramic view across the river to the massive towers of the United States Military Academy at West Point, as well as historic Sleepy Hollow and Bear Mountain Ridge to the south. Possessed of as many lives as the proverbial cat, it is a mansion which some might say has been literally "resurrected from the grave," and remains a role-model for preservationists. Once sold to a housewrecker for thirty-five dollars, then reduced to small parts for storage, the twenty-room structure has been reborn through the most ingenious efforts of historians and philanthropists who, together, enabled it to rise again on a new site fifteen miles north of its original one.

The public's enthusiasm for Boscobel stems largely from its classic Federal architecture. Historians call it one of the finest examples in the United States of eighteenth-century sophistication. Architects rate it as one of the most outstanding houses of the period. To scholars it is a jackpot for the study of the customs and culture of the past. For generations to come it will be a public exhibit, showing how families of affluence lived in the era of elegance after the Revolutionary War.

Restored to its original beauty and furnished with early nineteenth-century rugs, paintings, furniture, and chandeliers, Boscobel stands tall and stately on a knoll 200 feet above the east side of the Hudson River near Garrison, New York. It occupies a tract of thirty-five acres. Originally it occupied one of several hundred acres at Crugers, in Westchester County. The name Boscobel (the Italian bosco bello means "fair wood") was taken by Mr. Dyckman from an estate in Shropshire, England, where King Charles II hid in a giant hollow oak while evading the Roundhead pursuers after his defeat by Cromwell in the Battle of Worcester.

States Morris Dyckman, whose Dutch-given name had been Staats until he Americanized it, began construction of the mansion in 1804. A determined Tory, he had fled to England during the Revolution. Later he returned to this country to regain stature, marry Elizabeth Corne, who was a member of a distinguished Mohawk Valley family, and build Boscobel. The resurrection of Boscobel on its present site was completed in 1961.

Mr. Dyckman, frail and arthritic but with a will of iron, had a lifelong dream of building a beautiful home overlooking the river he loved. An ancestor, Jan Dyckman, had been one of thirty Dutch freeholders on Manhattan who received large grants of land in 1666. States grew up in an inn that his father operated at the Manhattan end of the old Farmers' Bridge over the Harlem River. There he experienced the turbulent days before the Revolution. He was twenty-one-years-old when the Declaration of Independence was signed in 1776.

States, a Tory by conviction, worked as a clerk for Sir William Erskine, a British Army commander in New York. In 1779 he traveled to England with Sir William and resided there for nine years, exposed to the elite living standards and luxuries of Sir William's friends. Returning to New York in 1788, Dyckman had an annuity of 100 pounds from Sir William but found it to be insufficient security. His kinsfolk had been ruined financially and socially by the war and he undertook to help them. In 1794 he married Elizabeth Corne, the granddaughter of another prominent Hudson River Valley Tory, and wrote to a friend: "Late in life my happiness has begun." States was thirty-nine and his bride was eighteen. They had two children, Peter and Letitia.

In a struggle to continue collecting his annuity, Dyckman traveled to England in 1800 and remained there for four years, arguing with the arbitrators, while planning Boscobel and buying its furnishings. One of his legal advisors was William Adam, a nephew of the famous Scottish architect and designer Robert Adam(1728-92), who is known to have brought about a revolution in architectural design. Together, William and Robert became experts on the "Adam-style," characterized by an addition of lightness and freedom in the use of classical elements of design.

The large entrance hall of Boscobel was intended to impress visitors. Photo by Joe Larese.

Dyckman returned to this country in 1804, having won a big financial settlement on his claim. His daughter Letitia had died during his absence, but he was joyously reunited with his wife and son. Upon his homecoming, he unfolded the plans for Boscobel and immediately began construction of his dream-house. In preparation, Dyckmann had purchased china, glass, silver, as well as a library; items which he had shipped home to his wife from London. He had only just begun construction of the house when he died in 1806. His widow and son Peter continued building Boscobel with the aid of States' cousin, master builder William Vermilyea. The family moved into the newly constructed residence in 1808 and lived there until the death of Mrs. Dyckman in 1823, fifteen years later. Her son died one year later of pneumonia.

Boscobel, still unfinished, fell into disrepair until a granddaughter of Mr. Dyckman - Eliza Letitia - married John Peach Cruger. After that, the house was restored, completed, and given new life as the Dyckman-Cruger mansion. It became a social center of the Hudson Valley, with appearances by women in party gowns, smartly dressed men on fine horses, and later leaders of the valley driving up in some of the first horseless carriages. The Crugers were the last family to live in Boscobel while it was a private residence.

The Westchester County Park Commission bought the house and its large acreage in 1923 for Crugers Park. The county planned to raze the building but a storm of protest arose from the Westchester Historical Society, the Hudson River Conservation Society and other groups. Soon after, a group led by Harvey Stevenson, who was architect in residence when Boscobel was restored, saved the house by leasing it and making essential repairs that would protect it from the elements. Yet no one knew quite what to do with the house on a permanent basis.

After World War II, the park commission sold the house and acreage to the federal government for use with the new Franklin Delano Roosevelt Hospital for neuro-psychiatric veterans. The red-brick buildings of the hospital soon towered beside Boscobel. The Veterans' Administration promised to preserve the mansion but soon discovered it was too expensive to maintain as a reception center. While the house fell into disrepair, mentally challenged patients from the neighboring hospital considered its spring house a good place to hide from doctors. Neighboring boys found that the front hall could be flooded with water in winter to produce ice for skating.

In 1955, the federal government declared Boscobel surplus property and signed its death warrant. Not even the National Trust, chartered by Congress for historical preservation, could save Boscobel from imminent destruction. The mansion was sold to a housewrecker for thirty-five dollars. Some of the choicest woodwork and exterior trim were carted off to a house that was being built on Long Island, although these parts were soon retrieved.

Historians were highly indignant when they heard of the sale. They felt the purchase price of thirty-five dollars was an absurdity matched only by Peter Minuit's purchase of Manhattan for twenty-four. Spearheaded by the efforts of Benjamin Frazier, a member of the Putnam County Historical Society, the mansion was literally defended by force, with strong-armed men hired to surround Boscobel until a court order was issued to stop the demolition.

The bizarre battle was abruptly halted for a month by a government order. Just as the month was running out, historians collected $10,000 to move Boscobel, but they

The front drawing room at Boscobel features elegant Federal furniture attributed to Duncan Phyfe, a Wilton carpet, and decorative arts of the Federal period. Photo by Matt Flynn.

The upstairs drawing room features original volumes acquired by States Dyckman in London.
Photo by Matt Flynn.

had no property to put it on. Undaunted, 125 organizations and friends of Boscobel made plans to dismantle the crumbling structure and store pieces of it in locations around the nearby area, rather than attempt to move the building intact.

A central problem was finding a suitable site to recreate the mansion. There was one piece of property that was ideally suited - sixteen acres of rolling land in Garrison, New York, with sweeping views of the Hudson River and an unsurpassed view of West Point and Constitution Island. The property appeared to be similar to Boscobel's original construction site - which was a key reason for its selection.

One of the early supporters of Boscobel was Mrs. Lila Acheson Wallace of Mount Kisco, New York, who, with her husband, DeWitt, founded the *Readers Digest* in 1922. Declaring Boscobel a "rare work of art" that should be preserved forever, she donated $595,000 for its initial restoration. Mrs. Wallace provided adequate financial assistance for the reconstruction and furnishing of the house, and for the landscaping of the new location. The *Reader's Digest* Foundation, led by Mrs. Wallace and her husband until 1973, would later donate millions of dollars for the perpetual operation of Boscobel. Generous contributions were also made by seventeen national and regional organizations and many individuals. Boscobel was formally dedicated on May 21, 1961, and opened to the public.

Boscobel's dismantling required five months, but its reconstruction on the new site took several years and was not finished until 1961. The reconstruction time was kept to a minimum largely due to the efforts of three architects who made detailed drawings of the house in 1932. Unusual things were found behind the plaster. There were sixty-foot beams running the entire length of the house, hand-split lathing and a huge main beam spanning the arches of the entrance hall. Many of the most established carpenters of the Hudson Valley had never before seen such timbers. The parts of the great jigsaw puzzle were stored in many widely separated buildings, including an icehouse, sheds, warehouses and uninhabited castles of the valley. John McNally, a local house-mover, devised an orderly system of numbering all the studs, beams, sills, baseboards, moldings and even the stones of the foundation as they were removed. Sections of the plaster cornices and ceiling medallions were carefully cut so they could be accurately reproduced later.

With the exception of a change in the color of the home from blue to yellow-ochre, the exterior of the newly reconstructed home remains largely the same. On the front of the mansion the classic Doric columns have lengthened capitals. The frieze and pediment are softened and lightened by the unusual swags across the upper portico. The proportions of the windows, the spacious interior, the decorative motifs and fireplaces achieve a harmonious relationship in synchrony with the Adam design that Dyckman favored.

One of the most startling innovations of the period in which Boscobel was built is the vast area given to windows. Persons are accustomed today to see walls of glass, but in 1805, when homes relied on fireplaces for heat, such natural illumination was rare in this country. More than one-third of the south façade of Boscobel is glass.

The wide entrance hall is flooded with sunlight on bright days. The combined height of the eleven-and-a-half foot ceilings produces an effect of spaciousness seldom found in early American houses.

Beyond a triple arch of the entrance hall a great wooden staircase rises towards a ten-foot Palladian window centered above a landing. Here again, natural illumination plays upon exquisite ornamentation to produce an unusual effect of light and shadow. The majestic stairway leads to a second floor that is less elegant. The library, twenty-two feet square, is located at the head of the stairs, and commands a spectacular view of the river valley below. Mr. Dyckman possessed a large library which he placed next to the bedroom in which he had intended to sleep. About 200 books from Mr. Dyckman's original book collection still remain.

The interior exemplifies the attention that Dyckman's advisor, William Adam, gave to detailed decorations. The woodwork, the mantels, the framing of windows and doors, the ceiling medallions and cornices were individually designed for each room. In the dining room, an oval sunburst at the mantel is repeated over windows, doors, and arches.

The front parlor has a melding of patterns. Corinthian columns frame the fireplace, two types of fretwork adorn the mantel; oval and round medallions are blended to complete an impression of unity in the room.

The Wedgewood pottery, the glass and all the other decorative arts typify the classical revival in the arts initiated by Robert Adam. Much of Dyckman's china and silver have been returned. There is, however, only one piece of original Dyckmann furniture. As a result of funding provided by Mrs. Wallace, examples of New York Federal furniture have been collected to more accurately reflect the period of Dyckman ownership. Significant documentary research into all historical records available to the curators of the mansion has also resulted in the addition of interior and exterior paint colors, floor coverings, and wallpapers which accurately reproduce

Boscobel's formal garden features over fifty varieties of roses. Photo by Joe Larese.

the classical style. Paintings by Benjamin West and John Watson, as well as a variety of English prints, also grace the rooms.

The enthusiasm generated by the restoration is exemplified by this comment of the Society of Architectural Historians upon the opening of Boscobel to the public: "The house was one of those rare monuments which casts its shadow forward to influence the architecture of the next several decades. It possesses a charm and grace seldom equaled."

Boscobel is surrounded by historical sites of noteworthy importance, including Sleepy Hollow to the South, Hyde Park (the home of Franklin D. Roosevelt), and the Vanderbilt mansion. The neighboring village of Cold Spring - to the north - is also the home of the Foundry School Museum, which features exhibits of the West Point Foundry, as well as Hudson River lore. Together or separately, they are legends of American history.

• • • • •

Boscobel is located beside State Route 9-D of Garrison, about fifty miles from New York City. It is open to the public from April through December, with the exception of Tuesdays, Thanksgiving, Christmas, and New Year's Day. Tours begin at 9:30 a.m. and continue until 3:15 p.m. in November and December and end at 4:15 April-October. Admission is charged. Children under 6 and members of Boscobel are admitted free. For further information, call: (914) 265-3638 or visit the Boscobel website at http://www.boscobel.org.

Photos courtesy of Boscobel Restoration, Inc.

A Permanent Memorial

Arlington House

ARLINGTON • VIRGINIA

ROBERT E. LEE once stated of Arlington House in 1854 that "my affections and attachments are more strongly placed there than at any other place in the world." Overlooking Washington, D.C. and the Potomac, the former Civil War hero's home is now maintained and kept open to the public by the National Park Service as a permanent memorial to the man many still consider one of the greatest military leaders in history.

The structure is of Greek Revival design and parts of it have dominated the tract on the Virginia side of the Potomac River since 1802. Construction was begun in that year by George Washington Parke Custis, the adopted son of General Washington and the grandson of Martha Washington by her first marriage. Custis was a farsighted agricultural pioneer, painter, playwright and orator. He constructed the house in memory of his stepfather, filling it with Washington memorabilia for all, including Robert, to see. Although the interior was never completed according to plan and the rear was left unstuccoed, "Arlington House" was soon considered one of the finest residences in Washington.

In 1804, Custis took his bride, the former Mary Lee Fitzhugh, to his new home. Young Robert E. Lee, whose mother was a cousin of Mrs. Custis, frequently visited Arlington. It was a place of solace to him during his youth, which was scarred by the desertion of his father when Robert was a boy of six. Henry "Lighthorse Harry" Lee, a dissipated Revolutionary War hero, had left his family greatly in debt, with Robert left to care for an ailing mother and sister throughout his teenage years. As a child Robert was a favorite in the Custis household and the frequent playmate of Mary Custis, George Custis' only surviving child. Robert and Mary are said to have planted some trees surrounding the house when they were young. Childhood friendship turned to love and the couple became engaged soon after Robert E. Lee graduated - second in his class - from West Point. The Lees were married at Arlington House in 1831 and led a pleasant plantation life there until the tragedy of the Civil War overtook them.

Arlington was Lee's first formal home, even though he had to share it with his father and mother-in-law for the first twenty-six years of his marriage. Marriage to Mary Custis produced seven children in rapid succession and when all of the Lees were in residence, at least nine people slept in four bedrooms on the second floor of the house. Robert's in-laws kept rooms in the north wing (first floor) of the house after their daughter's marriage. This was the same area that they had lived in during the early years of their marriage when the wings were the only portions of Arlington House yet built.

Lee fit easily into the quiet way of life at Arlington and enjoyed his time there immensely, despite the fact that he was rarely at home. The future colonel advanced rapidly in rank during his early military career and was greatly admired for his outstanding service in high government circles. Yet he was fretful and guilt-ridden when away from his native state and family, a fact encouraged by the frequent illnesses of his wife and the death of his in-laws in the 1850s. He once confided to a friend in the army: "I am waiting, looking and hoping for some good opportunity to bid an affectionate farewell to Uncle Sam."

It was at Arlington that Lee was forced to confront the greatest dilemma of his life in April 1861. On the night of April 19, the mansion was ablaze with lights while people talked noisily about states' rights, slavery and secession. Finding it impossible to think about his problems amid the excitement, Lee went into the gardens to pace back and forth alone. Still undecided, he returned to the house and went into his bedroom. Overhead, guests could hear him pacing, stopping only to kneel in prayer. It was after midnight when Lee went to his desk and wrote his resignation from the U.S. Army.

To his son he wrote: "It is the principle I contend for. I can anticipate no greater calamity for the country than a dissolution of the Union. Still, a Union that can only be maintained by swords and bayonets has no charm for me. I shall mourn for my country and the welfare and progress of mankind." Two days later he would leave his home for Richmond, where he would begin mobilizing southern military forces for the Confederate army. Lee would never spend time at his beloved Arlington again, and only once would he have a glimpse of it, from a passing train, several years after the war.

Mrs. Lee - forced to flee Arlington House the next month - stripped the mansion of its treasures as best she could. Family portraits were stored, family silver was hidden, mementos and furniture of George Washington - the mansion had at that time the greatest such collection in the world - were put away in packing cases. So were mementos of famous persons who had stayed in the house as visitors, including Sam Houston, Marquis de Lafayette, Andrew Jackson and Daniel Webster.

Mrs. Lee and her daughters endured a nomadic lifestyle for the next three years - living with friends and relatives before also settling in Richmond near the end of the war. A wartime law required that property owners in areas occupied by Federal troops appear in person to pay their taxes. Unable to comply with this rule, Mrs. Lee saw the Federal government take title to the mansion and its 1,100 wooded acres in 1864.

The house became a military headquarters for the Union army. Overnight, what had been a quiet country estate was transformed into a vast military encampment. The possessions that had been George Washington's disappeared so rapidly that finally the remaining treasure-trove was removed to vaults for safekeeping. The mansion fell into disrepair, and for need of a burial ground for dead Union soldiers, the grounds were converted into a cemetery. Some people believe this was done in contempt for Lee. The mansion became an office for the cemetery and remained such until 1925.

For a time following the Civil War, General Lee hoped to regain possession of Arlington for his wife, but he died in 1870 without having recovered it. Mrs. Lee died three years later, and her eldest son Custis then took legal action to obtain ownership of the property. In 1882 the United States Supreme Court ruled in his favor. By that time, thousands of graves of soldiers rimmed the mansion, hardly a cheering prospect for a home. Custis Lee finally made the decision to sell the entire property back to the government for $150,000.

Originally "Arlington House" had been famous for its associations with George Washington, but after 1865 it became even more widely known as the Confederate commander's home, and throughout the following years it became known as the "Lee mansion." When the War Department undertook the first restoration of the mansion in 1928, few of the original furnishings and mementos were returned, but copies were made of portraits and pieces appropriate to the period. By 1933, much of the initial restoration was completed and the Lee mansion was transferred to the National Park Service. Careful research has now made the rooms appear much as they were in 1861.

The real size of the mansion is not apparent until seen close at hand. The central

The White Parlor, Arlington House.

part of the building is two stories high, sixty-feet wide, and forty-feet deep. One-story wings, each forty-feet long and twenty-five feet wide, extend to the north and south, making the length of the entire building 140 feet. The wings are identical except that the north one, the first to be built, is divided into small rooms.

The Greek Doric portico of the mansion is one of the finest in the country. It has eight columns that are twenty-five feet tall and five feet in diameter at the base. Authorities disagree as to whether George Hadfield, the young English architect who designed the mansion, derived the design of the portico and its massive pediment from the well proportioned Greek temple Theseum in Athens or the temple known as Neptune in Paestum, Italy.

The building is of the most solid construction throughout. Timber cut on the premises and bricks made of local clay were used in the construction. The walls, two-feet thick with a covering of stucco, are grooved so that they appear to be made of large blocks of cut stone. Joists, studs, and rafters are of hewn timber and are neatly mortised together or pinned with wooden pegs; scarcely any nails were used.

A wide center hall extends throughout the main part of the house, on both the first and the second floors. Characteristic of Greek temples, arched doorways open from the first-floor hallway into the drawing room.

Robert E. Lee added significant improvements to Arlington House, despite his frequent absences. Before leaving for service in 1855, he had a large unfinished room off the main hall refurbished and made into a drawing room, complete with marble mantelpieces and crystal chandeliers (the design of the oak leaf motif in the decor and on the mantelpiece is Lee's own). He also had a hot-air furnace installed at this time to heat the house. After the death of his father-in-law in 1857, the grounds outside of the mansion, long neglected, were found in a decrepit state. Lee as executor, took a leave of absence from the Army until 1860 to begin necessary agricultural and financial improvements.

The family parlor was the favorite gathering place of the Lees and the Custises, who entertained most of their guests here even after the large drawing room was completed. Each Christmas it was the family custom to kindle the great yule log in the fireplace with the remains of that from the previous year. The wedding of Robert E. Lee and his wife took place in this room as well. A great deal of entertaining also took place in the family dining room. When he was at home, it was General Lee's custom to gather rosebuds in the garden each morning and place one beside the plate of each of his daughters, the youngest getting the smallest bud, and so on up to the eldest.

The mansion has an office that both Custis and Lee used. Avocational painters, Custis and his daughter also used it as a studio. A desk in the corner was frequently used by General Lee as well as a traveling chess set and a plain pine stand. Mr. Custis and his daughter also used the dining room to manage the affairs of the household.

Flowers were an important part of life at Arlington House. The conservatory was large enough to keep all the rooms in constant supply. Mrs. Custis called the conservatory her "camelia house" and spent much of her time working there when not taking on outside duties for the Episcopal church, to which she was devoted. The floor

The family parlor at Arlington House. An avocational painter, Custis also used it as a studio.

of this room has been restored, but the door, woodwork, and most of the windows are original.

Mrs. Lee acquired her mother's interest in gardening and had her own flower beds in a plot south of the mansion. Each of her daughters were also given separate plots in which to grow their favorite blooms. Roses of different types predominated, intermingled with a variety of flowers and plants. North of the mansion was a "kitchen garden" where a variety of fruits and vegetables were grown. Grapevines said to have been planted by Mrs. Lee are still bearing fruit at its north and east sides.

Following restoration work, the Lee mansion was transferred to the National Park Service of the Department of the Interior. By an act of Congress in 1955, the mansion was designated an official memorial to Robert E. Lee. On June 30, 1975, the mansion's name was changed to Arlington House. Today, over a million tourists per year visit the site, a number exceeded only by those touring the White House and George Washington's Mt. Vernon. A few hundred feet down the hill from Arlington House is the eternal light and memorial of former President John F. Kennedy and his wife Jacqueline, the Tomb of the Unknown Soldier, and the graves of numerous Medal of Honor recipients and former high ranking federal officials. Many people who visit the cemetery also visit the mansion and its gardens to relive history and get the sweeping view of Washington this historic home commands.

· · · · ·

Arlington House, in Arlington National Cemetery at Arlington, Virginia, is located off of U.S. Route 50 and may be reached by way of the Arlington Memorial Bridge. The mansion is open to the public daily, from 9:30 a.m. to 4:30 p.m. The memorial is closed Christmas and New Year's Day. Robert E. Lee's birthday is recognized in January and the Lees' wedding anniversary is observed June 30 with special events. Admission is free. For further information, please contact the visitor center at: (703)557-0613, or visit the museum website at http://www.nps.gov.

Photos courtesy of the U.S. Department of the Interior, National Park Service, Arlington House.

Old Hickory's House

The Hermitage of Andrew Jackson

NASHVILLE • TENNESSEE

ANDREW JACKSON is one of history's most complex and controversial characters. Self-confident, energetic, honest, and straightforward, he was also a very proud man who loved a good fight. His home, The Hermitage, now presents the public with a model image of a Southern gentleman; at the same time he lived there, it afforded Jackson a sanctuary from the world. The very name Hermitage means a secluded place of residence.

In the public's eye, Jackson was best known as the Hero of New Orleans and as the country's Seventh President. Early in his public career, a hot temper and indomitable will earned him the popular nickname "Old Hickory," but it also resulted in a somewhat undeserved reputation as a duelist. Later, Jackson's fame grew with his con

The Hermitage 305

There are over 600 original books in the Hermitage library, many of which were signed by the author. Jackson spent many hours here towards the end of his life.

quests over such foes as the British, the Second United States Bank, and the National debt.

Jackson's private life was often as tumultuous as some of the more famous battles he led. Born in South Carolina in 1767, he never knew his father. He lost two brothers and his mother in the Revolutionary War, in which he was called to duty at the age of fourteen. While serving in the war, his fiery refusal to clean a British officers' shoes while under capture earned him a saber slash across the face that left a permanent scar into adulthood. His experiences in this war left a distaste for Britain that would remain with him through life.

Admitted to the North Carolina bar in 1787, Jackson soon established a successful career as an attorney in the area of Tennessee now known as Nashville. In 1791 he married Rachel Donelson, daughter of one of Nashville's most prominent citizens, only to discover later, to the amazement of all concerned, that her estranged first husband had not finalized divorce proceedings. In 1794, after a divorce decree had finally been issued, Jackson went through the formality of remarrying Rachel. The marriage was an extraordinarily happy one - Jackson was deeply devoted to his wife and adopted son. Yet the unintentional irregularity of its beginnings was long used against Jackson, especially in the bitter Presidential campaign of 1828, when he defeated John Quincy Adams despite the so-called scandal.

By 1804, Andrew Jackson enjoyed a solid reputation in Tennessee, which he had established as the state's first member of the House of Representatives and its second Senator. Privately, Jackson was so mired in debt that he was forced to retire from public life. To find a solution, he decided to liquidate his farm, Hunter Hill, then his most valuable asset. Soon after, he bought a much smaller 425-acre farm named The Hermitage. Jackson and his wife Rachel began their life there in a very humble, but

Dining room, the Hermitage. The brilliant Prussian blue wall color was the height of fashion in Jackson's day. An original portrait of Jackson by Ralph E.W. Earl hangs above the sideboard.

The double parlors were used to entertain guests. The curtains, originally $300, were the most expensive single purchase in the house. The furnishings, including the portraits, are original.

nicely furnished log cabin, which later grew over the course of time into a larger, plantation-style home.

Within the next few years, Jackson's financial difficulties had begun to rally and his public career was about to undergo a major transformation. A new generation of American leaders had been elected to Congress and they were determined to put a stop to Great Britain's lack of respect for the United States. They declared war on Britain in 1812, but over the next three years were continually frustrated by defeat and stalemate.

Jackson, however, was able to make a name for himself early into this war through a series of battle victories that would promote his position from a general in the Tennessee militia to that of major general in the United States Army. In January of 1815, Jackson, although heavily outnumbered, halted a British invasion aimed at New Orleans. The Battle of New Orleans was an important strategic victory, more so for the significant psychological boost it gave the fledgling republic. The United States had finally defeated a veteran British Army with no help from other countries. Andrew Jackson reaped the benefits of this victory and his popularity soared among his countrymen, who affectionately labeled him the "Hero of New Orleans."

After 1815, Jackson's personal and public fortunes continued to grow and his name was frequently mentioned in high political circles. Aware of his new position in society, Jackson decided to use a portion of his growing wealth to build a more substantial home. In 1819, with twenty slaves to assist him, Jackson began construction of a rather plain two-story brick mansion in the Federal style. Bricks used in the structure were made on the property and the timbers were cut from nearby forests. Beside his home, Jackson had a formal English garden installed for Rachel, who was an avid gardener. In 1823, Jackson also donated two acres of his property and funds to build a Presbyterian church for his wife and community living near his new home.

By 1824, Jackson began his third decade of residence at The Hermitage. The old General would have been content to simply retire and live out the rest of his days at his Southern home, but popular demand motivated him to run for president. Although Jackson won the popular vote, he failed to win a majority of electoral votes. The election, which was tied, was therefore decided in the House of Representatives where Henry Clay directed his support to John Quincy Adams. Adams was elected president and he subsequently named Henry Clay as his secretary of state. Jackson denounced the "corrupt bargain" that Clay and Adams apparently struck and vowed to unseat Adams in the next election.

The Hermitage became the headquarters of Jackson's 1828 campaign, in which Jackson at last succeeded in overthrowing Adam's bid for a second term. The effects of his victory were muted, however, for one month later, Jackson suffered the death of his beloved wife after a prolonged illness. Jackson laid Rachel to rest in the garden that she loved and in time had a more appropriate Greek-inspired tomb built over her grave. The President-elect left for Washington a few weeks later, but despair over

Jackson's bedroom contains the bed on which he died as well as his chairs, bureau, wardrobe and washstand. The bedcurtains and draperies are exact reproductions of the originals.

Rachel's death and overall poor health left many wondering if Jackson would live through his first term as President.

While Jackson was in Washington, major changes took place at the Hermitage. In 1831, two wings and first-and second-story porches were added, which combined to give the home a Palladian appearance. Jackson also built a new kitchen, a smokehouse, and a tomb in the garden for Rachel. In 1834 a fire destroyed the roof and much of the interior of the mansion. The sturdy brick walls were not badly damaged, except for discoloration by smoke. Jackson set about remodeling the Hermitage in the more fashionable Greek Revival style. Repairs to the house were completed in 1836, with the addition of an attractive pediment entablature and six Corinthian columns. Jackson's daughter-in-law Sarah furnished the home with fine French wallpapers and American Empire style furniture.

Jackson returned to The Hermitage in 1837 to live out the remainder of his days. The old General stayed active in politics, but his health often confined him to his bed. Jackson enjoyed the comforts of home and family, especially his three grandchildren. Remaining true to a promise he made to his wife before her death, he joined the Presbyterian Church and attended services as his health allowed. On June 8, 1845, Andrew Jackson died at the age of seventy-eight. Shortly before his death, he expressed his assurance to his family and to his slaves that he would meet them in heaven.

After his father's death, Andrew Jackson Jr. was forced to meet the challenges of financial management alone. An extremely unsuccessful businessman, he was forced to sell The Hermitage to the State of Tennessee for $48,000 in 1856. The state intended to found a "West Point of the South" at The Hermitage, but the oncoming Civil War quashed that notion. The Jackson family initially moved to Mississippi where Andrew Jackson Jr. owned two other plantations, but those farms failed as well. In 1860, he returned to The Hermitage as a tenant and died there five years later from an infection caused by an accidental gunshot wound. His widow, Sarah Jackson and her sister, Mrs. Marion Adams, would remain on the property while sons of both women served duty in the Confederate army.

After Sarah's passing in 1887, the state was forced to make some disposition of The Hermitage. The Tennessee General Assembly awarded The Hermitage mansion and the twenty-five acres surrounding it to the Ladies' Hermitage Association which was inspired by Mrs. Andrew Jackson III in 1889. The remainder of the property was handed over to the management of the Tennessee Confederate Soldiers' Home for use as a veteran's home. When the Soldiers' Home closed in 1933, all of the property was entrusted to the LHA.

Today, the LHA continues to operate The Hermitage, making it one of the oldest house museums in the United States. The mansion is exhibited as it appeared from 1837 to 1845, which corresponds to Jackson's retirement years. There are large verandahs, a wide center hallway with a superb spiral staircase, all flanked by double rooms and supplemental wings. The eleven rooms are spacious, designed for elegant living with a bevy of servants. Between 1992 and 1997, the LHA completed a major restoration that has brought the home much closer to its appearance during Jackson's final eight years of life. So even today, visitors are afforded a rare glimpse into the private and public lives of Andrew Jackson.

Unlike many such shrines, The Hermitage is furnished largely with original furniture and curios. The home still contains six wallpapers from Paris that were installed after the 1834 fire. In the front parlor are a crystal chandelier, French vases, an Italian marble mantle, French Porcelain urns, a Japanese bronze clock, mahogany chairs, Bohemian glass, Victorian carpets and other objects that belonged to the Jacksons. However, the lace curtains and red brocatel draperies are reproductions of the originals. In the back parlor, the furnishings are original, except for those that had to be duplicated over the years as a result of deterioration.

Jackson's bedroom still contains the bed upon which he died, as well as his chairs, bureau, wardrobe, washstand, shaving paraphernalia, candlesticks and mirrors. Even pictures that he owned while in residence still hang on the wall. Curiosities also include a silver cup presented by Martin Van Buren to his godson, Andrew Jackson III, candles, hatboxes, sewing boxes and silver luster vases rumored to be from the Royal Court of Russia.

In the dining room, an oaken floor that replaced the original one has been torn up by the ladies' association, and a poplar one of the Jackson era has been installed. There is a table at which nine presidents have dined, some in recent years. The Hermitage was a favorite mansion of Franklin D. Roosevelt.

Near the mansion, the gardens that Rachel Jackson planted still remain, as well as The Hermitage Church, which was restored in 1969. An Easter sunrise service is held there annually and the church remains in use for private weddings.

• • • • •

The Hermitage is located twelve miles east of Nashville off Old Hickory Boulevard in Hermitage, which is easily accessible from Interstate 40, exit 221, or Interstate 65, exit 92. The home is open every day of the year, except Thanksgiving, Christmas, and the third week of January. Admission prices are $9.50 for adults, $8.50 for senior citizens, $4.50 for children ages 6-12, and free admission for children under the age of six. Special group and family rates are available. For further information call: (615)889-2941 or visit the Hermitage website at http://www.thehermitage.com.

Photos courtesy of the Hermitage.

Home of the Nation's "Most Hated Man"

Jay Gould's Lyndhurst

TARRYTOWN • NEW YORK

A TYPICAL LATE NIGHT at the turn of the 1870s saw multi-millionaire Jay Gould pacing the library of his well-appointed Fifth Avenue townhouse on Manhattan's west side. A tee-totaling insomniac who never quelched his emotions with liquor or tobacco, the financier's conscience was weighed down by concerns for his wife and six children. Jay was devoted to his family and saw to it that their every need was provided for. Husband and wife were happily married and the pair were considered an attractive couple with impeccable manners. Life should have been carefree. Yet only forty-two, Jay was the most hated man in New York, and his closest loved ones were outcasts from society.

To compensate for his unfortunate situation, the young financier acquired a magnificent new home in 1880 which he named Lyndhurst. Located on 110 acres at Irvington-on-Hudson, Gould had previously rented the forty-room Gothic Revival estate for use in the summer months from New York merchant George Merritt. The home was a swallow's paradise, complete with turrets, bays, buttresses, trefoils, filials, traceries of stone and crenellated roofs. Inside the stained-glass windows, the house was dimly lit, but it contained all the luxurious living space a gentleman's family could require. To Jay Gould, the mansion's finest feature was its location, for no longer popular among New York's upper crust, the Hudson River Valley was a perfect hiding place to escape the snubs and taunts of the social whirl.

In appearance, Jay Gould did not appear to be a man with enemies. The financier stood barely five-feet-four, weighed 110 pounds, and looked more like a bright-eyed boy than a capitalist baron. Yet as president of the Erie Railway, the soft-spoken financier used his power to weave intricate speculative webs that drove many of New York's most prominent members to the point of bankruptcy. Considered a leading force in the financial panic known as Black Friday, Gould's manipulation of the stock market in 1869 led to many of the laws that today protect investors. He was also seen as the financial power behind William Marcy Tweed, the boss of Tammany Hall, whose corrupt regime had all but obliterated the rule of law in New York. Gould surrounded his offices in New York with an iron portcullis, and paid gangs from the West Side docks for protection. Threats never ended, and he lived constantly with the fear of death.

Lyndhurst is located twenty-five miles up the Hudson from Manhattan and has a panoramic view of the river. The forty-room stone mansion is one of the finest Gothic Revival castles in America. Completely furnished, it features vaulted ceilings, a huge tower, and custom-designed furniture by the mansion's architect, Alexander J. Davis (1803-92). The grounds include one of the largest private greenhouses in America, a carriage house that could hold up to fifteen vehicles, and a dock, which supplied easy access to the Hudson River by private yacht or steamboat.

The estate was owned by the Gould family for eighty-one years and was bequeathed to the public by Mr. Gould's youngest daughter Anna (1875-1961), the former Duchess of Talleyrand-Perigord, who divided her time between a residence at the Plaza Hotel and Lyndhurst after returning to the United States in 1938. Under her will, the National Trust for Historic Preservation became the owner, and in 1964 it dedicated the property as its most elegant possession in the nation. The National Trust reduced the original acreage to sixty-seven acres, by selling superfluous acres at a price sufficient to restore the mansion and make necessary accommodations for public visitation.

This was not achieved without considerable opposition from many Tarrytown officials and residents, who contended that a shrine should not be maintained for a "robber baron" - especially since it entailed local tax exemption. The opposition was finally overcome by arguments that a great Gothic Revival mansion of Sleepy Hollow was being honored, not Mr. Gould. Tarrytown officials joined in the dedication cere-

Rebuilt greenhouse, after 1880.

monies. And the National Trust talked of how stables and other buildings on the property could be restored and used for community functions.

Here at Lyndhurst, Mr. Gould spent many happy hours with his children, gathering them together to plant trees and shrubs. The setting provided a distinct contrast to the intrigues of his business life, which included scheming with judges and legislators and daily fights for control of 15,854 miles of railroad. Mr. Gould controlled the Missouri Pacific system, the Texas and Pacific, the New York and New England Railroad, the Wabash system, the Manhattan Elevated, and large holdings in Union Pacific. By 1881, he also gained control of Western Union Telegraph Company, major portions of the New York City transit lines and a newspaper - *The New York World*. Mr. Gould played the business game like a master plays chess, and at the time of his death it is reported that he was the second richest man in the nation.

Lyndhurst, under another name, really began its life as a romantic estate in 1838 when Jason Gould was two years old, the youngest child and only son of a farmer's family of six children from Roxbury, New York.

Starting in the 1800s, wealthy patrons looking to retreat from the growing industrialization of New York City, commissioned mansions in a variety of styles along the Hudson River Bluffs. Built as a small country villa in 1838, Lyndhurst, then known as "Knoll," was commissioned by General William Paulding, a former mayor of New York who was among the many who moved north at this time. His political opponents called it Paulding's Folly, partly because of envy and partly because its design was a radical departure from the classical Georgian, Federal and Greek Revival architecture that had long been popular in this country.

Americans had begun to travel extensively in Europe for pleasure and General

Paulding was among those who felt more inspired by the Gothic Revival castles than the white-pillared ones his neighbors at home had built. Of especial interest to him was the infamous castle of Britain's noted author Horace Walpole, Strawberry Hill of 1750. Another great influence were the romantic novels of Sir Walter Scott, with tales of chivalry, moats, turrets and towers. Consequently, the Paulding castle rose with asymmetrical layouts of towers, turrets, wings and bay windows, and with leaded glass windows, diamond-shaped panes, carved corbels, vaulted ribbed ceilings and ornate details that never would have harmonized with Georgian simplicity.

Alexander Jackson Davis (1803-92), the architect hired by General Paulding in 1838, drew the specifications for Paulding's mansion in a turreted tower of a building he had just completed for New York University at Washington Square. Mr. Davis, the foremost American

The entrance hall, looking north to the dining room. The busts of George Washington and the marquis de Lafayette were sculpted by Horatio Greenough.

architectural theorist of the day, was an artist and furniture designer, and he designed not only the mansion but its furnishings, which are still there. Davis closely supervised almost every aspect of Knoll's design, a great exception to the usual role of an architect in nineteenth-century America.

The tract General Paulding chose was just north of Washington Irving's Sunnyside (1836) and its "snuggery." The general chose to build a mansion that looked impressively big outside but had the interior coziness of Sunnyside; some architects have called it the biggest house with the least room they ever saw. Nearby neighbors also included Henry Sheldon, whose Gothic Revival cottage, Millbrook, was also designed by Davis.

The house broke dramatically from the traditional box form, projecting in virtually every direction. Limestone from the nearby town of Sing Sing, as Ossining was then known, was shipped downriver for the exterior. Arcaded open portals provided enticing vistas of the Hudson. Broad verandahs linked the house with the gardens

The cabinet room, a small room north of the library.

and subsidiary buildings. Mr. Davis believed in uniting the interior of the house with the lawns and gardens outside, as Frank Lloyd Wright and other designers of contemporary homes were to do later. Like Mr. Wright, Davis also felt that the furniture he designed for Lyndhurst were objects that could not be viewed out of the mansion's context.

When the Pauldings moved away, the estate was bought in 1864 by George Merritt (1807-73), a successful merchant and holder of a railroad car spring patent. Looking to establish himself among a growing upper class that demonstrated wealth with increas-

The Duchess's suite is filled with furniture and objects belonging to Anna Gould, Duchess of Talleyrand-Perigord.

ingly large residences, Merritt called upon Davis's services again to transform the property into a grand country estate. He also changed the mansion's name to Lyndenhurst, after the numerous Linden trees surrounding the property.

Davis added a large wing to the north, raised several of the roofs, built a porte-cochère and constructed a tower with impressive battlements. He added more vaulted ribbed ceilings and ornate chimney pieces, and designed more Gothic Revival furniture for the rooms. The Paulding library, a great two-story room with stained-glass windows and a musician's gallery, was converted into a billiard room/picture gallery, with new emphasis on the dining room as the focus of the house. The drawing room and the entrance hall were the only two rooms in which original architectural detail remained unchanged. The old and the new parts are totally harmonious and provide a balanced masterpiece of asymmetrical Gothic composition.

Horticulturist Andrew Jackson Downing (1815-52), who planned the grounds of the Capitol and the White House, gave advice about the development of the grounds while master gardener Ferdinand Mangold (1828-1905) oversaw the actual reshaping of the property. Mangold, a former park superintendent of German royalty, made sweeping improvements to the property, including a curving entrance drive, orchards, vineyards and a massive greenhouse and conservatory complex. His changes were enhanced by the addition of 110 acres to the property in 1870.

Merritt would only have six years to enjoy his new home before succumbing to Bright's disease, a kidney ailment, in 1873. Upon acquiring the mansion from the Merritt family for $250,000, Mr. Gould shortened the property's name to Lyndhurst and purchased an additional 320 acres of land. Out of respect for Lyndhurst's Gothic excellence, his changes to the property were not considered extensive; the new owner added more elaborate stained glass to the mansion's windows, expanded the property's collection of exotic trees and plants, and used the estate's dock to steam his 150-foot yacht to work at his office in New York City's financial district.

Creative interior flourishes Gould added included the installation of a broad, two-story-high, Tiffany-style stained-glass window in a room that was once the Paulding library. The window overlooks the Hudson, the lawns and gardens; it has leaded-glass decorations at the top and inset magnifying glasses eighteen- inches wide at shoulder level for closer viewing of the sights up and down the river. Mr. Gould then converted this room into a picture gallery, and in it now are hung his valuable collection of paintings by Corot, Rousseau and other nineteenth-century masters.

Soon after Mr. Gould obtained the property a fire swept through the main greenhouse, destroying it entirely. Undaunted, Mr. Gould had the structure rebuilt in the Gothic Revival style to match the house. He also added two wings, each eighty-feet long. The new greenhouse was divided into fourteen sections, including a rose area, a carnation area, cold houses for azaleas, rhododendrons, camellias, and flowering bulbs, an orchid house, and a croton house. Every morning Mr. Gould would rise early, and spend at least an hour puttering in his greenhouse before sailing down the Hudson to his Wall Street office.

Jay Gould died of tuberculosis at the age of fifty-six and Lyndhurst became the home of his eldest daughter, Helen (1868-1938), who was twenty-four at the time of her father's death. Her mother, Helen Miller Gould (1837-88), had died three years earlier of a stroke, and at her father's death, Jay Gould's eldest daughter became the guardian of her younger brother and sister. When Helen's youngest brother Frank reached maturity six years later, Helen bought the property outright from her siblings for $382,000.

Helen led a quiet life at Lyndhurst, making few changes to the house's interior. Following marriage in 1913 to railroad executive Finley Shepard, Helen adopted four children. Many changes she had recently made to the outside grounds would be to their benefit, including a two-lane bowling alley in a separate building overlooking the river (1894), a Roman-style swimming pool (1910-11), a laundry building and a children's playhouse (1916). Helen became known for her philanthropic works, both locally and nationally, providing a sewing school for the children of the Irvington-Tarrytown community and establishing a Lyndhurst clubhouse, where young people of Irvington could gather for recreation.

Following Helen's death, her younger sister Anna, who had married into the French nobility, continued her sister's charitable traditions, welcoming wounded servicemen to the property during World War II. Anna was an avid collector of French furniture and did little to the interiors except add pieces from her own furniture collection. The only rooms she changed completely were her bedroom and the guest bedroom next to it, known today as "the duchess's suite."

Today, more than 90,000 visitors a year come to Lyndhurst, enjoying the mansion with its extensive collection of decorative and personal objects from the estate's three families, or to stroll across rolling grounds that have been described as one of the finest remaining examples of nineteenth-century landscape. Preservation of the mansion's interior is ongoing. Work is also under way to restore the bowling alley and greenhouse to their original condition. Lyndhurst's restored 1865 carriage house now serves as the estate's welcome center; with a gallery, visitor information center, café and shop. Yearly events at Lyndhurst include concerts and lectures, rose gardening workshops, craft fairs and candelight holiday celebrations. True to its original legacy, the property still provides a welcome escape from the hustle-bustle of urban life.

• • • • •

Lyndhurst is located at 635 South Broadway, one-half mile south of the Tappan Zee Bridge on Route 9 in Tarrytown. Hours of operation are Tuesday through Sunday, 10:00 a.m. to 5:00 p.m., from mid-April through October. In winter the estate is open on weekends from 10:00 a.m. to 4:00 p.m. Regular cost of admission is $9.00 for adults, $8.00 for seniors, $3.00 for children 12-17; children under 12 are admitted free. Forty-five minute tours of the mansion are offered as part of regular admission. For further information call: (914)631-4481, or visit the Lyndhurst website at http://www.lyndhurst.org.

Photos courtesy of Lyndhurst.

The living room at Gillette Castle. Gillette had an elaborate system of mirrors installed so he could view the living room from his bedroom off the upper balcony.

The Sleuth's Home

William Gillette's Castle

HADLYME • CONNECTICUT

FAME IN THE THEATER is fugitive, but the name of William Gillette was emblazoned on marquees of the largest theaters across the country in the early part of the twentieth century. This versatile actor was something of a John Barrymore, Tyrone Power, Henry Fonda and Maurice Evans, all rolled into one. Known as "Mr. Sherlock Holmes," he starred as Conan Doyle's famous detective over 1,300 times during the period from 1899 to 1932, including numerous revivals with box office receipts of over a million dollars. He personally wrote thirteen plays and adapted seven others, touring the United States and England to play the leading roles. He performed with the most notable actors and actresses of his time, including Charlie Chaplin, Helen Hayes, and Ethel Barrymore.

William Gillette was born in Hartford, CT, on July 24, 1853, the son of a prominent Connecticut family. His mother was a descendent of Thomas Hooker (one of the

Gillette Castle's dining room. The table was placed on rollers so Gillette and his guests could sit by the fire while eating.

founders of Hartford), and his father was a U.S. senator from Connecticut during the mid-1850s. Gillette chose a career in acting from an early age, despite the social taboos against this profession. His ambition was to write, act and direct in his own plays, a desire which he achieved early in life. The first play in which he fulfilled these goals, "The Professor," opened in 1880, and received the financial help of Mark Twain.

In 1882 he married Helen Nickles of Detroit. They traveled together on tour while Gillette continued to write and act in the theater. One of his most successful plays, "Held by the Enemy," a Civil War play, was produced during this period, first appearing in 1886. In 1888, his wife died suddenly of a ruptured appendix, and Gillette stopped acting for five years. Upon his return to the theater, Gillette produced another highly successful Civil War play, "Secret Service," in 1895, and "Because She Loved Him So," in 1898. With Sir Arthur Conan Doyle's approval, Gillette's first appearance of "Sherlock Holmes," which he wrote and acted in, appeared in New York State in November, 1899. The play would appear before the King and Queen of England in 1902, and later variations would include such luminaries as Ethel Barrymore and Charlie Chaplin. In 1915 Gillette was elected to the American Academy of Arts and Letters.

Mr. Gillette had been considering a site for a mansion near Greenport, Long Island, in 1913, where he had begun to amass building materials. He is known to have had a change of heart shortly after taking a cruise along the Connecticut River on his houseboat the *Aunt Polly*. He had a natural fondness for Connecticut, having been born there, and soon after made a decision to begin construction along the shores of Hadlyme, where he purchased 122 acres of land on one of the seven hills along the river. He called his home Seventh Sister, after the name given this hill as a navigational marker. Mr. Gillette designed the castle, which was constructed by Porteus and Walker of Hartford. To transport building materials and workmen up the steep hillside, the actor built an automated tramway.

Construction of the castle began in 1914 and continued for five years. "Finish" work continued well into the 1920s, with a third floor added between 1923 and 1926. Mr. Gillette was reported to have spent $1,200,000 on the property. Twenty masons and carpenters were continuously busy following plans that the actor personally drew and frequently revised.

Walls of local fieldstone are four-to five-feet-thick and rise four stories. Timbers, doors and woodwork are of hand-hewn white oak. Similar material was used for garden arches and the narrow-gauge railroad that circled the property. Known as "The Seventh Sister Shortline," the railroad began at Grand Central Station and extended throughout the property. It consisted of a steam and an electric locomotive, an observation car that held twenty people, and several Pullman cars. The railroad tracks are now hiking trails. The electric train has recently been reacquired by the state of Connecticut from Lake Compounce in Bristol, CT. A volunteer group, "Friends of the

"Grand Central Station," which served Gillette's three-mile gauge railway.
Plans are underway to restore the station.

Gillette Castle," are planning on restoring and exhibiting it again to the public.

As the engineer of locomotives on his shortline, Gillette kept guests, including Dr. Albert Einstein and President Herbert Hoover, in nervous tension as the train plunged through tunnels, over high trestles and around curves with whistles screeching and bells clanging. It was perhaps fortunate for everyone that Gillette, who was a speed demon, could not nudge the locomotive into going more than twenty miles an hour.

Gillette's mansion resembles a medieval Rhenish fortress, with crenelated battlements and openings typical to an old-fashioned Hollywood film set. The structure consists of twenty-four main rooms, strung together in a maze-like configuration. Twenty of these rooms are currently open to the public; the largest is the living room. There are forty-seven massive wood doors, one weighing 300 pounds. They have hand-hewn bolts and latches of white oak. Some of the arms of the latches are three feet long and operate in unison with other arms. Electric fixtures are festooned with bits of colored glass that Mr. Gillette collected with the aid of friends. Gillette's interest in trains is visible in his decorating tastes; the light switches are made of chunks of wood resembling train switches. All of the light fixtures are original, the most valuable are the Tiffanies above each staircase. The mansion also features Quiosel fixtures on the living room ceiling, the mezzanie, the dining room and other locations throughout the house.

No paint has been used inside or outside of the mansion. Native stone and natural wood dominate the decorations, although Mr. Gillette often used red rugs to brighten the scene. The walls have panels of Raffia Matting, rumored to be designed by Mr. Gillette and tinted in red and green.

The living room, the largest room in the castle, is fifty-feet long and nineteen-feet high, with a balcony off the bedrooms overlooking it. There are three fireplaces located throughout the house; the largest one is six feet wide. A large stone fireplace located within the dining room was the gathering place at mealtime. A table on rollers faced the fireplace so that Mr. Gillette and his friends could sit by the fire while dining.

Much of the furniture throughout the castle was made by local carpenters to specifications drawn by Mr. Gillette. In the actor's study, a large armchair on rollers rests on a track, which enabled Mr. Gillette to move back and forth easily. The drawers of the desk in this room have a secret locking device. A large bar is located near the study, equipped with trick levers and panels, which gave Mr. Gillette personal control of the bottled items. The bar was installed in 1934 during Prohibition which provides the explanation for such a complicated locking system. The study also features an inconspicuous "secret doorway" located behind the desk (it actually leads to his basement), that was used by Gillette to gain quick access to his workshop.

A conservatory housed rare plants and goldfish as well as Mr. Gillette's pet frogs, Lena and Mike. Mr. Gillette was also a cat fancier - whether live cats or those made of ceramics, concrete and granite. At one time he had seventeen live cats in the Castle. "The cat," Mr. Gillette said, "is the only critic of the human race with courage to act on his feelings." He noted that dogs and other animals would lick the hand of a cruel person but that a cat, once deciding that a person was likable or detestable, would display either affection of disapproval.

Unknown to most visitors is a section of the third floor of the house, which was added to the house between 1923-26. Located here is an art gallery containing 110 paintings Mr. Gillette acquired over the course of his life. The display includes watercolors by Amelia Watson, as well as the works of Chalaner, John Whorf, Maxfield Parish, Paul Marny and William Richards. Gillette's tastes in art are easily discernible by the gallery's contents - he favored pastoral landscapes and seascapes.

The third floor contains a wealth of Mr. Gillette's personal and professional memorabilia, including pictures from the actor's plays, his priceless china collection, and family portraits. Located here too is Gillette's "Secret Room," accessible from a somewhat hidden, pull-down stairway. This room was Mr. Gillette's quiet retreat, very small and heated only by a small fireplace. It is hard to imagine the tall, lanky, elderly gentleman ascending up to this room.

Mr. Gillette's constant companion was a Young Japanese man named Yukitaka Osaki, who began his career with Gillette as a cabin boy on the *Aunt Polly*. He was also Mr. Gillette's valet during his theater days. Later, Osaki worked in the Castle and its gardens. He lived in a small house on the Castle grounds until his death in 1942. It was Osaki's brother who donated to the U.S. government three thousand cherry trees which now grace the tidal basin of Washington, D.C. He was mayor of Tokyo at the time.

Mr. Gillette, who died in 1937, was so worried about the future of his Castle that he left instructions to the executors of his estate "to see to it that the property does not fall into the hands of some blithering saphead who has no conception of where he is or with what surrounded." Upon his death he left the Castle to two nieces and a nephew, who did not have the financial resources to maintain it. His property was sold to the Connecticut State Park and Forest Commission in 1943 for $30,000 and opened as a State Park in 1944. The State sold the narrow-gauge railroad to Lake Compounce in Bristol, Connecticut for $3,000. It had originally cost Mr. Gillette $50,000.

Mr. Gillette's fondest wishes about the mansion were fulfilled. Now open to the public, the Castle and grounds are visited by more than 340,000 people a year.

• • • • •

The Gillette Castle is located at 67 River Road, East Haddam, CT. To arrive by car, take Route 9, Exit 7, and follow 82E or Exit 6 via Route 148 to the Chester-Hadlyme Ferry. The ferry operates spring through fall. The Park Grounds are open daily year round. The Castle will be operating on an indefinite renovation schedule. For further information call: (860)526-2336.

Photos by Alan Benner, courtesy of Gillette Castle State Park.

Acknowledgments

Hastings House would like to take this opportunity to gratefully acknowledge the painstaking cooperation received from the following mansion owners, foundation officials, archivists, curators and researchers who made revision of this book possible. Deep gratitude is expressed to all, and the wish is given that this book will help to perpetuate the mansions they represent.

Special thanks to the following: the staff of the Preservations Society of Newport County; Joyce Bimbo and John Horn of the Hearst Castle; the staff of Biltmore Estate; the staff of Shelburne Museum; William Allman, Asst. Curator: The White House; The Taliesin Preservation Committee; Patricia Kahle, Director: Shadows-on-the Teche; James Ryan, former Site Manager: Olana and David Seaman, Ph.D, Professor of Architecture, Kansas State University; Suzanne Coffman, Editor: Colonial Williamsburg; King Laughlin, Historical Curator: Mount Vernon for his writing and research assistance; Sally McDonough of Mt. Vernon's public relations department; Michelle Blomberg and Don Werling, archivists: The Fairlane Estate; Jennifer Rutledge, Operations Manager: San Francisco Plantation; Katherine Sheedy, Museum Technician: Sagamore Hill; Edgar Munhall, Curator: The Frick Collection; Rebecca Bowman, Research Historian: The Thomas Jefferson Memorial Foundation; Frederic Fischer, Exec. Director, Hillwood Museum & Gardens, the staff of the Gardner Museum; Amy Richardson, Site Administrator: the Society for the Preservation of New England Antiquities; the staff of Belle Meade Plantation; Gene Soivak, Director: Rosedown Plantation; Douglas Tarr, Reference Archivist: The Edison Estate at Glenmont; the staff of the Edison Winter Estate: Fort Myers, Florida; the staff of Historic Hudson Valley; Hillary Holland, Media Relations Manager: Winterthur Museum and Gardens; the staff of the FDR National Historic Site, Hyde Park, New York; Cate O'Hara, former Assoc. Curator of Public Programs and Publications: The Taft Museum; Abby Schwartz, Curator of Education: The Taft Museum; Donald Goss, Park Supervisor: Gillette Castle State Park; Anthony Guzzi, Curatorial Asst: The Hermitage; Carolyn Brackett: Marketing Director, The Hermitage; Hillary Sunderland, Special Events Coordinator: Shelburne Farms; The Staff of Shelburne Museum; Elizabeth Montgomery, Development Assoc. and the staff of the Lockwood-Mathews Mansion; Janene Charbeneau, Director of Marketing and Public Relations: the Museum of the Confederacy; Julia Weede, Mgr. of Resource Development: Lyndhurst; Charles Lyle, Exec. Director: Boscobel and Frederick Stanyer, former Exec. Director: Boscobel.

Bibliography

Articles

DeWan, George. "The House on the Hill." *Newsday* (Spring 1998): 1-17.

Gill, Brendan. "The Shelburne Museum." *Architectural Digest* (June 1995): 198-99.

Maurer, David. "The Lees of Stratford Hall." *Colonial Homes* (February 1997): 40 (8).

McCullough, David. "House as Autobiography." *House Beautiful* (February, 1997): 78 (8).

Nasaw, David. "Earthly Delights." *The New Yorker* (March 23, 1998): 66-79.

Nelligan, Murray H. "Lee Mansion National Memorial." *National Park Service Historical Handbook Series* (No. 6): 1-47.

Patton, Thomas W. "FDR's Trees." *Conservationist*. April, 1995: 26 (4).

Reid, Brian Holden. "General Lee's House." *History Today* (March 1997): 60-1.

Russell, John. "Restored Ringling Museum Opens in Subtropical Glory." *The New York Times* (January 22, 1991): C11.

Samuels, David. "The Confidence Man." *The New Yorker* (April 26/May3, 1999): 150-161.

Ward, Timothy Jack. "2000 and Then Some: A Shopping Odyssey." *The New York Times* (Sept. 9, 1999): F1, 6.

Books

Jules Abels. *The Rockefeller Billions*. New York: The Macmillan Co., 1965.

Neil Baldwin. *Edison: Inventing the Century*. New York: Hyperion Press, 1995.

Ann Benway. *A Guidebook to Newport Mansions*. Newport, RI: The Preservation Society of Newport County, 1984.

Fawn M. Brodie. *Thomas Jefferson: An Intimate History*. New York: W.W. Norton & Co.,

1974).

Rachel D. Carley and Rosemary Rennicke. *A Guide to the Biltmore Estate.* North Carolina: The Biltmore Company: 1995.

Barbara Carson. *The Governor's Palace: The Williamsburg Residence of Virginia's Royal Governor.* Williamsburg, VA: The Colonial Williamsburg Foundation, 1991.

Malinda Collier, John M. Coski, Richard C. Cote, Tucker H. Hill and Guy R. Swanson. *White House of the Confederacy: An Illustrated History.* Richmond, VA: Cadmus Marketing, Inc.

Peter Collier and David Horowitz. *The Fords: An American Epic.* New York: Summit Books, 1987).

_____. *The Roosevelts: An American Saga.* New York: Simon & Schuster, 1994.

_____. *The Rockefellers: An American Dynasty.* New York: Holt, Rinehart & Winston: 1976.

Nancy Curtis and Richard C. Nylander. *Beauport: The Sleeper-McCann House.* Boston: Godine Publishers, 1990.

Harvey Einbinder. *Frank Lloyd Wright: An American Genius.* New York: Philosophical Library, Inc., 1986.

John Foreman, Louis Auchincloss and Robbe Stimson. *The Vanderbilts and the Gilded Age: Architectural Aspirations, 1879-1901.* New York: St. Martin's Press, 1991.

Ernest B. Furgurson. *Ashes of Glory: Richmond at War.* New York: Alfred A. Knopf, 1996.

Mary Ann Harrell. *The White House: An Historic Guide.* Washington, D.C.: White House Historical Association with the cooperation of the National Geographic Society, 1995.

Lauren B. Hewes and Celia Y. Oliver. *To Collect in Earnest: The Life and Work of Electra Havemeyer Webb.* Shelburne, VT: The Shelburne Museum, 1997.

Edwin P. Hoyt. *The Goulds: A Social History.* New York: Weybright & Talley, 1969.

William Randolph Hearst, Jr. *The Hearsts: Father & Son.* New York: Roberts Rinehart

Publishers, 1991.

Graham Hood. *The Governor's Palace in Williamsburg: A Cultural Study.* Williamsburg, VA: The Colonial Williamsburg Foundation, 1991.

Gerry Van Der Heuvel. *Crowns of Thorns and Glory: Mary Todd Lincoln and Varina Howell Davis.* New York: E.P. Dutton, 1988.

Kathleen Eagan Johnson. *Washington Irving's Sunnyside.* New York: Historic Hudson Valley Press, 1995.

_____*Van Cortlandt Manor.* New York: Historic Hudson Valley Press, 1997.

Nancy E. Loe. *An Interpretive History of W.R. Hearst's San Simeon Estate.* California: ARA Leisure Services, 1994.

Anne Odom and Liana Paredes Arend. *A Taste for Splendor: Russian Imperial and European Treasures from the Hillwood Museum.* Art Services International, 1998.

Micheal Olmert. *Official Guide to Colonial Williamsburg.* Williamsburg, VA: The Colonial Williamsburg Foundation, 1985.

Joseph E. Persico. *The Imperial Rockefeller: A Biography of Nelson A. Rockefeller.* New York: Simon & Schuster, 1982.

Charles P. Roland. *The Confederacy.* Chicago: The University of Chicago Press.1960.

William Seale. *The White House: The History of an American Idea.* Washington, D.C.: The American Institute of Architects Press, 1992.

Joe Sherman. *The House at Shelburne Farms.* Middlebury, VT: Paul S. Erikson, Publisher, 1992.

Clarice Stasz. *The Rockefeller Women.* New York: St. Martin's Press, 1995.

Hudson Strode. *Jefferson Davis: Confederate President.* New York: Harcourt, Brace & Company, 1959.

A. Swanberg. *Citizen Hearst: A Biography of William Randolph Hearst.* New York: Charles Scribners' Sons: 1961.

Allan Tate. *Jefferson Davis: His Rise and Fall.* New York: Minton, Balch & Company, 1929.

Joseph J. Thorndike, Jr., ed. *Three Centuries of Notable American Architects*. New York: American Heritage Publishing Co., Inc., 1981.

Robert C. Twombley. *Frank Lloyd Wright: His Life and His Architecture*. New York: John Wiley & Sons, 1979.

Ginger Wadsworth. *Julia Morgan: Architect of Dreams*. Minneapolis, MN: Lerner Publications, 1990.

Mark R. Wenger. *Carter's Grove: The Story of a Virginia Plantation*. Williamsburg, VA: The Colonial Williamsburg Foundation, 1994).

Ridley Willis, II. *The History of Belle Meade: Mansion, Plantation and Stud*. Nashville: Vanderbilt University Press, 1991.

Susan Wizowaty, ed. *Shelburne Museum: A Guide to the Collections*. Shelburne, VT: Shelburne Museum, Inc., 1993.

INDEX

(Page numbers in italics refer to illustrations)

336

EAU CLAIRE DISTRICT LIBRARY